SE Worklife: How to Become a Sales Engineer

By: Kevin R Kunz

Disclaimers

The content in this book may not be reproduced, duplicated, or transmitted without direct written permission from the author or the publisher. Under no circumstances will the publisher or author be held responsible for any damages, reparations, or monetary loss due to the information contained within this book, whether directly or indirectly. You are responsible for your own choices, actions, and results.

Legal Notice

This book is copyright protected and intended for personal use only. You cannot amend, distribute, sell, use, , or paraphrase any part of this book without the consent of the author or publisher.

Disclaimer Notice

Please note that the information contained within this document is for educational and entertainment purposes only. Every effort has been made to present accurate, up-to-date, reliable, and complete information. No warranties of any kind are declared or implied.

Readers acknowledge that the author is not providing legal, financial, medical, or professional advice. The content within this book has been derived from various sources. Please consult a licensed professional before attempting any techniques outlined in this book. By reading this document, the reader agrees that under no circumstances is the author responsible for any direct or indirect losses incurred as a result of using the information contained within, including but not limited to errors, omissions, or inaccuracies.

Additional Notices

KDP, Kindle, Kindle Unlimited, and Kindle Select are all registered trademarks of the Amazon Corporation.

FTC Notice

Some links in this book are affiliate links, which means I will receive a small commission.

Registration # TXu 203430190 - SE Worklife
Copyright Kevin R Kunz 2022. All rights reserved.
Paper Back : ISBN: 9798362636432

Table of Contents

ACKNOWLEDGEMENTS **17**
   UNLOCK YOUR FUTURE IN SALES ENGINEERING 20
INTRODUCTION: **22**
   EMBARK ON YOUR JOURNEY TO SALES ENGINEERING EXCELLENCE 22
   WHY I AM WRITING THIS SERIES 23
PART 1: WHAT IS THE JOB **28**
CHAPTER 1: SEAC (S.E.A.C.) WORKLIFE **28**
   THE BEST JOB EVER 28
   INTRODUCTION 28
   WHAT IS THE ROLE? 30
   PERSONAL JOURNEY 31
   EVOLUTION OF ROLES 33
   MARKET MATURITY AND SKILL REQUIREMENTS 33
CHAPTER 2: JOB TITLES AND DESCRIPTIONS **35**
   SYSTEMS ARCHITECT 36
   SOLUTION ARCHITECT / ENGINEER 38
   SOLUTION CONSULTANT 43
   SALES ENGINEER / CONSULTANT 44
   TECHNICAL SPECIALIST 51
   EVANGELIST 56
   CONSULTANT 61
   ISR INSIDE SALES REPRESENTATIVE 63
   SOFTWARE ACCOUNT EXECUTIVE ROLE 67
   BUSINESS ANALYST - POST SALES 81
   CSM - CUSTOMER SUCCESS MANAGEMENT - POST SALES 84
   SUGGESTED WORKSHOP: FINDING YOUR IDEAL ROLE 89
   QUIZ: UNDERSTANDING YOUR IDEAL ROLE 92
CHAPTER 3: THE S.E.A.C. ROLES AND EXPECTATIONS **94**
   UNDERSTANDING S.E.A.C. EXPECTATIONS 94
   WORKSHOP: IDENTIFYING YOUR IDEAL ROLE IN SALES ENGINEERING ... 103
   QUIZ: UNDERSTANDING SEAC ROLES 104
   SEAC SKILLS 105
   TECHNICAL SALES OPERATIONS 108
   WORKSHOP: IDENTIFYING THE RIGHT ROLE FOR YOU 109
   RECOMMENDED BOOKS 111
   QUIZ: TEST YOUR UNDERSTANDING 111
   SEAC MANAGERS EXPECTATIONS 113
   WORKSHOP: EFFECTIVE MANAGEMENT PRACTICES 118
   QUIZ: TEST YOUR UNDERSTANDING 120
   RECOMMENDED BOOKS 122
   AE ACCOUNT EXECUTIVE EXPECTATIONS 124

- Recommended Books 127
- Quiz 128

PART 4 DAY IN THE LIFE (DIL) 130
CHAPTER 4: TYPICAL WORK BREAKDOWN 130
- Quiz 134
- The Other 26 Hours 136
- Recommended Books: 138

CHAPTER 5 : TIME IS THE DREADED ENEMY 141
- Q1 Kickoff 141
- Recommended Books 143
- Most Important Week - Week 6 146
- Q2 and Q3 - The Best Quarters 148
- Workshop: Prioritizing Tasks & Managing Week 6 149
- Recommended Books 150
- Quiz 151
- Q4 Game Time 153
- Recommended Books: 155
- QBR: Quarterly Business Review 158
- Workshop: Preparing for a QBR 160
- Quiz 161

PART 5 : REMEMBER YOU ARE A SALES PERSON! 163
CHAPTER 6: SALES METHODOLOGIES 163
- Examples of BMANTR Questioning: 165
- MEDDPICC 168
- Examples of MEDDPICC Questioning: 169
- Recommended Books: 172

CHAPTER 7: THE SALES JOURNEY - STEP BY STEP 175
- Recommended Books: 179
- Quiz: 180

CHAPTER 8: SALES STAGES IN DETAIL 182
- Step Zero 182
- Workshop: Account Planning and SDR Collaboration 183
- Recommended Books 185
- Quiz 186
- The First Stage 188
- Workshop: Customer Research and Discovery 191
- Recommended Books 192
- Quiz 193
- Sales Stages Two and Three - Your Breakdown 195
- Workshop: Effective Meeting Preparation 198
- Recommended Books 199
- Quiz 200

CHAPTER 9 – SALES METHODOLOGY & TOOLS 202

 Workshop: Utilizing Sales Tools Effectively 204
 Recommended Books 205
 Quiz 206
Chapter 10: Game Day **208**
 Workshop: Effective Customer Meetings 213
 Recommended Books 214
 Quiz 215
Part 8: Let's Get You a Job! **217**
Chapter 11: Job Search and Interview Process **217**
 Marketing 101 218
 Quiz 223
Chapter 12: Leverage SEO **225**
 Global Sales Engineering Recruitment 101 225
Chapter 13 Hiring Process **233**
Chapter 14: The Interview Day **239**
 Key Elements of Adobe and Oracle Interview Styles 243
 Quiz for Adobe and Oracle Interview Processes 245
Snowflake Interview Guide **248**
 Job Interview Setup 251
Chapter 15: What Should We Be Looking For? **257**
Chapter 16: The Things I Always Looked For and Why ...**261**
 Workshop 265
 Quiz 267
 Book Recommendations 268
Part 10: You Are Accepted **269**
Chapter 17: Compensation Plans **269**
 Workshop 279
 Quiz 280
 Books Recommended 281
Chapter 18: Sales Incentive Options **282**
 Workshop 285
 Quiz 286
Chapter 19: How Much Are You Worth **287**
Chapter 20: Let's Make a Deal **291**
 Offer Negotiation Stage 291
 Recommended Books 299
 Quiz 300
Part 9: You Got the Job – Now What **302**
Chapter 21: Congrats Day 1 - Ready to Start **302**
 Workshop 307
 Book Recommendations 309
 Quiz 311
Chapter 22: Having a Sherpa Program **313**

    THE WALKABOUT PROGRAM (TWC) 313
    WORKSHOP 318
    QUIZ 321
CHAPTER 23: THE REST OF THE ORGANIZATION **323**
    WORKSHOP: 328
    BOOKS TO RECOMMEND AND REASON: 329
    QUIZ: 330
CHAPTER 24: OFF YOU GO ! **332**
    HOLD ON TO THE SAFETY BAR 332
SUMMARY AND WHAT IS NEXT **334**
    WHAT'S NEXT: 335
GLOSSARY OF TERMS AND ACRONYMS **336**
SE WORKLIFE - MY JOURNEY **343**
DISCLAIMERS **344**
    LEGAL NOTICE: 344
    DISCLAIMER NOTICE: 344
ACKNOWLEDGEMENTS **345**
SE WORKLIFE **348**
    A JOURNEY THROUGH TECH LEADERSHIP 348
    OVERVIEW: 348
    WHY YOU SHOULD READ THIS BOOK: (REVIEWERS INSIGHT) 348
INTRODUCTIONS **350**
CHAPTER 1: MODEL HOMES **351**
    LESSONS LEARNED: MODEL HOMES 357
    APPLYING LESSONS TO MODERN BUSINESS CULTURE 357
    WORKSHOP TOPIC: BUILDING STRONG TEAMS 359
CHAPTER 2: CRAZY BOBS **362**
    CRAZY BOB'S COOKIE STORE: LEARNING THE BASICS 362
    STARTING CRAZY BOB'S COOKIE STORE 362
    THE BEST LEARNING EXPERIENCE 363
    DEALING WITH LOCAL POLITICS 363
    TRAINING AND OPERATIONS 364
    FACING ENVIRONMENTAL CHALLENGES 364
    LESSONS LEARNED: CRAZY BOB'S COOKIE STORE 365
    WORKSHOP TOPIC: NAVIGATING LOCAL POLITICS AND REGULATIONS 368
CHAPTER 3: CSR **371**
    STARTING THE CORPORATE JOURNEY 371
    STARTING AT CSR 371
    CUSTOMER RELATIONSHIPS AND PRODUCT KNOWLEDGE 371
    THE VALUE OF MENTORSHIP 372
    NAVIGATING CORPORATE POLITICS 372
    THE POWER OF PERSISTENCE 372
    BALANCING TERRITORIES 372

- Adapting to Different Markets 373
- Technical Passion and Process Improvement 373
- Lessons Learned: CSR 375
- Workshop Topic: Building Strong Customer Relationships 377

CHAPTER 4: MOORE **380**
- Moore Business Forms: 380
- Moore Business Forms: Expanding Horizons 380
- Production on Demand 382
- From Print to Digital 383
- Lessons Learned: Moore Business Forms 387
- Workshop Topic: Handling Difficult Situations and Objection Handling 389

CHAPTER 5: JETFORM **392**
- The Transition to Technical Sales 392
- **Jetform: The Transition to Technical Sales** 392
- Lessons Learned: Jetform 395
- Compensation Models 396
- The SE and AE Working Relationship 398
- Another Great Working Relationship 400
- Lessons Learned: Jetform 412
- Corporate Confidential: Why You Should Read It! 416
- Workshop Topic: Mastering Negotiations and Solution Selling .. 419

CHAPTER 6: ADOBE **422**
- Navigating Corporate Culture & Innovation 422
- Fortunate Beginnings and Uncertain Mergers 422
- Tech Insights: Measuring What Matters for the SE Community .. 425
- Macromedia Acquisition Impacts 426
- Sometimes Things Are Out of Your Control 427
- Lessons Learned 428
- **Applying Lessons to Modern Business Culture** 430
- Workshop: How to Measure Value in Sales Engineering 431

CHAPTER 7: INVOLVER **434**
- Embracing the Startup Mindset 434
- Lessons Learned 436

CHAPTER 8 : ORACLE **438**
- Merging Ambitions and Cultivating Change 438
- Lessons Learned 440
- Lessons Learned: Oracle 444
- Workshop Title: Navigating Mergers and Acquisitions 446

CHAPTER 9: ELASTIC SEARCH **456**
- Embracing Open Source 456

CHAPTER 10 SNOWFLAKE **462**
- Embracing Challenges and Building a Future 462

LESSONS LEARNED 467
WORKSHOP: BUILDING RELATIONSHIPS IN A REMOTE WORLD 469
PERSONAL NOTE: 474
CONCLUSION: LESSONS LEARNED FROM MY JOURNEY 474
INTRODUCTION 474
THE IMPORTANCE OF FAMILY 475
CUSTOMER-CENTRIC APPROACH 475
VALUING EMPLOYEES 477
EFFECTIVE LEADERSHIP 477
THE IMPACT OF PROFESSIONAL RELATIONSHIPS 478
MANAGING POST-IPO CHALLENGES 479
APPLYING LESSONS TO MODERN BUSINESS CULTURE 479
FINAL THOUGHTS 481
CONNECT AND CONTINUE THE JOURNEY 481
IF YOU NEED HELP, GIVE ME A CALL – I CAN HELP 483
RECOMMENDED READING LIST 485

Book Review: (External Reviewer)

SE Worklife: How to Become a Sales Engineer

Rating: ★★★★★ (5/5)

"SE Worklife: How to Become a Sales Engineer" by Kevin Kunz offers an unparalleled deep dive into the world of sales engineering. With over three decades of industry experience, Kunz brings a wealth of knowledge, practical advice, and personal anecdotes that make this book an essential read for anyone interested in this dynamic and rewarding career.

Comprehensive and Insightful

One of the book's standout features is its comprehensiveness. Kunz covers every aspect of becoming and thriving as a sales engineer, from the initial job search and interview process to the intricacies of day-to-day responsibilities and long-term career development. The detailed onboarding checklists, robust glossary of terms and acronyms, and practical tips on navigating corporate structures provide readers with the tools they need to hit the ground running.

Real-World Application

What sets this book apart from other career guides is its focus on real-world application. Kunz doesn't just tell you what skills you need; he shows you how to develop them. The inclusion of innovative programs like the Sherpa and Walkabout programs highlights the importance of mentorship and continuous learning. Readers will appreciate the step-by-step approach to mastering essential sales techniques such as storytelling, objection handling, and deal qualification.

Engaging and Relatable

Kunz's writing style is engaging and relatable, making complex concepts easy to understand. The book is peppered with personal stories and humor, which keep the reader entertained while driving home important points. His candid discussion of successes and failures provides a realistic view of what it takes to succeed in sales engineering.

Valuable for All Career Stages

Whether you're a recent graduate exploring career options, a seasoned professional looking to transition into sales engineering, or an experienced SE seeking to advance your career, this book has something for you. Kunz's insights into compensation negotiation, career progression, and the transition from technical roles to leadership positions are invaluable.

Practical Tools and Resources

The book is packed with practical tools and resources, including workshop exercises, quizzes, and self-assessment tools that reinforce learning and help readers track their progress. The suggested reading list and additional resources provide further opportunities for professional development.

A Must-Read for Aspiring and Current Sales Engineers

"SE Worklife: How to Become a Sales Engineer" is more than just a guide; it's a roadmap to a successful and fulfilling career in sales engineering. Kunz's expertise and passion for the field shine through on every page, making this book a must-read for anyone serious about excelling in this profession. It's not just about learning the ropes; it's about mastering the craft and becoming a standout sales engineer in today's competitive market.

In summary, "SE Worklife: How to Become a Sales Engineer" is a definitive guide that combines in-depth knowledge with practical advice, making it an indispensable resource for both aspiring and current sales engineers. Highly recommended!

Acknowledgements

I must start by acknowledging Anne Kunz for putting up with my workaholic drive and its impact on our family. She has always been by my side when I needed her the most, and I want to thank her for convincing me to retire early, take my 30 years of experience, and do something meaningful with it. Not to mention, having three amazing children early in our journey provided me with real-world experience in applying family management skills to everyday work. Exceptional leaders often have a supportive family behind them, serving as the proving grounds for leadership. I thank Lauren, Brian, and Heather, my three kids, for making my life and career journey as exciting as it has been so far. I am so proud of each of them for continuing in their parent's footsteps: Lauren leading a team of pre-sales engineers at Veeva Software, Brian coding solutions for a consulting organization, and Heather starting her career as a human resources lead for a software startup. Great job to all of you!

A huge thank you to those individuals who took a risk on me and made a huge difference in my career as leaders: Seth Lewis at CSR; Dan Shea, Warren Lederer, Steve Corwin, Steve Zimmerman, and Tracey Lyons at Moore Business Forms; Rick Allen, Tony Bishop, and John Hogerland at JetForm; David Antila, Don Beck, Stacey

Box, Johne Brennan, Gloria Chen, Bill Hippenmeyer, John Hogerland, Keith Johnson, Nicole Kealey, Thomas Loane, Tracey McDonald, Josee Murray, Karen Richter, Hugh Shannon, Steve Trombetta, Kumar Vora, and Donna Zontos at Adobe; Don Beck at Involver; Tanya Bragin, Anne Krechmer, Steve Mayzak, and Ryan McGinty at Elastic; and Brian Daniels, Michael Keaveney, and John Sapone at Snowflake. To keep the book under eighty thousand words, I only selected those in leadership circles. Many more people have influenced my career direction and have been left off this list. The key takeaway is that your village will become larger over time, and you will quickly discover who is there to help you and who is there to help themselves. As Yoda wisely said, "Truly wonderful, the mind of a child is." This sentiment extends to all those who have guided and nurtured my growth.

To my review team, who inspired me to start this book series and have painstakingly put in the work reviewing, adding, and editing this content. You, the readers, all benefit from each of these leaders' experience, and when you combine this team's talent, you are looking at over 274 years of combined experience. Don't worry; I have a few 25-year-olds in the mix to keep it relevant. Thanks, Jason Barnett, Anne Kunz, Andrea Middleton, Greg Robinson, Tracey Sacht, Bill Van Hout, Neal Wadhwani, and others. You are all remarkable leaders in your roles, and I am deeply humbled by your support in this effort.

As you will see from my career journey section, my father and sister had a huge impact not just on my life but on how I accelerated my career. The understanding that the people who work for an organization are far more valuable than the executives is a fundamental principle my father lived by. Take the time to understand what each person works for and how you can help them get there as a leader. Also, understand that hard times will cycle, and you may need to make tough choices by letting people go for the business's survival. But don't stop there; use your network to find those people jobs. In my father's business, he would find jobs for people if he had to reduce work, and I followed this same approach during my Adobe career. Thanks, Dad and Sister, for being there when it counted the most. As Steve Jobs once said, "The people who are crazy enough to think they can change the world are the ones who do." This book is for those who dare to think differently and act boldly.

Unlock Your Future in Sales Engineering

Embark on a transformative journey with "SE Worklife: How to Become a Sales Engineer." This comprehensive guide provides aspiring and experienced sales engineers with the tools, techniques, and insights needed to excel in one of the most dynamic careers in tech.

In this book, you will discover:

- **Proven Strategies for Success:** From understanding the core responsibilities of a sales engineer to mastering advanced sales techniques, this book covers it all. Learn how to navigate compensation negotiations, develop critical skills, and become a trusted advisor to your customers.
- **Real-World Insights:** Benefit from the author's 30+ years of industry experience and candid advice. Explore detailed case studies, practical examples, and personal anecdotes that reveal the unfiltered realities of a sales engineering career.
- **Step-by-Step Onboarding:** Get ready for your new role with comprehensive onboarding checklists, essential HR guidelines, and tips for setting up your communication tools and profiles.
- **Innovative Programs:** Discover the value of the Sherpa and Walkabout programs, designed to enhance your skills through mentorship and real-world shadowing experiences.
- **Interactive Learning:** Engage in workshops, quizzes, and self-assessment tools to reinforce your learning and track your progress.
- **Future Growth:** Plan your career path with guidance on transitioning from sales engineering to leadership, balancing

work and personal life, and continuously developing your professional network.

Whether you're just starting out or looking to advance your career, "SE Worklife: How to Become a Sales Engineer" is your ultimate resource for achieving success and making a lasting impact in the tech industry. Get ready to embrace the challenges, celebrate the victories, and become a standout sales engineer in today's competitive market.

Unlock your potential and start your journey today with "SE Worklife: How to Become a Sales Engineer." Your future in sales engineering awaits!

Introduction:

Embark on Your Journey to Sales Engineering Excellence

Welcome to "SE Worklife: How to Become a Sales Engineer." You're about to embark on an enlightening and transformative journey that will equip you with the knowledge, skills, and insights necessary to excel in the dynamic world of sales engineering. This book is not just a manual; it's a comprehensive guide designed to navigate you through the multifaceted landscape of this crucial profession. Whether you're a novice stepping into the field for the first time or a seasoned professional looking to refine your craft, this book has something valuable for you.

This is my "I just got an ice-cream" headshot! - Ocean City, NJ Boardwalk

This book will follow a step-by-step process to help you start and further your career in the sales engineering world. You will find that you can enter this career at various technical skill levels, from almost no technical skills to highly technical, provided you have the charisma, drive, and interpersonal capability to tell great stories. The one goal is to become that trusted advisor for your customer and identify the critical business and technical issues you can solve.

Why I Am Writing This Series

I am writing a series of books focused on SE Worklife, starting with the first of the series, "My Journey - Lessons Learned," – which you will find at the back of the book as part of this purchase, followed by "How to Become a Sales Engineer," then "SE Worklife - Living the Job," and lastly, "SE Worklife - Leadership vs. Management." No other books on the market today offer the combined experience of my thirty years and the years contributed by this team, ranging from legacy on-prem software solutions to current consumption-based solutions. You will read the unfiltered, pure, and honest direction on the ins and outs of this career. I will not ask for forgiveness for how blunt I will be, and there will be no sugar-coating of successes and failures.

The first book, "SE Worklife - My Journey," is about my career, including all the successes and lessons learned over this thirty-year journey. The second book, "SE Worklife - How to Become a Sales Engineer," will take you on a backstage tour of how organizations hire, what they look for, and how they measure one candidate versus another. I will help you understand the job, how to get the job, and the onboarding experiences. The third book, "SE Worklife - The Day in the Life of a Sales Engineer," will cover several key elements to become a world-class Sales Engineer, Solution Architect, and Solution Consultant. We will work through understanding where you want to be in five years, both professionally and personally. We will cover all the promotional levels with real examples and guides to play the career chess game and move up that ladder. You will learn how to mutually work with your sales leaders, with roles, rules, and responsibilities outlined for success. We will workshop important sales tools and skills tailored for the position: Brainstorming; DISC profiling; Storytelling; Lead SE Training; Negotiation; Objection Handling; and how not to do Proof of Concepts.

The last book, "SE Worklife - Leadership vs. Management," will pull all this together and show how to migrate your career to leadership, not just management. I have had the honor of developing amazing leaders throughout my career and have outlined the steps necessary to help you get there. Once there, you will need to know how to balance your first-line relationships and manage them throughout the organization. The chess game just became more complicated and more political. We will cover how to hire, manage, and place people on plans and let people go. We will have an entire section on the delta between IPO and Corporate America and how to handle the complex transition from a private to a public company. We will discuss how to measure success or failure through the lead lifecycle and how to report data and make sense of that reporting. I am most excited about this book, as we will go deep into the secret backstage of business, revealing how ugly this beast can be. As Elon Musk says, "When something is important enough, you do it even if the odds are not in your favor." This book series is for those willing to navigate the challenges and triumphs of a sales engineering career.

Why This Book Matters

In today's rapidly evolving tech industry, the role of a sales engineer (SE) is more vital than ever. The complexity of modern technology, coupled with the fierce competition within the data cloud/platform market, demands sales engineers who are not only technically proficient but also skilled in the art of selling. The days of relying solely on product education are over. Now, you must sell alongside account executives, using a blend of technical knowledge and strategic sales techniques to drive growth and success.

This book aims to bridge the gap between technical prowess and sales acumen. We'll delve into essential concepts such as storytelling in presentations, objection handling, give-gets, challenger selling, deal qualification, and proper Discovery. These are not merely buzzwords but critical skills that will set you apart in a crowded marketplace.

What You Will Learn

Throughout the chapters, you'll find a blend of theoretical insights, practical advice, and real-world anecdotes that bring the content to life. You'll explore:

- **Compensation Strategies**: Understand the nuances of compensation matrices, negotiation techniques, and the importance of on-target earnings. Learn how to maximize your earning potential and make informed decisions about your career.
- **Day 1 Essentials**: From writing your bio for your boss to setting up email filters and communication tools, we'll guide you through the crucial steps to ensure your first days are smooth and productive.
- **The Sherpa Program**: Discover the value of mentorship and shadowing programs. Learn from the best in the field and see firsthand what excellence looks like in sales engineering.
- **Training and Professional Development**: Engage with training organizations, professional services, and support teams to enhance your skills and build valuable relationships.
- **Consumption Economics**: Gain insights into the consumption-based model and how it impacts your role and strategies in presales.

Get Ready for the Ride

As you turn each page, you'll find detailed checklists, interactive workshops, quizzes, and recommended readings designed to deepen your understanding and reinforce key concepts. The hands-on activities will ensure that you don't just read about best practices—you'll actively engage with them.

This book is more than just a guide; it's a call to action. Embrace the challenges, learn from your failures, and celebrate your successes. By the end of this journey, you will be equipped not only to meet the demands of today's sales engineering roles but to exceed them.

A Final Thought

In the words of Yoda from Star Wars, "Do or do not, there is no try." This book will arm you with the tools to "do" and to do it exceptionally well. So, buckle up, hold on to the safety bar, and get ready for an exciting ride into the world of sales engineering. Your journey to becoming an exceptional sales engineer starts now. Welcome aboard!

Enjoy the journey and let the learning begin!

Part 1: What is the Job

Chapter 1: SEAC (S.E.A.C.) Worklife

The Best Job Ever

"In a world where technology changes by the minute, the role of a Sales Engineer is to ensure the bridge between innovation and practical application remains strong and effective." – Steve Jobs

Introduction

Welcome to the next chapter in your career. Before we get started, strap yourself in and prepare for your life's best ride. I have over 30 years of experience in this field, starting as a salesperson, becoming a top-performing pre-sales engineer, and rounding out my career in several leadership roles. Here is my LinkedIn profile and my website for podcasts, tools, and access to information you will not find anywhere else:

- LinkedIn Profile https://www.linkedin.com/in/kevinrkunz/
- SE Worklife Website (www.seworklife.com)

To give you a preview of the following few chapters:

- What is the Role?
- What Skills do I Need?
- Why Should I Consider this Role?
- Typical Day in the Life (Week)
- How Do I Make Money?
- Job Searching
- Interviewing
- Negotiating
- Onboarding 30/60/90
- Best Practices

What is the Role?

Okay, here we go! I am confused a little; what is this role about, what do you do, and why does this role exist? Can you help me with all the various titles in this career? Let's start with a fundamental understanding of a "presales engineer." For now, we will use SE as a Sales Engineer, and you will see how this gets muddy later in the book. A presales engineer (SE) is a special kind of individual who has a unique combination of sales, technology, and the ability to lay a customer on a couch, ask them about their mother and get them to buy stuff.

The primary function of a successful SE is to help the sales team convince the customer that the vendor's technology will solve the customer's issues and offer value beyond their competitors. I use the term "issues" lightly, as this can range from specific technical issues to the other side in solving business-related problems. A masterful SE turns this into an art form, and the rush you get from a technical win becomes a bit addicting.

If you are a significant introvert, have minimal technical skills, are not passionate about solving business problems, and are not excited by winning, guess what? This job is not for you! Don't be too disheartened; you could always go into marketing or potentially consulting. I have seen several incredible transformations with people moving from sales, marketing, and consulting into this presales role. Aren't you glad I had this as one of my first paragraphs?

You may be asking, do I have enough sales or technology experience to be a good fit for this role? The reality is that it "depends," but it's okay if you do not have a solid technical background for certain types of point solutions. In many cases, this can be an advantage as it allows you to learn more about technology. The hardest thing to find is technical people with great charisma, presentation ability, appearance, and genuine curiosity.

Depending on the sales motion, many early-career individual contributors may not have a solid technical background but bring strong interpersonal skills and see technology as a hobby. Hiring managers may also forgive your technical experience levels if you have industry domain experience. Remember, the goal here is to build relationships with prospects. If you can relate to their industry challenges, your story will be more convincing since you have lived it.

Personal Journey

When I first started in this role, I was a salesperson with a tenured computer passion and a motivation to solve problems through automation. You can read a free copy of "SE Worklife in the back of this book. In 1993, the dot com world created a new breed of sales and sales support. Remember that most of the automation back then came from mainframe solutions. I know that at the fourth basement level inside the Prudential Insurances building on Washington Street, Newark, NJ, they are still running a series of mainframe applications called "Profs," one of the first email solutions. They have a legacy application that receives an automated email queue control to kick it off.

Understand that the first packaged software on-prem solutions were costly and required teams of people to install. To sell the technology, you need to know more than just the FAB's (Features, Advantages, and Benefits). You had to know so much more about the implementation details. What kind of operating system, any load balancers, and what version of WebLogic 3.01 A or B? If it's B, we don't support that solution. You had to involve database admins, network admins, desktop teams, infrastructure, building operations, and in some cases, the building power providers.

I remember showing up to do a conference room pilot, and the Database admin changed all our privileges just because he woke up on the wrong side of the bed and was not notified of our visit. So be lucky you are not in the 90s.

Evolution of Roles

The early pre-sales profiles were very technical and would have been called architects in the day. We had to know the implementation requirements to ensure we could sell the technology to the customer. However, one of the challenges for many technical people was not to confuse selling with implementation details. Fast forward to 2018, and I noticed several parallels to the 90s with open-source companies like Elasticsearch, MongoDB, and Redhat. We sold to the technical teams, bottom-up, and to have credentials, you had to know as much or more than the person on the other side of the table. We called our new architects "Solution Architects." After 20 years, you would think marketing would have fancy branding. Understand the customer technical staff had veto power, but no to limited decision power. But the technical team did influence the business.

Market Maturity and Skill Requirements

As mentioned above, we have just started to look at a few and where the role mix requirements are. Interestingly, it has been my experience that even a well-matured IPO and post-IPO will have a wide skill requirement related to its market penetration. As you can see on this chart below, typically, North America matures quicker, EMEA next, Asia Pac, and LATAM or South America. This is especially important if you read this book from a territory outside North America. You want to remember that your skill set matches where the company is today and where it is headed. You can position yourself well in EMEA and Asia Pac for leadership roles.

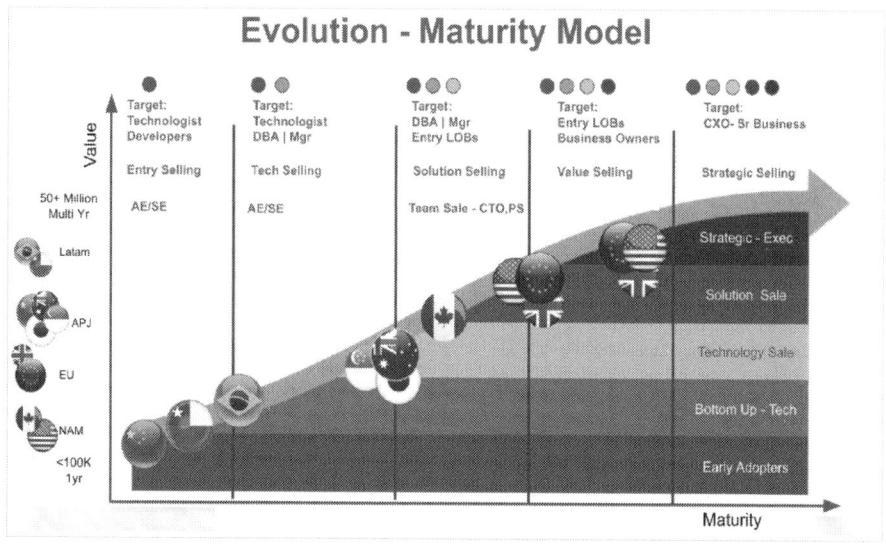

Early adopters will typically target technologists and developers. You will find that the sales teams will only need Account Executive (AE) and SE relationships. You will need several proof offerings and heavy technical relationship lifting. As you can see on the Maturity curve, a very early startup will typically be to the far left. As you move across the curve, the EU and the US have moved to the solution sale in this example. As a result, we have broken out into verticalization, and product packaging focused on solving the customer's challenges. At this stage, the sales motion shifted from entry selling to Solution Selling to Value Selling and finally to Strategic Executive-level Selling. Keep this chart handy; I will include the JPEG since you might want to use it in an interview or pre-interview questioning the company where they think they are on this curve. It will impress them that you will know and appreciate the bigger global picture.

Chapter 2: Job Titles and Descriptions

Skills Tech / Business	Coder	Product Manager	Enterprise Architect	Solution Architect	Sales Engineer	Sales consultant	Technical Specialist	Evangelist	Business Analyst	Consultant	CSM	Tech Account Manager	Inside Sales	Account Executive
90/10	X	X	X	X										
80/20	X	X	X	X	X	X	X	X	X	X				
70/30	X	X	X	X	X	X	X	X	X					
60/40					X	X		X	X	X	X	X		
40/60					X	X			X	X	X	X	X	
20/80									X	X	X	X	X	X
10/90										X	X	X	X	X

Skills Tech / Business	Coder	Product Manager	Enterprise Architect	Solution Architect	Sales Engineer	Sales consultant	Technical Specialist	Evangelist	Business Analyst	Consultant	CSM	Tech Account Manager	Inside Sales	Account Executive
Intravert	X	X												
Love Code	X	X												
Love learning	X	X							X	X				
Efficienty	X	X	X						X	X				
Organized	X	X	X	X					X	X	X			
Routine	X	X	X	X	X	X	X		X	X	X			
Chess Player		X	X	X	X	X	X	X	X	X	X	X	X	X
Extravert			X	X	X	X	X	X	X	X	X	X	X	X
Therapyst				X	X	X	X	X	X	X	X	X	X	X
Competitive					X	X	X	X	X	X	X	X	X	X
Dominate							X	X	X	X	X	X	X	X
Stong Ego							X	X	X	X	X	X	X	X

Let's move into some definitions you should be familiar with as you move through the book. First, we will start with the job titles and descriptions you will find there.

Systems Architect | Enterprise Architect | Solution Architect | Sales Engineer | Sales Consultant | Technical Specialist | Evangelist | Consultant | Inside Sales | Account Executive | Technical Account Manager | Business Analyst | Customer Success Management

Systems Architect

A systems architect is an information and communications technology professional who defines the architecture of a computerized system to fulfill certain requirements. This includes a breakdown of the system into components, the component interactions and interfaces, and the technologies and resources used in its design and implementation. The systems architect's work should seek to avoid implementation issues and readily permit unanticipated extensions/modifications in future stages. Typically, a very senior technologist with substantial but general knowledge of hardware, software, and similar (user) systems takes on this role.

By the way, you can always tell a systems architect because they will have a ton of stickers plastered all over their laptop and probably be very calm. However, they will be very sure of themselves, so

D - dominant High,

I - Influential Low - they will think they are more influential than they are.

S - Steady - Low. They will not be patient when they want something.

C-compliant, Very High complaint - focused on analytics, conscientious, and cautious.

I know I did a quick DISC profile on the architect; you might want to know what DISC is - I have a workshop and podcast for this - here is a taste.

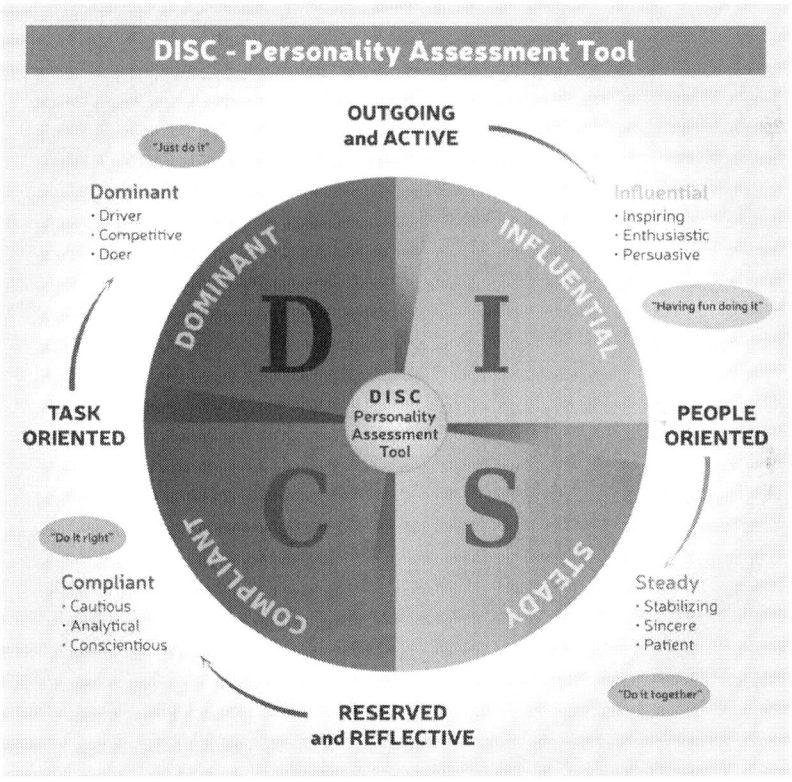

Solution Architect / Engineer

Scaled Agile (2020) describes a Solution Architect/Engineer as responsible for defining and communicating a shared technical and architectural vision across a "Solution Train" to ensure the system under development is fit for its intended purpose. According to Gartner (2013), a solution architecture (SA) is an architectural description of a specific solution, combining guidance from different enterprise architecture viewpoints (business, information, and technical), as well as from the enterprise solution architecture (ESA).

A typical property of Solution Architecture, in contrast to other flavors of Enterprise Architecture, is that it often seeks to define a solution within the context of a project or initiative. This close association with actual projects and initiatives means that solution architecture is the means to execute or realize a technology strategy. According to Forrester Research, Solution Architecture is one of the key components by which Enterprise Architecture delivers value to the organization. It entails artifacts such as; solution business context, solution vision and requirements, solution options (e.g., through RFIs, RFPs, or prototype development), and an agreed optimal solution with build and implementation plans ("road-map").

Here is an Elastic Search Job Description –

Solution Architect

Location: [Insert Location]

Company Overview: Elasticsearch, part of the Elastic Stack, is the most popular enterprise search engine and offers a robust, scalable solution for real-time search and analytics. Our mission is to enable the world's data to solve the world's problems. At Elasticsearch, you will work with a dynamic team dedicated to building cutting-edge technology that is transforming industries.

Position Overview: We are seeking a Solution Architect who will be a key technical leader responsible for driving the adoption and integration of Elasticsearch products within customer environments. The ideal candidate will have a strong technical background combined with excellent communication and problem-solving skills. You will work closely with customers to understand their requirements, design tailored solutions, and ensure successful implementation and adoption of our products.

Key Responsibilities:

- **Customer Engagement:** Partner with customers to understand their business needs and technical requirements, and design solutions leveraging Elasticsearch products.
- **Technical Leadership:** Provide architectural guidance and best practices for deploying, managing, and scaling Elasticsearch clusters.
- **Solution Design:** Develop comprehensive solution architectures that address customer needs and integrate with their existing systems.
- **Implementation Support:** Assist customers with the installation, configuration, and optimization of Elasticsearch solutions.
- **Training and Enablement:** Conduct workshops, webinars, and training sessions to educate customers on Elasticsearch capabilities and best practices.
- **Collaboration:** Work closely with sales, product management, and engineering teams to ensure customer

success and feedback incorporation into product development.
- **Documentation:** Create and maintain detailed documentation on solution designs, implementation steps, and best practices.
- **Technical Pre-sales:** Support the sales team with technical presentations, product demonstrations, and proof-of-concept engagements.
- **Community Engagement:** Participate in community events, conferences, and meetups to represent Elasticsearch and share knowledge with the broader community.

Qualifications:

- **Experience:** 5+ years of experience in a technical role such as Solution Architect, Systems Engineer, or similar, preferably in a customer-facing capacity.
- **Technical Expertise:** Proficiency with Elasticsearch, the Elastic Stack (Kibana, Beats, Logstash), and related technologies.
- **Programming Skills:** Strong coding skills in languages such as Java, Python, or similar.
- **Cloud Experience:** Experience with cloud platforms (AWS, Azure, GCP) and containerization (Docker, Kubernetes).
- **Architectural Knowledge:** Deep understanding of distributed systems, data architectures, and real-time analytics.
- **Problem-solving:** Excellent analytical and problem-solving skills with a focus on delivering customer-centric solutions.
- **Communication:** Strong verbal and written communication skills, with the ability to articulate complex technical concepts to technical and non-technical audiences.
- **Certifications:** Relevant industry certifications (e.g., AWS Certified Solutions Architect, Microsoft Certified: Azure Solutions Architect Expert) are a plus.
- **Education:** Bachelor's degree in Computer Science, Engineering, or a related field; advanced degree preferred.

Preferred Skills:

- Experience with DevOps practices and tools.
- Knowledge of security best practices for data systems.
- Familiarity with industry verticals such as healthcare, finance, retail, and government.

Why Elasticsearch?

- Work with innovative technology and a passionate team dedicated to solving real-world problems.
- Opportunity to make a significant impact on the adoption and success of Elasticsearch products.
- Competitive compensation and benefits package.
- Continuous learning and professional development opportunities.

How to Apply: Interested candidates should submit their resume and a cover letter outlining their qualifications and interest in the role to [insert application link or email]

The DISC on a Solution Architect:

- **D - Dominant**: Medium, they need to provide a credible relationship with the customer technical side.
- **I - Influential**: Higher, as they are working for a vendor and will have a business mindset; they tend to be good influencers at the customer.
- **S - Steady**: High. This is their primary value; they are dependable and capable of working the time necessary to get it right.
- **C - Compliant**: Medium, they are not product managers who live to a code; we are still selling and need to be flexible in our approach - focused on analytics, conscientious, and cautious.

My first introduction to a Solution Architect role was at Oracle and then Elasticsearch. Now you will find some overlaps in these positions; in many cases, the dividing line is technical versus business problem-solving. You will see this broken down as percentages - a

Solution Architect will be 90/10 - 80% Tech / 20% Business, and an Enterprise Architect - 90% Tech / 10% Business. Interestingly, early pre-sales engineers had to have a good amount of architecture knowledge, as mentioned. Over time, the traditional pre-sales position morphed into two roles, and soon I will show how it's about to morph again with major consumption sales impacting requirements.

Solution Consultant

The purpose of the job is to help potential customers understand, compare, and contrast the solutions that are available for purchase (the pre-sales role); to troubleshoot problems with their implementations—that is, to help ensure that the solutions work successfully once a purchase is made (the post-sales role); and to maximize sales for the sales engineer's employer by providing help to customers.

Solution Consultants are very much like the Solution Architect with one caveat: the architect focuses on the implementation plumbing, whereas the solution consultant will look at the end-to-end impacts across all implementation levels. These individuals are best for large complex technologies like ServiceNow, Workday, SAP, EMC, and Oracle solutions. If you are in the consulting business today and want to open opportunities in this career track, the solution consultant is a fantastic area to migrate to. Due to their business aptitude and logistical mind, I have successfully hired several consultants to convert them into solution consultants.

The DISC on Presales - Solution Consultant:

- **D - Dominant**: Medium, personality is one of relationship building; they are welcoming and not off-putting with their presence. They are coaches, mentors, and technical advisors.
- **I - Influential**: Medium, in the advisor role, they need to be good influencers, not overbearing but more credible. It would be best if you stood tall in your position with the grace of accepting you may not have all the answers.
- **S - Steady**: High. No doubt here, you need to be reliable, steady, and trustworthy in your relationship with the external customer and your internal customer/partner, the account executive.
- **C - Compliant**: High. We are in sales, so you need to understand not to confuse selling with implementation details. The implementation is with professional services. Though you need to ensure you are not lying. It's better to say sorry, I don't know, versus making untruthful statements. The solution consultant has the skills related to a project manager, who has the confidence and credentials to back up what they are reviewing for the entire business.

Sales Engineer / Consultant

Sales engineering is a sales and engineering hybrid in industrial and commercial markets. An Engineering degree is not mandatory for a sales engineer; as long as they have sales knowledge and sufficient technical knowledge of the service or product, they are called a sales engineer. Buying decisions in these markets are based more on technical information and rational analysis and less on style, fashion, or impulse. Therefore, selling in these markets cannot depend on consumer-type sales methods alone, and instead, it relies heavily on technical information and problem-solving to convince buyers that they should spend money on the seller's products or services, in order to meet a business need (that is, to satisfy a business case).

Sales Engineers are thus both "a salesperson that understands and can apply engineering" and "an engineer that understands how to sell engineered systems". They thus not only sell but also provide advice and support. They provide this service to various internal or external customers, and they may work for a manufacturer (servicing its industrial-account/business-to-business customers), for a distributor (which in turn services the industrial-account/business-to-business customers), or for a third party such as an engineering consultancy or a systems integrator.

Sales Engineers are a critical sales team member in many companies and industries around the world. They are more than just technical experts in their respective industries. Highly successful sales engineers must build and maintain parallel expertise in "soft skill" disciplines such as business acumen, presentation skills, building customer relationships, developing an engagement strategy, and having a thorough understanding of the targeted industry. Many companies have difficulty finding people who possess these qualities plus have extensive technical knowledge.

I see the sales engineer as closer to the 60/40 split between technical and sales business mindset. A sales consultant works very well for those technologies that lend themselves to more lines of business applications, such as Service Now, Workday, and even desktop software like Adobe Creative Suite and Microsoft Office. In my early years, I considered my work at JetForm as this type of role. I sold point solutions such as electronic forms, document management solutions, workflows, and security solutions. When I was managing solution architects at Elastic, they were more 80/20 mix.

Interestingly, as we migrated past the IPO and started to navigate closer to those who held the money, we needed to present business solutions. The Solution Architect at Elastic was morphing into a sales engineer/consulting role as the company migrated to the line of business sale. I reference this position as a split between sales 'Engineering and Consultant' because this role can take on a consulting mindset to help the customer understand the implementation impacts. This was also true for Snowflake, which started as a technical sell and is now post-IPO migrating to business verticalization.

You can see the differences between these job descriptions – if you notice no need for certifications, like you see in the Elastic Search requirements –

Presales Engineer – Adobe Experience Manager (AEM) and Workfront

Location: [Insert Location]

Company Overview: Adobe is a leader in digital media and digital marketing solutions. Our creative, marketing, and document solutions empower everyone – from emerging artists to global brands – to bring digital creations to life and deliver immersive, compelling experiences to the right people at the right moment. Adobe Experience Manager (AEM) and Workfront are integral parts of our mission to revolutionize how businesses manage content and collaborate on work.

Position Overview: We are seeking a highly skilled and motivated Presales Engineer with expertise in Adobe Experience Manager (AEM) and Workfront. In this role, you will partner with our sales team to understand customer needs, provide technical expertise, and deliver compelling product demonstrations that showcase the value of Adobe solutions. You will play a critical role in driving customer adoption and satisfaction by demonstrating how our technologies can solve complex business challenges.

Key Responsibilities:

- **Customer Engagement:** Collaborate with the sales team to understand customer requirements, develop tailored solutions, and present Adobe's AEM and Workfront capabilities effectively.
- **Product Demonstrations:** Conduct in-depth product demonstrations that highlight the unique value propositions of AEM and Workfront, addressing customer pain points and business objectives.
- **Technical Expertise:** Provide deep technical knowledge of AEM and Workfront, including content management, digital asset management, workflow automation, and project management.
- **Solution Design:** Develop comprehensive solution architectures that integrate AEM and Workfront with existing customer systems and workflows.
- **Proof of Concept (PoC):** Lead the development and delivery of PoCs to validate solution designs and demonstrate feasibility to customers.
- **RFP/RFI Responses:** Assist in the preparation of responses to Requests for Proposals (RFPs) and Requests for Information (RFIs) by providing technical content and solution descriptions.
- **Training and Enablement:** Conduct workshops and training sessions for customers and partners to enhance their understanding and usage of AEM and Workfront.

- **Collaboration:** Work closely with product management, engineering, and customer success teams to ensure customer feedback is incorporated into product development and to support successful customer implementations.
- **Technical Documentation:** Create and maintain technical documentation, including solution designs, integration guides, and best practices.

Qualifications:

- **Experience:** 5+ years of experience in a presales, solutions consulting, or technical sales role, with a focus on enterprise content management and project management solutions.
- **Technical Expertise:** Proficiency with Adobe Experience Manager (AEM) and Workfront, including hands-on experience with implementations and integrations.
- **Programming Skills:** Familiarity with programming languages and web technologies such as Java, JavaScript, HTML, and RESTful APIs.
- **Cloud Platforms:** Experience with cloud platforms (AWS, Azure, GCP) and understanding of SaaS and PaaS models.
- **Solution Architecture:** Strong knowledge of solution architecture principles, including the design of scalable and secure systems.
- **Problem-solving:** Excellent analytical and problem-solving skills with the ability to translate customer requirements into effective solutions.
- **Communication:** Strong verbal and written communication skills, with the ability to explain complex technical concepts to both technical and non-technical audiences.
- **Certifications:** Relevant certifications in AEM, Workfront, or cloud platforms are a plus.

- **Education:** Bachelor's degree in Computer Science, Information Systems, or a related field; advanced degree preferred.

Preferred Skills:

- Experience with Agile methodologies and DevOps practices.
- Knowledge of digital marketing and content strategy.
- Familiarity with other Adobe products, such as Adobe Analytics, Adobe Target, and Adobe Campaign.

Why Adobe?

- Work with cutting-edge technologies and a talented team dedicated to creating exceptional digital experiences.
- Opportunity to make a significant impact on the success of Adobe's enterprise solutions.
- Competitive compensation and benefits package.
- Continuous learning and professional development opportunities.

How to Apply: Interested candidates should submit their resume and a cover letter outlining their qualifications and interest in the role to [insert application link or email]

The DISC on a Sales Engineer/Consultant:

- **D - Dominant**: Medium, they need to provide a credible relationship with the customer technical side.
- **I - Influential**: Higher, I see this role as more influential than a solution architect. You are on the edge of a full-time sales rep. This is a good role for those who may not be too technical and have strong interpersonal skills.
- **S - Steady**: High. This is their primary value; they are dependable and capable of working the time necessary to get it right.
- **C - Compliant**: Medium. This is close to a Solution Architect, though with a little grayer in their positioning technology to business owners. At no role level are we going to lie to a customer? We cannot get stuck in the implementation details at this role level and pivot to business value.

Technical Specialist

The technical specialist is an individual who is a master Jedi; yes, get used to Star Wars and Star Trek references; you are in the technology industry. Check out my friend Marcel: [LinkedIn Profile](https://www.linkedin.com/in/marcelboucher/). https://www.linkedin.com/in/marcelboucher/ Please do, since I want him to get piles of InMail - sorry, Marcel, Kunz lives on. Marcel and I both worked at Adobe, and he has had the entire technical career path from presales to technical specialists to evangelists to product manager. He was our go-to person for Lifecycle enterprise at Adobe. He had 301 knowledge and a direct line to product management. He was also our voice from the field to product marketing and engineering to ensure we didn't build a pet project but instead built products customers wanted. He was our go-to person for doing roadmaps. A note on roadmaps: NEVER have a product manager give a roadmap pitch. They love to talk about futures, and as a pre-salesperson, you never want to extend a sales cycle in the hope that a solution feature will launch on time (LOL). Rarely!

Here is a great job description for Oracle Marketing Cloud Technical Specialist –

Technical Specialist – Oracle Marketing Cloud

Location: [Insert Location]

Company Overview: Oracle is a global leader in cloud solutions, providing a comprehensive and fully integrated stack of cloud applications, platform services, and engineered systems. Oracle Marketing Cloud helps modern marketers optimize their marketing efforts, personalize customer experiences, and drive revenue through innovative and scalable cloud solutions.

Position Overview: We are seeking a skilled and proactive Technical Specialist to join our Oracle Marketing Cloud team. The ideal candidate will possess deep technical knowledge of marketing automation and customer experience solutions and have a strong ability to translate customer requirements into effective and innovative solutions. As a Technical Specialist, you will play a critical role in driving customer success by providing expert technical guidance and support throughout the implementation and integration of Oracle Marketing Cloud solutions.

Key Responsibilities:

- **Customer Engagement:** Collaborate with customers to understand their marketing and business requirements, providing expert technical advice on Oracle Marketing Cloud solutions.
- **Solution Design:** Design and architect Oracle Marketing Cloud solutions that meet customer needs, ensuring scalability, performance, and security.
- **Implementation:** Lead the technical implementation of Oracle Marketing Cloud solutions, including configuration, customization, and integration with other systems.
- **Technical Support:** Provide advanced technical support and troubleshooting assistance to customers during and after implementation.
- **Best Practices:** Develop and promote best practices for using Oracle Marketing Cloud, including the creation of technical documentation, guidelines, and training materials.
- **Innovation:** Stay current with the latest Oracle Marketing Cloud features and technologies, providing

recommendations for leveraging new capabilities to benefit customers.
- **Collaboration:** Work closely with the sales, product management, and engineering teams to ensure the successful delivery of Oracle Marketing Cloud projects.
- **Mentorship:** Mentor and guide junior technical team members to enhance their skills and knowledge of Oracle Marketing Cloud solutions.

Qualifications:

- **Experience:** 5+ years of experience in a technical role involving the implementation and support of marketing automation and customer experience solutions.
- **Technical Expertise:** Deep knowledge of Oracle Marketing Cloud, including Eloqua, Responsys, BlueKai, and other related modules.
- **Programming Skills:** Proficiency in programming languages and technologies such as JavaScript, SQL, REST APIs, and HTML/CSS.
- **Certifications:** Oracle Marketing Cloud certifications are highly desirable.
- **Cloud Platforms:** Experience with cloud computing platforms such as Oracle Cloud, AWS, Azure, or Google Cloud.
- **Solution Architecture:** Strong understanding of solution architecture principles and the ability to design scalable and secure systems.
- **Problem-solving:** Excellent analytical and problem-solving skills with the ability to troubleshoot complex technical issues.

- **Communication:** Strong verbal and written communication skills, with the ability to explain technical concepts to both technical and non-technical audiences.
- **Education:** Bachelor's degree in Computer Science, Information Technology, Marketing, or a related field; advanced degree preferred.

Preferred Skills:

- Experience with Agile methodologies and DevOps practices.
- Knowledge of marketing strategies and best practices.
- Familiarity with integration technologies such as REST, SOAP, and API management.

Why Oracle?

- Work with a leading cloud platform and innovative solutions that are transforming the marketing landscape.
- Opportunity to make a significant impact on the success of Oracle Marketing Cloud customers.
- Competitive compensation and benefits package.
- Continuous learning and professional development opportunities.

How to Apply: Interested candidates should submit their resume and a cover letter outlining their qualifications and interest in the role to [insert application link or email].

The DISC on Specialists:

- **D - Dominant**: Medium is very supportive and knows you will not waste their time when you call them.
- **I - Influential**: High. I would bring in a specialist to help gain access to power as a good Give / Get. Understand

customers don't want to make a bad decision; they want a person to pin the decision on.

- **S - Steady**: High. They are ready for all arrows thrown their way by a customer; too often, a customer sees the meeting as an opportunity to stump the chump. You have to have thick skin in this position. They are reliable; you call them, and it's like calling 911.
- **C - Compliant**: Medium - they are in sales and understand how far to take things. But, they know NEVER to talk about their futures.

Evangelist

A technology evangelist is a person who builds a critical mass of support for a given technology and then establishes it as a technical standard in a market that is subject to network effects. The word evangelism is borrowed from the context of religious evangelism due to the similarity of sharing information about a particular concept with the intention of having others adopt that concept. This is typically accomplished by showcasing the potential uses and benefits of technology to help others understand how they can use it for themselves.

Platform evangelism is one target of technology evangelism, in which the vendor of a two-sided platform attempts to accelerate the production of complementary goods by independent developers (e.g., Facebook encourages developers to create games or develop mobile apps that can enhance users' experiences with Facebook). Professional technology evangelists are often employed by firms seeking to establish their technologies as de facto standards. Their work could also entail the training of personnel, including top managers so that they acquire skills and competencies necessary to adopt new technology or new technological initiative. There are even instances when technology evangelism becomes an aspect of a managerial position.

Open-source evangelists, on the other hand, operate independently. Evangelists also participate in defining open standards. Non-professional technology evangelists may act out of altruism or self-interest (e.g., to gain the benefits of early adoption or network effect).

Evangelism is an exciting concept, and I feel it is closer to product marketing than I would say in the sales team. At Adobe, we had several "Evangelists" who would draw thousands to an auditorium to listen to what they had to say. I remember Ben Forta at one of our user conferences. There was a line of people out the door to get their Ben Forta t-shirts signed by this guy. Oh, and the T-shirt was just a picture of Ben's face. Another outstanding individual was Terry White, who was all about photography and what to do with Photoshop. He also would draw a crowd; now, he has a full-time business as an evangelist for creative tools. Adobe had the best evangelists; the customer base had a religious relationship with the Adobe brand. Oracle also has its series of evangelists, sure the products are significantly different and attract more technical than creative personas. But nevertheless, these people would pack a room and, like Ben, have collateral with their names on it. These folks are technical rockstars in their industry.

Job Title: Photoshop Evangelist

Location: [Insert Location]

Company Overview: Adobe is a global leader in digital media and digital marketing solutions. Our creative, marketing, and document solutions empower everyone—from emerging artists to global brands—to bring digital creations to life and deliver immersive, engaging experiences to their customers. At Adobe, we're passionate about changing the world through digital experiences.

Position Overview: We are seeking an enthusiastic and dynamic Photoshop Evangelist to join our team. The ideal candidate will be a creative professional with deep expertise in Adobe Photoshop and a passion for sharing knowledge and inspiring others. As a Photoshop Evangelist, you will engage with the creative community, demonstrating the power and versatility of Photoshop through various channels and events.

Key Responsibilities:

- **Community Engagement:** Actively engage with the creative community through social media, blogs, forums, and live events to inspire and educate users about Adobe Photoshop.
- **Content Creation:** Develop and deliver high-quality tutorials, webinars, blog posts, and other content that highlights the features and capabilities of Photoshop.
- **Public Speaking:** Represent Adobe at industry conferences, workshops, and meetups, delivering keynote presentations and hands-on sessions to showcase Photoshop's tools and workflows.
- **Customer Advocacy:** Gather feedback from the community and work with product teams to inform the development of new features and improvements.
- **Partnerships:** Collaborate with industry influencers, educational institutions, and creative organizations to promote Adobe Photoshop and build strategic partnerships.
- **Training and Support:** Provide training and support to creative professionals, helping them to fully leverage Photoshop in their workflows.
- **Innovation:** Stay updated with the latest trends in digital art and design, ensuring Adobe remains at the forefront of creativity and innovation.
- **Storytelling:** Share compelling stories and case studies that demonstrate the impact of Photoshop on the creative process.

Qualifications:

- **Experience:** 5+ years of professional experience in graphic design, digital art, photography, or a related creative field.
- **Technical Expertise:** Mastery of Adobe Photoshop, with extensive knowledge of its tools, features, and applications.
- **Communication Skills:** Exceptional verbal and written communication skills with the ability to present complex technical information in a clear and engaging manner.
- **Public Speaking:** Proven experience as a public speaker or presenter, with the ability to captivate and inspire an audience.
- **Content Creation:** Strong portfolio of content creation, including tutorials, articles, videos, and social media engagement.
- **Community Involvement:** Active presence in the creative community with a passion for helping others and sharing knowledge.
- **Problem-solving:** Creative problem-solving skills and the ability to think on your feet.
- **Education:** Bachelor's degree in Graphic Design, Digital Art, Communications, or a related field.

Preferred Skills:

- Experience with live streaming and video content creation.
- Knowledge of other Adobe Creative Cloud tools.
- Familiarity with emerging technologies in digital art and design.

Why Adobe?

- Work with a team of passionate, creative professionals in a dynamic and innovative environment.

- Opportunity to influence the development of industry-leading tools and technologies.
- Engage with a vibrant and diverse community of creative professionals.
- Competitive salary and benefits package.

If you are a Photoshop expert with a passion for creativity and a talent for teaching and inspiring others, we invite you to join our team as an Adobe Photoshop Evangelist. Apply today and help us shape the future of digital creativity!

The DISC on an Evangelist:

- **D - Dominant**: High. They are rock stars; name me one rock star who is not a little ego - right!
- **I - Influential**: High. Yeah, this is the job description - turn nonbelievers into believers.
- **S - Steady**: Medium. I gave them a medium; sometimes, you run across a Prima Donna who has it in their head that they are more critical than the CIO of Citibank.
- **C - Compliant**: HAHAHA, No! They make the rules.

Consultant

The reality is these are individuals with a set of skills deployed by a project manager through an SOW - statement of work. Many of these engagements are either Fix or Time and Materials contracts. Consulting resources typically will not be provided to an unfunded exercise as they have their Profit and Loss requirements.

Professional services consultants are critical for those complex technology solutions. If your solution is a little unstable, the last thing you want is your customer kicking the tires or trying to implement the solution themselves. This is a recipe for disaster, and potential risks to other future Lines of business cross-sell and upselling. You want to build a strong working relationship with this team.

As a leader, I used to pair up the professional services teams with the SE organization. In certain technologies, I would require that a pre-salesperson not take on sales till they have done a professional services tour of duty. I would loan my team out as an unfunded element to shadow or do all the grunt work. This became very valuable later in their role, as they could always reference - Oh, when we deployed this at XYZ brand, our services team did this and encountered that. When asked by the client oh, were you on that deployment team? Hoping for the answer - no to show up the SE - yes, this has happened too often. You just smile and say oh, of course, it is a requirement as an SE to participate in implementation so I can understand firsthand how we position the technology. It is GOLD! Building relationships with the delivery team allows you to vet who is good and so-so. You don't want the so-so folks on the lighthouse deals. Lighthouse deals are companies like Merck, which other pharma companies will follow. Lastly, and I am NOT condoning this without following proper procedures, a great opportunity to have some of these consultants join your team as a career transition - NO POACHING - you don't want it to happen to you, then you DON'T do it! Get it!

Another fun consulting story, a few years ago, several technologists ran into an employee title conflict with the term Consulting. Adobe, Oracle, Salesforce, and a few other companies had traditional field consultants who were charging customers hourly for their time, travel, and expense. The last two were the fine points of detail that a class action lawsuit came about. A series of sales consultants were conducting consulting-level work, funded in some cases and unfunded in others. The argument was if the vendor is billing the company for time, travel, and expenses for those consultants and not paying them more than their salary, there is an issue. So the consultants won the lawsuit against the vendors. This is why Oracle pays their consultants overtime if they go over a 50 hr. work week. I knew several employees who would make more on overtime than on commission. Of course, this does not support the proper behavior to shorten sales cycles. If anything, it promotes extending sales cycles. So, a lesson learned, if interviewing for a California-based tech giant, find out if they pay overtime.

The DISC on Consultants:

- **D - Dominant**: Medium. They are confident and take charge of projects.
- **I - Influential**: Medium. They need to influence clients without appearing too salesy.
- **S - Steady**: High. Dependability is key, and they often handle intense client scrutiny.
- **C - Compliant**: High. Accuracy and attention to detail are crucial.

ISR Inside Sales Representative

Inside Sales can be synonymous with Business Development Managers with a twist. In most cases, Inside Sales are the first step in an account executive career. These are typically entry-level people who have an amazing ability to spend all day dialing for dollars. This is a grinding work week, where you have a territory mapped to an account executive team. They will take the account list and spend most of the time calling with a 90% rejection response. So it is safe to say you must have very thick skin to get hit all day and wake up the next day to go back to calling.

I have seen some situations where the ISR, Account Executive, and SE have a weekly call to verify what accounts to call on, what to ask for, where to look and how to leverage resources in an effort to qualify in or out customer leads. This is a critical planning relationship; otherwise, you end up wasting time on customer meetings that should have never happened. Unfortunately, the ISR teams are compensated on how many meetings they get; as you can see, this does not mean qualified meetings. It is very tempting for an ISR to give away several things like access to you as an SE to get a meeting. This can be disastrous for an SE, as time is the dreaded enemy. Note you will hear this from several Sales VPs. I think it is in the first chapter of the "how to be a sales manager" book. But it is correct; you should consider becoming very close to your ISR. I remember a few ISRs at Elasticsearch who were rock stars. I would have a number of my new SE hires spend one-on-one time with the ISR during a typical work week. This allowed the SE to see how hard it was to achieve a qualified meeting. It also allowed them to hear the sales elevator pitch, objection handling, and closing. For the ISR, it allowed an immediate resource on a call to pitch some technical answers to questions and or allow a sounding board for the

ISR to verify that this would be a good customer to push to the sales team.

If you are an ISR today, have a technical edge, and feel that a long-term account executive role may not be in the cards, I highly recommend interviewing for an SE position. Sure, you may not have a full technical background, but you will have the full sales side with a technical aptitude.

Job Title: Inside Sales Representative

Location: [Insert Location]

Company Overview: Elastic is a search company built on a free and open source foundation. We help people and organizations explore and analyze their data differently using the power of search. Whether it's uncovering hidden insights in logs, security events, or system metrics, Elastic products are engineered to help customers innovate quickly and gain actionable insights in real time.

Position Overview: We are seeking a highly motivated and results-driven Inside Sales Representative to join our dynamic sales team. The ideal candidate will have a strong background in sales, excellent communication skills, and a passion for helping customers solve complex problems using Elastic's suite of products.

Key Responsibilities:

- **Lead Generation:** Identify and qualify new sales opportunities through inbound lead follow-up and outbound cold calls and emails.
- **Customer Engagement:** Build and maintain relationships with potential customers, understanding their needs and how Elastic's solutions can address them.

- **Sales Process Management:** Manage the sales process from initial contact to closure, ensuring accurate and timely updates in the CRM system.
- **Product Knowledge:** Maintain a deep understanding of Elastic's products, solutions, and competitive landscape to effectively communicate value propositions.
- **Quota Achievement:** Consistently meet or exceed monthly and quarterly sales targets and quotas.
- **Collaboration:** Work closely with field sales, sales engineers, and marketing teams to drive sales growth and share best practices.
- **Reporting:** Provide regular reports on sales activities, pipeline status, and forecast to sales management.
- **Market Feedback:** Collect and communicate market and customer feedback to internal teams to help shape product development and marketing strategies.

Qualifications:

- **Experience:** 2+ years of inside sales or related experience, preferably in the technology or software industry.
- **Sales Skills:** Proven track record of meeting or exceeding sales targets. Strong negotiation and closing skills.
- **Communication:** Excellent verbal and written communication skills with the ability to build rapport quickly.
- **Technical Aptitude:** Ability to quickly learn and understand technical products and solutions. Experience with search technologies, big data, or analytics is a plus.
- **CRM Proficiency:** Experience using CRM software (e.g., Salesforce) to manage sales processes and track performance.
- **Education:** Bachelor's degree in Business, Marketing, or a related field is preferred.

- **Team Player:** Ability to work effectively in a team-oriented, collaborative environment.
- **Motivation:** Highly motivated, self-starter with a strong work ethic and a drive to succeed.

Preferred Skills:

- Familiarity with Elastic's suite of products, including Elasticsearch, Kibana, Beats, and Logstash.
- Experience selling open source or SaaS solutions.
- Knowledge of the enterprise software sales cycle and customer buying processes.

Why Elastic?

- Join a company built on a foundation of free and open source, with a global community of users and developers.
- Work with a talented team of professionals in a dynamic and innovative environment.
- Opportunities for professional growth and development.
- Competitive salary and benefits package.

If you are a driven sales professional with a passion for technology and a knack for building relationships, we invite you to join our team at Elastic. Apply today and help us drive the future of search technology!

The DISC on ISR - Inside Sales Rep:

- **D - Dominant**: Medium. You have to be a strong personality to accept rejection over and over.
- **I - Influential**: Medium. This is a tough role, and you need to be able to influence people without going over the line. When working with an ISR, understand that they are under the gun, a very high-pressure job, and some will look to offer your time up in exchange for a meeting. You would only want to provide your time in scarce situations without offering it to the ISR.
- **S - Steady**: High. It is about numbers and waking up each day to finish them. It is one of the hardest sales jobs, and for a good reason. This is the stepping stone to a full account executive.
- **C - Compliant**: Low. Like the account executive, it is a careful line to walk; you do not want to over-promise and under-deliver with a customer as you will need that customer when you become an account executive.

Software Account Executive Role

What is a Software Account Executive?

A Software Account Executive (AE) is a critical role within a software company, responsible for driving sales, managing client relationships, and ensuring customer satisfaction. The position demands a combination of sales expertise, technical knowledge, and strong interpersonal skills. AEs are often the bridge between the company and its clients, working to understand client needs, present software solutions, negotiate contracts, and close deals.

How Challenging is the Role?

The role of a Software Account Executive is both challenging and rewarding. It requires:

- **Sales Skills:** The ability to identify potential clients, pitch products effectively, and close deals.
- **Technical Understanding:** A good grasp of the software being sold, including its features, benefits, and how it addresses client needs.
- **Client Management:** Building and maintaining strong relationships with clients, understanding their business needs, and providing exceptional customer service.
- **Problem-Solving:** Addressing client concerns, managing objections, and finding solutions that meet both client needs and company goals.
- **Time Management:** Juggling multiple clients, sales cycles, and internal responsibilities requires excellent organizational skills.

A Typical Week for a Software Account Executive

A Software Account Executive's week is dynamic, involving a mix of client interactions, internal meetings, strategic planning, and administrative tasks. Here's a look at what a typical week might entail:

Monday:

- **Morning:**
    - **Team Meeting:** Participate in a sales team meeting to discuss weekly goals, share insights, and align on strategies.
    - **Client Outreach:** Start the day by reaching out to potential clients, scheduling meetings, and following up on leads from the previous week.

- **Afternoon:**
    - **Product Demo:** Conduct a virtual product demonstration for a prospective client, highlighting how the software can solve their specific business challenges.
    - **Internal Collaboration:** Meet with the marketing team to discuss upcoming campaigns and provide feedback from the field.

Tuesday:

- **Morning:**
    - **Account Management:** Check in with existing clients to ensure they are satisfied with the software

and to explore opportunities for upselling or cross-selling.
- **Proposal Preparation:** Work on crafting detailed sales proposals for new prospects, including pricing, implementation plans, and support options.

- **Afternoon:**

  - **Client Meeting:** Meet with a new prospect to understand their business needs, present the software solution, and discuss potential next steps.
  - **Training Session:** Participate in a training session to stay updated on new features or updates to the software.

Wednesday:

- **Morning:**

  - **Follow-Up Calls:** Make follow-up calls to clients who attended demos earlier in the week, addressing any questions or concerns they may have.
  - **Market Research:** Spend time researching market trends and competitor activities to refine sales strategies.

- **Afternoon:**

  - **Deal Negotiation:** Engage in contract negotiations with a potential client, working to close the deal while ensuring mutual satisfaction.
  - **Strategy Session:** Join a strategy session with the sales team to brainstorm new approaches for difficult-to-close accounts.

Thursday:

- **Morning:**
    - **Client Presentation:** Deliver a formal presentation to a prospective client's executive team, demonstrating the software's ROI and strategic value.
    - **Pipeline Review:** Review the sales pipeline, updating CRM systems with the latest client interactions and deal statuses.

- **Afternoon:**
    - **Networking Lunch:** Meet with industry contacts or clients for a networking lunch to strengthen relationships and explore new opportunities.
    - **Client Training:** Organize a training session for a new client, ensuring they understand how to use the software effectively.

Friday:

- **Morning:**
    - **Weekly Reporting:** Prepare and submit weekly sales reports to management, summarizing activities, achievements, and areas needing attention.
    - **Client Follow-Up:** Follow up with clients to confirm next steps, schedule future meetings, and ensure ongoing satisfaction.

- **Afternoon:**

- **Planning:** Plan for the following week, setting priorities, scheduling meetings, and identifying new prospects to target.
- **Wrap-Up:** Wrap up the week by ensuring all administrative tasks are completed, emails are answered, and everything is set for a smooth start on Monday.

Is this Role Right for You?

If you thrive in a fast-paced environment, enjoy building relationships, and have a passion for technology and sales, the role of a Software Account Executive could be a great fit. It offers the excitement of closing deals, the satisfaction of helping clients solve problems, and the opportunity to continually learn and grow in the ever-evolving tech industry. However, it requires resilience, adaptability, and a relentless drive to succeed. If you're up for the challenge, this role can be incredibly rewarding both personally and professionally.

Personal Opinion

Let me tell you, the job is very hard and your employment risks can be very high. Account executives deal with the pressures of deadlines, sales quotas, relationships, and general work stresses. The most successful account executives are very competitive, and could work up to 80 hours a week during the crush time, Week 6. This is the week in a quarter where you will have to have your forecast buttoned up for the end-of-the-quarter targets. Too often, the account executive is only viewed as a transaction arm of the sales process. Typically, they are out dining, going to football games, golfing with customers, and generally doing a great job. When in fact, many external variables can impact their success.

I know the stigma for salespeople: they don't work, go out to dinners, golf, and have an easy life. This is true as these individuals play hard and work hard. Though think about trying to manage your checkbook on half your salary and wonder if you have done enough work to get the other half paid. This is a constant battle; the pressures in the role are tremendous. Sometimes you get lucky, and the product is so fantastic that the sales process is easy. But nine out of ten times, you will find so many technologies that just don't meet the mark, and this becomes a sales rep's nightmare. When at Adobe, our LiveCycle ES solution was hardly an enterprise and battle-tested technology. Yet, we were still able to make our number and, in some cases, overachieve that number. This is done through a tremendous amount of work from the sales support teams, the sales reps, and the back office teams to make it all work. However, if we don't hit that number, no one on that list will be let go except for the sales rep. They are on the hook to make it happen; if not, they are let go. They take on all the risks, and for that, they take on the monetary reward, but it is a gamble.

If you decide to become a pre-sales person as a career, take the time and ask the sales rep to shadow them from end to end. You will see firsthand how hard it is to get a qualified meeting and how hard it is to get deals past your own sales prevention teams like Finance and Legal. Now with SaaS solutions, you cannot just sell a solution, take your money, and walk away. Now you need to ensure that what you sell is not just delivered and implemented, it has to be successful, or you run the risk of losing a renewal.

Several solution engineers have complained that they do all the work and are not rewarded equally. The account executive shows up and hands the meeting to the sales engineer to run the entire meeting. The SE has to do all this follow-up work or a full proof of concept and yet doesn't end up going to the club. I have heard all the complaints, and unlike many sales engineers, I was a sales executive and understood what they did not. I remember some of these folks would request to become sales reps. Since I knew the role and the individual, I would tell them no problem, though I would keep the position open for one quarter if they wanted to return to the role. As expected, many would come back with new complaints. I didn't realize how hard it is to get a meeting. I didn't realize that getting the deal's legal T&Cs approved with our internal legal team was harder. I didn't realize how hard it was to get the deal through my own finance department. I would privately say, I told you so, and publicly pull them back into the role. Many of those returned became some of my best SE's in the field. They tasted the other side and realized how difficult; they immediately respected their business partner. In some cases, like Joe Chiaro, he became an amazing account executive: Joe Chiaro LinkedIn.

It is important to understand your business partner and respect each other; like patrol officers riding in a car, their partner assumes risks. Some more risks than others, but you will succeed together or fail together. In addition, you may find this path rewarding, and a great entry point into an account executive role is the sales engineering path.

If you are an account executive reading this book today and are interested in presales, I would highly recommend it. I have hired several salespeople who understand where they fit in the 70/30 split. Many enjoy the technology more than the week six forecast calls looking for an end-of-quarter blood number. If considering this position, look in the mirror and check your competitive levels. You will be the one who is taking less risk in your partnership with a salesperson. As you know, salespeople do not like to be schooled by others, and you could find yourself in a contentious relationship if you do not know your place in that relationship.

I have had the luxury to have worked with so many great account executives, to name a few: Kevin Maher, John Kessler, Tom Papp, Steve Trombetta, Tiffany Weisert, Mark Solazzo, Michael Harvat, David Wondolowski, Julia Towne, Alex Weinstein, Ray Deutschbein, Jenny Hay, Lindsay Hill, Charles Bernoskie, Dan Schapiro, Holger Rabe, Jimmy Barens, Julie Coe, Jay McDonald, Scott Ziegler. My list is so large, I know I left off many here in the book. I will ensure to provide my entire list on my site.

The big takeaway from understanding this role is that it is hard, and you, as a sales support arm to the process, should respect them in what they do. Now, this is a two-road street, and they, too, need to understand your challenges so they respect your role. Later you will find a list of minimum requirements I would place on my SE and SEM's to see what is expected of these teams. I will also include the sales expectations review to see what is required on that part of the org.

Job Title: Account Executive

Location: [Insert Location]

Company Overview: Snowflake enables every organization to mobilize their data with Snowflake's Data Cloud. Customers use the Data Cloud to unite siloed data, discover and securely share data, and execute diverse analytic workloads. Wherever data or users live, Snowflake delivers a single and seamless experience across multiple public clouds.

Position Overview: We are looking for a highly motivated and experienced Account Executive to join our growing sales team. The ideal candidate will have a proven track record of success in B2B software sales, excellent communication skills, and a passion for driving customer success with data-driven solutions.

Key Responsibilities:

- **Sales Strategy:** Develop and execute a strategic sales plan to achieve or exceed sales targets within an assigned territory or vertical.
- **Lead Generation:** Identify, qualify, and develop new business opportunities through inbound lead follow-up and outbound cold calls and emails.
- **Customer Engagement:** Build and maintain strong relationships with key decision-makers and stakeholders at targeted accounts.
- **Solution Selling:** Understand customers' business needs and challenges, and effectively communicate how Snowflake's Data Cloud can address them.
- **Sales Process Management:** Manage the entire sales cycle from prospecting to closure, including proposal creation, negotiation, and contract execution.
- **Collaboration:** Work closely with internal teams, including Sales Engineering, Product, Marketing, and Customer Success, to ensure a seamless customer experience.
- **Market Feedback:** Collect and communicate market and customer feedback to internal teams to help shape product development and marketing strategies.
- **Reporting:** Provide regular reports on sales activities, pipeline status, and forecast to sales management.

Qualifications:

- **Experience:** 5+ years of experience in B2B software sales, preferably in the data, analytics, or cloud industry.
- **Sales Skills:** Proven track record of meeting or exceeding sales targets. Strong negotiation, closing, and account management skills.
- **Communication:** Excellent verbal and written communication skills with the ability to build rapport quickly.
- **Technical Aptitude:** Ability to quickly learn and understand complex technical products and solutions. Familiarity with data warehousing, analytics, and cloud technologies is a plus.
- **CRM Proficiency:** Experience using CRM software (e.g., Salesforce) to manage sales processes and track performance.
- **Education:** Bachelor's degree in Business, Marketing, Computer Science, or a related field is preferred.
- **Team Player:** Ability to work effectively in a team-oriented, collaborative environment.
- **Motivation:** Highly motivated, self-starter with a strong work ethic and a drive to succeed.

Preferred Skills:

- Familiarity with Snowflake's Data Cloud and related data and analytics technologies.
- Experience selling cloud-based solutions and understanding of cloud architecture.
- Knowledge of the enterprise software sales cycle and customer buying processes.

Why Snowflake?

- Join a leading company in the data cloud industry, driving innovation and customer success.
- Work with a talented team of professionals in a dynamic and collaborative environment.
- Opportunities for professional growth and development.
- Competitive salary, commission structure, and benefits package.

If you are a results-driven sales professional with a passion for data and cloud technologies, we invite you to join our team at Snowflake. Apply today and help us revolutionize the world of data analytics!

The DISC on Account Executive:

- **D - Dominant**: High. Account executives need to be very competitive, though there needs to be a balance so as not to be viewed as a used car dealer. You must play to their competitive nature when working with a high-D individual. They will resist suggestions, and you must allow them to get to your idea naturally.
- **I - Influential**: High. Of course, you want someone influential. Though I find the really good reps like Tom Papp, Kevin Maher, and John Kessler are all very high I's, they are relationship builders. All three I worked directly with during my early years, and they could string together relationships from previous jobs to new jobs. These customers followed them from one software vendor to the next.
- **S - Steady**: Medium. Unfortunately, not many are steady; some can be considered to be a bit lazy and enjoy the fun part of the job way too much. Then some are disciplined. I remember working with Rob Silva, SE manager and now Director at Snowflake, who used our technology to analyze the sales teams' Google calendars to identify a trend pattern. We were not too surprised to see those who had a full week's worth of work and activity over-achieving their numbers and those who would have nothing on a Friday or a Monday be on a plan. We had some surprises in the analysis, but Rob is a master at SQL, and Snowflake technology is magical concerning these types of analysis.

- **C - Compliant**: Low. Many account managers can be noncompliant, and I understand the lack of commitment in this area. It is tough to be compliant and disciplined with record-keeping or forecast discipline. The strong reps understand not to wait till the end of the week to write up notes; they do it in the car, on the train, bus, or during lunch each day.

Business Analyst - Post Sales

A business analyst (BA) processes, interprets, and documents business processes, products, services, and software through the analysis of data. The role of a business analyst is to ensure business efficiency increases through their knowledge of both IT and business functions. Some tasks of a business analyst include creating detailed business analysis, budgeting and forecasting, planning and monitoring, variance analysis, pricing, reporting, and defining business requirements for stakeholders. The business analyst role is applicable to four key areas/levels of business functions – operational, project, enterprise, and competitive focuses. Each of these areas of business analysis has a significant impact on business performance and assists in enhancing profitability and efficiency in all stages of the business process and across all business functions.

A business analyst's job description tends to include "creating detailed business analysis, outlining problems, opportunities, and solutions for a business, budgeting and forecasting, planning and monitoring, variance and analysis, pricing, reporting, and defining business requirements and reporting back to stakeholders". There are many business activities in which the business analyst is involved. Some areas in which business analysts can have an important role are in financial analysis, quality assurance, training, business policy and procedures, organizational development, and solution testing. More specifically, business analysts are required to use the data which is gathered for the purpose of analysis and interpret greater meaning for the business. This can then be used to improve business performance through identifying areas for potential growth, cost reduction, understanding customer behavior, and observing economic trends and forecasts, and then reacting appropriately.

Successful business analysts should influence the business environment by providing reliable guidance in decision-making for the future through observing data that reflects the business's past behavior. Business analysts are essential at all business levels, as tactical and strategic planning requires analysts who help with "incremental improvements to products, business processes, and applications".

A business analyst is a perfect entry into a presales role. I used to hire several business analysts, especially those with vertical experience. These folks are very good at breaking down complex challenges. Typically, a BA will be part of the consulting organization and, as such, a funded resource. At Adobe, I used to position the BA as an excellent opportunity for consulting to seed a customer for post-sales implementations. You have to work with Sales VPs and build those relationships to pull these kinds of deals out of the hat. Some organizations will charge back the costs to the sales org as a natural part of doing business.

Using BA's to gain access to power

I have successfully used BAs in the field when selling complex solutions. We would tell the customer that we would come in for two weeks to conduct a mini baseline or baseline analysis. Then, we would deliver a comprehensive overview that the customer can take to the board to gain access to funds. The costs would be $10K; typically, this was just below authority requirements for the sponsor we worked with. The understanding was if they went with the business, we would blend in the costs to the deal, and they would not have to pay for the analysis.

To get to the fundamental critical business issues, the consulting team and my presales team would partner up to give the sales team access to all people involved in the business issue. I used to print money with these types of deals. We essentially had a wolf in sheep's clothing asking all individuals involved in a workflow process. I remember one meeting with NY Life. We are all in the room with one conference line open with a few department heads. We walked through the workflow - department by department, on how a business conducts its underwriting process approval workflows. We are about to take a break; the giant whiteboard is filled with arrows and names. Some of the arrows are pink, blue-black, oh, and evil Red. By the way, as a best practice - use blue for text, red for pain or costs, and green for good to go or money, and try to only use black for box lines, etc. More on that later with best practices. Sorry for the squirrel! - So, climax moment - I ask what happens here with the workflow? Does it hit a system or a person? Dead silence in the room, finally after a minute that felt like an hour, a voice appeared on the speaker, "that would be Jackie " in that department. I asked, "do you know what she does at this point in the workflow?" and she said no. In a quick defeat, the room says okay, let's take a break. Nope, we asked if we could call Jackie? Sounds reasonable. So to the shock of the room, we call Jackie and explain where we are in the workflow. So Jackie, what do you do with this request? Wait for it!! - "Oh, I rekey all this data into a spreadsheet to report on that." Oh, so Jackie, how long does that take you? About 1 hr. each request. Oh, that's a long time, how many do you do a week? About 15 a week? Okay, so Jackie, if you could create a utopia, what would you like to see - I kid you not - "ah, not to have to rekey all that data." So many more questions came from that one moment. Doing the math on that one part of the process - 1hr x 15 = 15hrs a week, x 51 weeks figure holidays = 765 hrs. at 250.00 FTE costs per hr. BOOM - 191,250.00 a year wasted on that one process - ah folks, the solution is priced at 500K - solving that one problem would ROI in less than two years. That came from a Baseline analysis. I highly recommend it! - I will provide some samples in the back. See how important it is to ask questions; that's the value of a pre-sales person. I have another book to make more money off of you - SE Worklife - Day in the Life that will cover more of the details.

Check out - [Guy Warwick LinkedIn](). Hi "Guy" - great times, he was a master at this back in the day, I learned so much from him.

The DISC on Business Analyst:

- **D - Dominant**: High is very good at providing structure; personality is one who is in control, especially during a project. You want an individual who can be excellent at project and people management.
- **I - Influential**: Low. I don't view the BA as a very influential personality, yes they are influential but not salesy. In fact, it's best to have a BA who is not trying to bend the bar but keeps it straight and honest.
- **S - Steady**: High. They are dependable people; their mind is focused on getting the task completed and accurately.
- **C - Compliant**: High. You want them to be very disciplined and compliant. Business Analysts are there to ensure we are not running the business incorrectly and live up to a set of standards.

CSM - Customer Success Management - Post Sales

The CSM Customer Success Manager role has been a key role in a post-sales support transition role. With the subscription and renewal business growing, so did the Customer Success Manager role. Typically the CSM role comprises either legacy customer support individuals or account managers who function more like farmers vs hunters on the front line.

The CSM role is a very complex role requiring several requirements. As you would expect, the primary objective is to create a healthy customer relationship, be the brand ambassador evaluate the customer needs, onboard new clients, train, and be that voice of the customer back to the vendor with product enhancements. They are not directly responsible for solving bug or customer support issues, though they are there to broker the conversations with support and escalate if necessary. CSMs are not considered to be purely account executives, though as part of building client trust and advocacy. They are there to help provide insight on new product releases, solution cross-sell and upsell. Some CSMs are compensated as individual contributors with a base salary and an MBO (Manager Business Objective) to reach certain customer goals and, if achieved, rewarded through a bonus. Some are compensated as an Account Executive would be compensated for not just expansion but also professional services and training.

Suppose you believe this is a good role for you. In that case, you will need strong project management skills, the ability to negotiate escalations, and be the mediator between your company and the client. This job is not for everyone, and unfortunately, in many organizations, it can be viewed as a subservient job from the sales side of the house.

Interestingly, CSMs became more important as the industry shifted from on-premise installations to that SaaS or no software solutions. The industry understood that it took months, if not years, to acquire a customer and only seconds to lose a customer over poorly managed customer relationships.

The stock market began to evaluate the renewal rates with many of these SaaS customers and noticed that several clients would not renew after 18 or 24 months. To combat this evolution, some savvy reps would sell three and five-year contracts to lock in the customer. This presented a negative brand relationship, but to the account rep, they closed the business, received their commission check, and were off to another vendor.

The CSM role became increasingly important to ensure renewal rates and land and expand opportunities for renewal, with growth becoming the trend. The CSM was designed to ensure the renewal success. Unfortunately, the disconnect between the selling side and the implemented nurturing caring side became a wide gap. Much of this was because a CSM's roles, rules, and responsibilities were very muddy. To add to this challenge, the compensation model did not incent the proper behavior. Are you there to sell more or to keep the customer happy? Which is it? It is hard to do both.

Frank Slootman, known for his success at Service Now, decided to eliminate the CSM role at Snowflake and place this burden on the sales team, including the SE organization. At first, I was surprised at this move, but in hindsight, it was the right move. Though I would have implemented it differently. Understand we still have the classic compensation dictates behavior, and we have behavioral factors that need to be understood. We have hunters and farmers in the sales culture. Ideally, the hunters should be pulling down the new customers and expanding the footprint inside accounts. However, Yelp-level reviews for customer implementation, onboarding, and support will impact future brands you hunt, and incumbent lines of business will steer away.

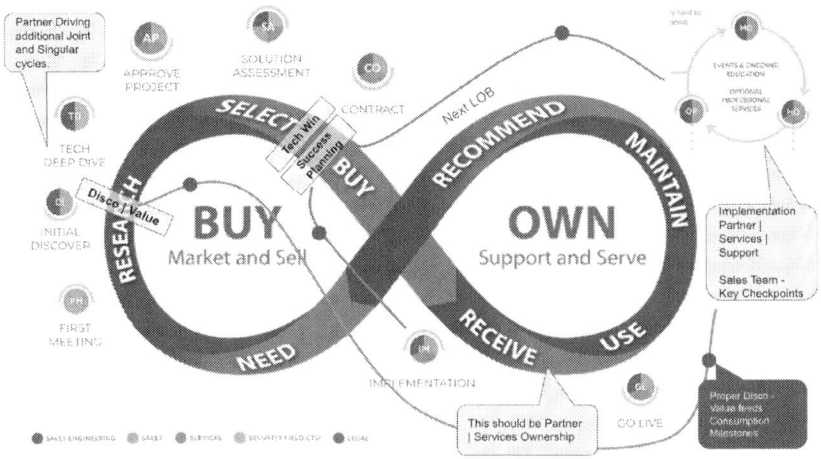

I modified a chart from Oracle called Buy and Ownership Loop to represent the importance of having a symbiotic relationship between the buy and ownership sides. I agree with Frank that CSMs need to be redefined, but customer success is critical for positive advocacy to encourage future buyers to partner with your organization. The solution combines established communication rules inside the organization between departments. To encourage this behavior, the compensation plan needs to motivate all these key individuals to cooperate.

A quick explanation of this chart is to relate it to something you may have purchased. Let's take a car, for example. You identified a need starting on the buy side, realized you needed to research the car, and discovered the star rating for the reviews on the dealer or car itself. You finally take a test drive, decide with the dealer and purchase the car. They tell you that you can pick up the car in a few days. You show up at the dealer at the scheduled time, and the front desk doesn't even know you are a customer. You wait for a bit, the sales rep is nowhere to be found, and the customer support person shows up to give you the keys to the car. You pick up the car, and a light comes on after driving a few blocks. You bring it back to the car dealership and are told sorry, you didn't buy the loner car option and are told you will need to take an Uber home. After waiting a few days, you call them to find out what is happening. They continue to push you off and finally come clean and tell you they don't know what the issue is. Still no access to a loner car, though. Finally, you get your car; they provide no apology. You are not likely to recommend the car or vendor, and hopefully, your review will help someone else in the Need buy cycle.

Selling a product to a SaaS customer is just the beginning of hopefully a very long profitable journey. It can be even more critical to have a successful customer onboarding than the actual purchase process. This buy and ownership loop is a living entity inside the SaaS customer and vendor relationship. In all the roles mentioned, you will need to continue viewing your customer through this buy and ownership lenses. If you do that, you will be very successful in the new SaaS sales world.

I wanted you to fully understand all the role options you may look at during this career review. Understand that having all these options is unlike any other role in the market, and you will benefit from entering and exiting any of these roles if you decide to become a sales engineer. This has been the most rewarding and flexible job you will find in the market.

Suggested Workshop: Finding Your Ideal Role

To help you determine which role suits you best, we suggest conducting a workshop designed to explore your strengths, interests, and career aspirations. Here's a step-by-step guide:

Workshop Materials

- Post-it notes
- Voting dots
- Flip chart or whiteboard
- Markers
- Role profiles (printed summaries of each role)
- Self-assessment questionnaires
- Career interest inventories (e.g., Holland Code (RIASEC), MBTI)
- Notebooks and pens for participants

Duration

Approximately 2-3 hours

Step-by-Step Instructions

1. Introduction (15 minutes)
    - Begin with an overview of the workshop's objectives: to identify the role that aligns best with each participant's skills, interests, and career goals.
    - Briefly describe the different roles discussed in the chapter (e.g., Sales Engineer, Solution Architect, Account Executive, etc.).
2. Self-Assessment (30 minutes)

- Distribute self-assessment questionnaires and career interest inventories.
- Allow participants time to complete these assessments.
- Encourage them to jot down their thoughts and reflections in their notebooks.

3. Role Exploration (45 minutes)
   - Provide printed summaries of each role.
   - Ask participants to read through the profiles and highlight the responsibilities and skills that resonate with them.
   - Use Post-it notes to write down key aspects they find appealing or relevant.

4. Group Discussion (30 minutes)
   - Form small groups and discuss the findings from the self-assessments and role exploration.
   - Share insights and listen to feedback from peers.
   - Use the flip chart or whiteboard to categorize common themes and interests.

5. Voting and Prioritization (30 minutes)
   - Each participant places voting dots on the role profiles that interest them the most.
   - Discuss the results as a group and see which roles have the most interest.
   - Encourage participants to consider why they chose certain roles and if they align with their self-assessment results.

6. Action Planning (30 minutes)
   - Based on the roles with the most votes, participants create an action plan for pursuing their chosen role.

- This plan should include steps such as further research, skill development, networking, and setting career goals.
- Participants share their plans with the group for feedback and support.
7. Wrap-Up (15 minutes)
    - Summarize the key takeaways from the workshop.
    - Encourage participants to continue exploring and refining their career paths.
    - Provide resources and contacts for further guidance and support.

Recommended Books

To further assist you in identifying the best role for your career, here are some recommended books:

1. "StrengthsFinder 2.0" by Tom Rath
    - This book helps you identify your strengths and how to leverage them in your career.
2. "Designing Your Life" by Bill Burnett and Dave Evans
    - A guide to using design thinking to build a fulfilling career and life.
3. "The Pathfinder: How to Choose or Change Your Career for a Lifetime of Satisfaction and Success" by Nicholas Lore
    - Provides practical advice and exercises to help you find a career that fits your passion and skills.
4. "What Color Is Your Parachute? 2022: Your Guide to a Lifetime of Meaningful Work and Career Success" by Richard N. Bolles
    - A comprehensive guide to career planning and job searching.

5. "Drive: The Surprising Truth About What Motivates Us" by Daniel H. Pink
   - Explores what truly motivates people and how to use this understanding to achieve career satisfaction.

Quiz: Understanding Your Ideal Role

1. What combination of skills do you possess?
   - a) Technical and sales skills
   - b) Project management and problem-solving skills
   - c) Relationship-building and negotiation skills
   - d) Analytical and data interpretation skills
2. Which work environment do you thrive in the most?
   - a) Dynamic and fast-paced with constant client interaction
   - b) Collaborative and solution-focused with cross-functional teams
   - c) Competitive and goal-driven with clear targets
   - d) Structured and data-centric with a focus on analysis
3. What motivates you in a job?
   - a) Helping clients solve technical issues and seeing them succeed
   - b) Designing and implementing effective solutions
   - c) Achieving sales targets and closing deals
   - d) Improving business processes and efficiencies
4. How do you prefer to interact with clients?
   - a) Providing technical demonstrations and support
   - b) Consulting on system architecture and integration
   - c) Building long-term relationships and managing accounts

- d) Analyzing their needs and recommending solutions
5. What kind of career growth do you envision?
    - a) Moving into a leadership role in sales engineering
    - b) Becoming a senior solution architect or consultant
    - c) Advancing to a top-performing account executive
    - d) Leading a team of business analysts or becoming a data scientist

Answer Key:

- Mostly A's: Consider a career as a Sales Engineer or Technical Specialist.
- Mostly B's: You might excel as a Solution Architect or Solution Consultant.
- Mostly C's: An Account Executive or Inside Sales Representative role could be a good fit.
- Mostly D's: Look into opportunities as a Business Analyst or Customer Success Manager.

This workshop, along with the recommended readings and the quiz, will help you pinpoint the role that aligns best with your skills and career aspirations.

Chapter 3: The S.E.A.C. Roles and Expectations

Understanding S.E.A.C. Expectations

Sales workflows and stages are critical elements in the sales process, providing a structured path from initial contact to closing the deal. Understanding these workflows and stages helps sales engineers (SE), solution architects (SA), and solution consultants (SC) align their efforts with broader organizational goals. This section outlines the sales workflow stages and how they relate to the expectations and roles of SEAC professionals.

Salesforce.com CRM Sales Stages for a Software Company

Salesforce.com CRM is widely used for managing sales processes. Here are the typical sales stages for a software company:

1. Lead Generation
    - **Description:** Identifying potential customers through various channels such as marketing campaigns, referrals, and industry events.
    - **Key Activities:** Collecting contact information, qualifying leads based on initial criteria, and entering leads into the CRM system.
2. Qualification
    - **Description:** Determining if a lead is worth pursuing based on budget, authority, need, and timeline (BANT criteria).

- **Key Activities:** Conducting initial calls or meetings, understanding customer needs, and assessing the potential for conversion.
3. Needs Analysis
    - **Description:** Deep diving into the customer's specific requirements and pain points.
    - **Key Activities:** Conducting detailed discovery sessions, documenting customer requirements, and mapping them to potential solutions.
4. Proposal/
    - **Description:** Preparing and presenting a formal proposal or that addresses the customer's needs.
    - **Key Activities:** Drafting a detailed proposal, outlining the solution, pricing, and implementation plan, and delivering the proposal to the customer.
5. Negotiation/Review
    - **Description:** Engaging in discussions to address any objections and finalize the terms of the deal.
    - **Key Activities:** Negotiating pricing, terms, and conditions, revising proposals as needed, and getting internal approvals for discounts or special terms.
6. Closed/Won
    - **Description:** The deal is finalized, and the contract is signed.
    - **Key Activities:** Preparing contract documents, obtaining signatures, and updating the CRM to reflect the closed deal.
7. Closed/Lost
    - **Description:** The deal is not won, and the sales process is terminated.

- **Key Activities:** Documenting reasons for the loss, updating the CRM, and planning follow-up activities for future opportunities.
8. Implementation/Delivery
    - **Description:** Delivering the product or service to the customer and ensuring a smooth onboarding process.
    - **Key Activities:** Coordinating with the implementation team, managing customer expectations, and providing initial training and support.

SEAC Expectations:

Below is an example of the early days at Adobe for relationships and requirements between groups. This group was called TSO Technical Sales Operations. Oddly enough, twenty years later, these departments have not changed much. You find the expectations are also in line with today's requirements.

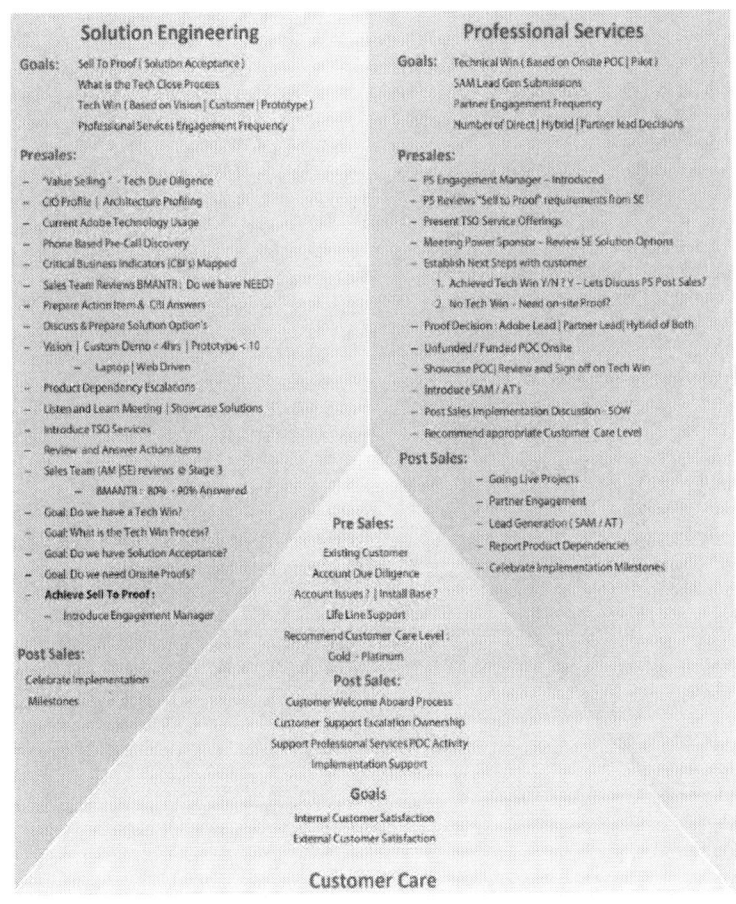

From understanding the various roles within the sales engineering landscape, we now delve deeper into the specific expectations and relationships that shape the daily experiences of SEAC professionals. This section provides a comprehensive look into the structured expectations that drive success in these roles.

"Innovation distinguishes between a leader and a follower." – Steve Jobs

Since this book focuses on the bundle "Sales Engineering/Consulting - pre and post," here are some expectations I drew up for several companies like Adobe and a few startups. These are what I would consider the minimum expectations for an individual contributor to perform. I always found it odd that companies did not have minimum expectations. After pushing this out to a few other companies, HR was very sensitive to a document like this. I thought this was odd since much of it came from hiring these folks' job descriptions. When you become a manager, I would not recommend you push a formal document out, as it could get you in some hot water. Though, I would recommend that everyone understands the baseline requirements, and you will find that most if not all are still applicable today.

The primary objective for the SEAC team is to drive revenue into the organization in alignment with our budgeted objectives. These expectations target three main areas: Value Selling Objectives, Solution Consulting, and Technical Sales operations. It is a listing of required activities and skills that are fundamental to the success of each SC. It is expected that the SC can adequately document their performance of the required activities as outlined and possess the fundamentals of the Solutions Engineer job description.

Value Selling Objectives:

Pipeline Development

The SEAC is expected to assist the assigned account teams or region in building a pipeline that is 3X to 4X their annual quota. This critical objective is necessary for "meeting and exceeding" the current fiscal revenue plans. This means each SEAC needs to work with their assigned account teams or region to build a pipeline as outlined by your manager. The SEAC should look for ways to position multiple technologies within each opportunity while solving the customer's business problems.

Adherence to Engagement Model: Account Due Diligence

Account due diligence starts with account planning, and account planning starts with you working with your sales counterpart to identify what accounts will be our premier accounts. As soon as we have filtered through the account lists, divide those accounts that will be run by inside sales, and partners and those that will not be worked on. For each account plan that the SEAC and Account Executive are preparing, the SEAC is to construct a full technical account plan to be delivered during the quarterly review. We will have the advantage of engaging other members of our internal vendors during this process. These vendors are Consulting, Partners, Customer Care, Technical Marketing, and Marketing business units. The SEAC will orchestrate the collection of data associated with each account plan. We expect that you will receive your company's and partner-led project updates associated with the plan from professional services. We will look to our Customer Care counterparts for details surrounding the install base and any relative escalation issues. The SEAC will be held accountable to pull these details together, along with all relative details around the technical leadership and overall critical technical business issues.

Engagement Model:

The SEAC will have responsibility for the account relationship through the entire sales engagement process. The SEAC will provide significant account leadership starting in sales stage 1 through stage 4 (Circle of Influence). The SEAC primary objective is to achieve a "Sell to Proof" or a "Technical Win" within these stages. You will do your best to pull the Consulting Engagement Managers earlier in the sales process. Consulting will have a targeted list of accounts, and in those accounts, we are to Inform | Invite | and Participate after the sales team has achieved the necessary Need qualifiers and has passed sales stage 2. For those accounts outside the primarily targeted list, the SEAC will work with the sales manager to coordinate the introduction of a partner in a similar engagement process and timing.

Proof Offerings:

SEAC will be responsible for showcasing the brand's technology through either a hosted site or via their laptop. The SEAC has three options for proof offerings; vision demo, custom demo (<4hrs), and prototype (<10hrs). The SEAC will have access to the "Technical Win Team" POC Team in a limited fashion for any work beyond 10 hours. At Adobe, we had a proof of concept team that would assist the SEAC team. I am surprised that other companies do not support this type of model. If the SEAC cannot achieve a "Technical Win" and the onsite proof is required, the account team will need to submit a requirements document for additional resource approval. This last line is critical for leadership to negotiate properly. Too often, we just throw resources at the customer on a HOPE that we will get something. This is why a technical close plan with some give/get requirements will prove to be more successful if used.

Customer Care Escalations

SEAC will continue all facets of the customer relationship. The SEAC will be responsible for escalation to their customer care escalation contact based on the technology involved. It is the expectation that the customer care escalations contact will own follow-up and communication with the account manager. This will enable the SEAC to focus efforts on building pipelines and Customer Care to be accountable for the post-sales relationship issues. This has changed over time, and the brand you are working for may have a customer success team. The responsibilities do not change much; you cannot abandon your customer and what you need to do is work with the CSM Customer Success Management teams. In cooperation, you may use them to manage the relationship. I would recommend understanding who manages those most important accounts you depend on for upsell, cross-sell, and renewals.

Personal Story

When I first started implementing these expectations at Adobe, the SE team was initially overwhelmed. However, once we integrated these structured goals and practices, the clarity it brought was transformative. I remember a particular instance where an SE, initially hesitant about the account planning process, found that the thorough preparation allowed him to close a major deal with Prudential. The structured approach of account planning, engagement models, and proof offerings not only streamlined our operations but also significantly boosted our success rates. This methodology has continued to prove effective across various companies and startups I've been involved with.

Workshop: Identifying Your Ideal Role in Sales Engineering

Objective:

Help participants determine which sales engineering role best fits their skills and career goals.

Materials Needed:

- Role definition worksheets
- DISC assessment tools
- Flip chart and markers
- Role-playing scenarios

Duration:

90 minutes

Step-by-Step Instructions:

1. Introduction (10 minutes):
    - Introduce the workshop and its objective.
    - Provide an overview of the various roles within sales engineering.
2. Self-Assessment (20 minutes):
    - Distribute role definition worksheets.
    - Have participants complete the DISC assessment to understand their personality types.
3. Role Exploration (30 minutes):
    - Discuss the different roles: SE, SA, SC, and others.
    - Match DISC profiles to the roles and discuss the fit.

4. Role-Playing Scenarios (20 minutes):
   - Provide scenarios for each role.
   - Have participants role-play to get a feel for each position.
5. Q&A and Wrap-Up (10 minutes):
   - Open the floor for questions.
   - Summarize key takeaways and encourage participants to continue exploring roles.

Quiz: Understanding SEAC Roles

1. What is a primary objective for the SEAC team?
   - a) Drive revenue into the organization
   - b) Handle customer complaints
   - c) Develop marketing materials
   - d) None of the above
2. What is the importance of account due diligence?
   - a) To understand the customer's business issues
   - b) To close deals quickly
   - c) To avoid interacting with the customer care team
   - d) None of the above
3. What should the SEAC focus on during the engagement model stages?
   - a) Achieve a "Sell to Proof" or a "Technical Win"
   - b) Skip proof offerings
   - c) Focus only on post-sales activities
   - d) None of the above
4. Which proof offering is intended to take less than 4 hours?
   - a) Vision demo
   - b) Custom demo
   - c) Prototype
   - d) Technical Win Team support

5. What is the role of customer care escalations in SEAC responsibilities?
    - a) To ensure SEAC can focus on pipeline building
    - b) To handle all sales activities
    - c) To manage all technical issues alone
    - d) None of the above

Answers:

1. a) Drive revenue into the organization
2. a) To understand the customer's business issues
3. a) Achieve a "Sell to Proof" or a "Technical Win"
4. b) Custom demo
5. a) To ensure SEAC can focus on pipeline building

SEAC Skills

In the previous section, we explored the various roles within the sales engineering and solution consulting landscape. Now, it's time to delve deeper into the specific skills and expectations required to excel in these positions. Understanding these core competencies will help you navigate your career path effectively and achieve professional success.

"Success is not the result of spontaneous combustion. You must set yourself on fire." — Arnold H. Glasow

Introduction

Understanding the required skills and expectations for Sales Engineers (SE), Solution Architects (SA), and Solution Consultants (SC) is critical for success in these roles. This chapter provides a detailed overview of the necessary technical and soft skills, industry knowledge, and operational requirements. By mastering these areas, you will be well-equipped to meet and exceed the demands of your position.

Application of Technology

Each SEAC must possess and maintain industry knowledge, quickly assess a customer's business needs, and articulate how your brand's solution could be used to solve them. Each SEAC is expected to maintain current and complete familiarity with all your brand's enterprise products and be able to articulate the technical details and associated value propositions.

Requirements (Reviewed Annually with Management)

- Your ability to present the current elevator pitch
- Demonstrate the foundation of the brand's technology, implementation, and support
- Conduct a Solution Conversation Whiteboard session
- Certifications: (Annual Requirement)
- Individual component best practices
- Submitting your own Customized Demonstration for review

Competitive Product Knowledge and Positioning

Each SEAC is required to develop and maintain knowledge of competing technologies and be able to position the brand's solutions against them competitively. This expectation includes viewpoints within specific assigned industries, geographic regions, and named accounts.

Industry Knowledge

The SEAC should have detailed knowledge of the industries associated with their assigned named accounts. This includes but is not limited to Life Sciences, Financial Services, Manufacturing, and the Public Sector. Depending on what stage your brand is at, you could not be at the verticalized level or market knowledge.

Soft Skills

Essential soft skills include PowerPoint, Whiteboarding, Public Speaking, Interpersonal Skills, Writing, Listening, and Consultative Questioning. SE Managers (SEM) will conduct random audits of these requirements during the year. The SEM will look to provide their SEAC with the necessary guidance, coaching, and training if identified concerns are surfaced during these audits.

Technical Sales Operations

SE Management Weekly Status Calls

The SEAC will be required to conduct a weekly "one-on-one" call with their SEM. This call will cover four fundamental categories: Pipeline forecast, Field Notebook discipline (insert your company's tracking system – Salesforce, Vivun, etc.), Product risk dependencies, and Career-related action items.

Field Notebook Usage | Reporting CRM

At Adobe, the SEAC were expected to use the Field Notebook to document key activities within targeted opportunities, assigned accounts, or solution partners. In the Field Notebook, each SEAC is expected to know the details of every deal they are working on and ensure that these deals are accurately reflected in the Field Notebook. This requirement will be inspected during every SEM and SEAC "one-on-one" session. If management feels you are not maintaining proper activity logging, you will receive an official warning.

Over the years, the expectation for salespeople has been the same for SEAC s in reporting your activity and sales actions. Unfortunately, many of the technologies that have existed since the field notebook are useful for leadership and not as much for the SE. I agree with metrics and data analytics as they can help support increases in headcount and alleviate wasting resource time chasing deals that do not have a chance to succeed. Lacking any tool, I would recommend if the sales team is using Salesforce, then modify Salesforce to include an SEAC section that collects the necessary details that can be shared not just with leadership, but those details that can help the SEAC organization as a whole. Like the Field Notebook we designed at Adobe, the byproduct or exhaust from a solution should benefit the leadership, and the actual functionality of the car should benefit the SEAC.

At Snowflake, we had a product called VIVUN to sit on top of Salesforce, though it also collected data outside the primary source of truth. We ended up with two separate data silos. Unfortunately, the SEAC teams had to straddle two software solutions to understand the account executives' elements in the deal cycle. This happens when you migrate from a startup to the beginnings of the corporate culture. You end up having executives from SAP, EMC, and Oracle pushing a division to drive power between the orgs. True, this doesn't happen often, but you will see it can happen too often in my journey. Leaders tend to lead through spreadsheets and dashboards versus being in the field to understand what is happening on the ground. I have been guilty of this in the past, but lessons have been learned.

Commissions

The SEM team will provide a new forum for commission review. We will have a formalized compensation escalation process. The SEAC will have up to three weeks from receipt of commission sheets for SEM escalation. The SEM team will have a scheduled call with the compensation team to voice all concerns and take necessary actions for all the agreed-upon changes.

Workshop: Identifying the Right Role for You

To help you determine which role (SE, SA, or SC) is the best fit for you, consider conducting the following workshop:

Materials Needed:

- Post-it notes
- Voting dots
- Markers
- Large sheets of paper or whiteboards

Duration:

- 1-2 hours

Steps:

1. **Introduction (10 minutes)**: Explain the purpose of the workshop and provide an overview of the SEAC roles.
2. **Self-Assessment (20 minutes)**: Have participants write down their skills, interests, and career goals on Post-it notes.
3. **Role Exploration (30 minutes)**: Divide participants into groups and assign each group a role (SE, SA, or SC). Each group discusses the specific skills and responsibilities of their assigned role.
4. **Role Matching (20 minutes)**: Participants individually match their skills and interests with the role that best fits them using voting dots.
5. **Discussion (20 minutes)**: Open the floor for a group discussion on findings and individual preferences. Provide feedback and guidance.
6. **Conclusion (10 minutes)**: Summarize the workshop and provide resources for further exploration.

Recommended Books

To further help you identify the aspects of each role and enhance your skills, here are some recommended books:

1. "The Sales Engineer Manager's Handbook" by John Care
2. "Mastering Technical Sales: The Sales Engineer's Handbook" by John Care and Aron Bohlig
3. "The Trusted Advisor" by David H. Maister, Charles H. Green, and Robert M. Galford
4. "Spin Selling" by Neil Rackham
5. "The Challenger Sale: Taking Control of the Customer Conversation" by Matthew Dixon and Brent Adamson

Quiz: Test Your Understanding

1. What are the three main areas of focus for SEAC roles?
    - A) Value Selling Objectives, Solution Consulting, Technical Sales Operations
    - B) Marketing, Sales, Customer Service
    - C) Financial Planning, Product Development, Market Research
2. What is the primary objective for the SEAC team?
    - A) Drive revenue into the organization
    - B) Manage customer complaints
    - C) Develop new products
3. Which soft skill is NOT listed as required for SEAC roles?
    - A) Public Speaking
    - B) Programming
    - C) Writing
4. How often should SEAC certifications be reviewed?
    - A) Monthly

- B) Annually
- C) Quarterly
5. What is the purpose of the Field Notebook?
    - A) To document key activities and details within targeted opportunities, assigned accounts, or solution partners
    - B) To track personal expenses
    - C) To store customer contact information

Answers:

1. A) Value Selling Objectives, Solution Consulting, Technical Sales Operations
2. A) Drive revenue into the organization
3. B) Programming
4. B) Annually
5. A) To document key activities and details within targeted opportunities, assigned accounts, or solution partners

SEAC Managers Expectations

Having explored the necessary skills and expectations for SEAC roles, it's essential to understand what is expected from those who manage these teams. If you aspire to move into a managerial position, this section will provide valuable insights into the responsibilities and expectations for SEAC managers.

"Management is doing things right; leadership is doing the right things." — Peter Drucker

Introduction

The role of a Solutions Engineering Manager (SEM) is critical in driving revenue, building a quality pipeline, and ensuring customer satisfaction. This section outlines the key expectations and responsibilities for SEMs, focusing on technical sales organization, value selling management, business partner engagement, and operational excellence.

Revenue Attainment

The primary responsibility of the SEM is to assist the Area VPs, Regional Directors, and District Managers in generating net new revenue opportunities from both current and prospective customers and to manage overall customer satisfaction. Each SEM is expected to meet or exceed their quarterly quota, with an expectation to meet or exceed the quarterly and annual M1 targets (100% of the assigned quota as outlined in the Compensation Worksheet).

Building a Quality Pipeline and Driving Sell to Proof Deliverables

The SEM is expected to align with Area VPs, Regional Directors, and District Managers to build a pipeline that is 3X to 4X their annual quota. This is necessary for meeting and exceeding quota. The SEM should ensure that their team is looking for ways to position multiple technologies within each opportunity while solving the customer's business problems. The SEM should also be using the STEPPS process (Sell to Proof | Tech Win | Engagement Manager | Proof Onsite | Product Dependency | Services) in each opportunity to ensure that the appropriate offerings are used at each sales stage to achieve the goal of Sell to Proof and a TSO Technical Win.

Value Selling Management

The SEM is responsible for leading the value selling process within their assigned team. This process helps identify risks associated with all current opportunities, which fall into three main categories: Delivery Partner, Product, and Supportability. The SEM must drive this effort to ensure the opportunities developed into technical wins.

Business Partner Engagement

The SEM must facilitate the required teamwork and collaboration between sales and business partners (Professional Services or Solutions Partners). This includes ensuring that their team communicates with the assigned engagement manager after achieving a successful sell-to-proof or technical win. The SEM will monitor communication with business partners throughout the sales process on all key opportunities within their assigned region or business. The SEM must also ensure that business partners are engaged with customers appropriately and early enough in the sales cycle. Additionally, the SEM must inspect that business partners (Professional Services or Solutions Partners) are proactive, including their SE teams in all implementation milestones and post-sales activity.

Promoting WW Best Practice Sharing

Each SEM will be assigned ownership of one major WW SE Team initiative per year. The project plan should be developed and submitted to your manager within 30 days of assignment. A quarterly review of project success will be conducted by management.

Recruiting

Core to the SE organization's success is its ability to attract new talent. The SEM Management Team needs to be in recruiting mode constantly, always having qualified targeted candidates in each major metro area within their assigned territories ready if a headcount opens. When headcount does become available, recruiting and hiring should happen within one quarter.

Coaching, Mentoring & Performance Management

Each SEM must actively coach and mentor their regional pre-sales teams. This includes providing constructive advice and counsel after customer calls and being active in their territories, facilitating deal structure, technical requirements, and technology issue escalations. The SEM must also manage SE performance in the region, meeting with employees at least twice a year to provide performance feedback and facilitate career development. This includes completing the mid-year and annual review processes.

Coordinating & Directing SEAC Development

SE Managers must take an active interest in developing regional SE capabilities. Each SEM must assess, develop, and implement a training plan for SEs in the region to balance regional and personal development goals, ensuring the region has a full set of capabilities across all products. SEMs will encourage using the new flex-based skills tool to allow visibility of their team's skills throughout the company.

Developing a Diverse Team

- Perform a critical skills analysis of each SE in the region. Determine SE strengths and weaknesses, evaluating both soft and technical skills. Soft skills include presentation, demo, account management, meeting management, and sales objection handling skills.
- Ensure the team has the soft and technical skills to succeed. Balance personal development goals with sales needs and develop written training plans for each SE resource to enhance their value within the region. Plans should be completed for each SE in the region no later than the second week of Q2.
- Implement training plans with SEs in the region to address skill deficiencies and SE development according to the written plan.

Competitive Knowledge and Positioning

The SEM is primarily responsible for the competitive intelligence within each region. The SEM must ensure that each SE develops and maintains knowledge of competing technologies and can competitively position the brand's solutions against them. This expectation includes viewpoints within specific assigned industries, geographic regions, and named accounts.

Customer Care Engagement

Each SEM is required to assist their Teams by facilitating the reporting of Customer Care issues in a timely manner. It is expected that Customer Care will own all pre and post-sales service requests, providing full ownership and accountability for follow-up and reporting case status. The SEM must escalate if this agreement has not been satisfied.

Operational Excellence

The SEM must ensure that all operational activities are completed fully and on time.

Field Notebook

It is required that the SEM inspects full Field Notebook participation.

KPI Data

With a 3:1 ratio, it is critical to keep a close watch on KPI reporting. This reporting will ensure the necessary changes as we move into the next year. The KPI data is driven by CRM tools such as Salesforce, Oracle Siebel, and others.

Customer Success Dashboard (CSD)

The CSD will provide an automated view of our new STEPPS process. The data must be updated 24 hours before our TSO weekly CSD reviews.

Budget

SEMs will report accurate budget forecasting on a bi-weekly basis to upper management, and all expenses must be submitted no later than two weeks after the expense has been incurred.

Personal Time Off

SEMs must provide adequate support and backup for employees on PTO or Sabbatical as outlined in our PTO policy.

Professionalism

All SEMs will showcase the utmost respect for all organized training and corporate events. This requires showing up on time, dressing appropriately, and being an active listener, participant, and professional.

Workshop: Effective Management Practices

Materials Needed:

- Post-it notes
- Markers

- Large sheets of paper or whiteboards
- Laptops or tablets (optional)

Duration:

- 1.5-2 hours

Steps:

1. **Introduction (10 minutes)**: Explain the purpose of the workshop and provide an overview of the SEM role.
2. **Self-Assessment (20 minutes)**: Have participants write down their current management practices, strengths, and areas for improvement on Post-it notes.
3. **Role Exploration (30 minutes)**: Divide participants into groups and assign each group a different aspect of SEM responsibilities (e.g., pipeline management, coaching, operational excellence). Each group discusses best practices and common challenges.
4. **Role Matching (20 minutes)**: Participants individually match their skills and practices with the SEM responsibilities using voting dots.
5. **Discussion (20 minutes)**: Open the floor for a group discussion on findings and individual experiences. Provide feedback and guidance.
6. **Conclusion (10 minutes)**: Summarize the workshop and provide resources for further exploration.

Recommended Books

To further help you understand and excel in the SEM role, here are some recommended books:

1. "The Sales Manager's Guide to Greatness" by Kevin F. Davis
2. "Drive: The Surprising Truth About What Motivates Us" by Daniel H. Pink
3. "Leaders Eat Last: Why Some Teams Pull Together and Others Don't" by Simon Sinek
4. "High Output Management" by Andrew S. Grove
5. "The Coaching Habit: Say Less, Ask More & Change the Way You Lead Forever" by Michael Bungay Stanier

Quiz: Test Your Understanding

1. What is the primary responsibility of an SEM?
    - A) Managing customer complaints
    - B) Generating net new revenue opportunities and managing customer satisfaction
    - C) Developing new products
2. Which process should SEMs use to ensure opportunities become technical wins?
    - A) BANT
    - B) MEDDPIC
    - C) STEPPS
3. What is the required ratio for pipeline building according to SEM expectations?
    - A) 2X to 3X annual quota
    - B) 3X to 4X annual quota
    - C) 1X to 2X annual quota
4. How often should SEMs meet with their team members to provide performance feedback?
    - A) Once a year
    - B) Twice a year
    - C) Quarterly

5. What should SEMs do if Customer Care does not meet their service request agreement?
    - A) Handle the request themselves
    - B) Escalate the issue
    - C) Ignore the issue

Answers:

1. B) Generating net new revenue opportunities and managing customer satisfaction
2. C) STEPPS
3. B) 3X to 4X annual quota
4. B) Twice a year
5. B) Escalate the issue

Recommended Books

To further help you understand and excel in the SEM role, here are some recommended books with explanations on why they are relevant to this chapter:

1. "The Sales Manager's Guide to Greatness" by Kevin F. Davis
    - **Reason**: This book provides practical strategies and insights for sales managers to drive performance and achieve sales targets, aligning with the SEM's role in revenue attainment and building a quality pipeline.
2. "Drive: The Surprising Truth About What Motivates Us" by Daniel H. Pink
    - **Reason**: Understanding what motivates team members is crucial for coaching, mentoring, and performance management. This book delves into the science of motivation and can help SEMs inspire their teams to excel.
3. "Leaders Eat Last: Why Some Teams Pull Together and Others Don't" by Simon Sinek
    - **Reason**: SEMs need to foster teamwork and collaboration within their teams and with business partners. This book emphasizes the importance of leadership that creates a sense of safety and trust, which is essential for a cohesive and high-performing team.
4. "High Output Management" by Andrew S. Grove
    - **Reason**: Grove's book is a classic on management practices that SEMs can apply to ensure operational excellence, from performance reviews to training and

    development. It provides actionable insights for managing both people and processes effectively.
5. "The Coaching Habit: Say Less, Ask More & Change the Way You Lead Forever" by Michael Bungay Stanier
    - **Reason**: Coaching is a critical component of the SEM role. This book offers practical advice on how to coach effectively by asking the right questions, which can help SEMs improve their coaching and mentoring skills to support their teams better.

AE Account Executive Expectations

Transitioning from the previous chapter on SEM expectations, where we delved into the roles and responsibilities of Solutions Engineering Managers, we now shift our focus to Account Executives (AE). Understanding the dynamics between AEs and SEs, and how their collaborative efforts drive sales success, is crucial.

"The only way to do great work is to love what you do." - Steve Jobs

This section will be an interesting exploration as I have worked with countless fantastic account executives. There is a careful, balanced relationship between the SEAC and the account executive. For sales to work, there must be mutual respect for each individual on the sales team. True, the account executive has the most risk, but this does not allow the account executive to dismiss the entire team's needs. I recently worked with a fantastic coach, Andrea Middleton, and we conducted a SaaS academy training session he renamed "How to Train Your Dragon." This was a team training where the SEAC and the AE were to participate together. We will have a podcast and webinar, and the second book will provide greater detail on how you, too, can workshop this when you are hired as an SEAC.

Fundamental Account Executive Expectations

Here are some fundamental account executive expectations, and then I will provide the SEAC expectations to help balance the respect and responsibilities. An Account Executive is responsible for fully understanding a client's needs and determining whether a business can meet those needs. An Account Executive oversees a team to ensure the company's products or services are delivered on time, on budget, and up to the client's standards. Some of the other duties an Account Executive is responsible for include:

- Gathering information about a project's scope, budgets, and timelines
- Meeting with other executives to discuss clients' project goals, progress, and outcomes
- Developing budgets and timelines for clients and the company they work for
- Coordinating teams to meet project milestones
- Assembling new teams to meet clients' or businesses' goals
- Reporting and recording all sales activities in a web-based CRM system
- Qualifying inbound leads and prospects via phone and email
- Organizing regular client meetings to ensure excellent customer service
- Prospecting new sales by cold calling businesses
- Holding virtual demonstrations with an end goal of earning a prospect's business
- Preparing and presenting proposals and bids
- Negotiating terms and conditions with clients
- Collaborating with key decision-makers to identify opportunities and develop ideas that deliver sales results
- Uncovering and understanding a company's needs
- Attending trade shows and hosting customer events

S.E.A.C Perspective on AE Requirements

From an SEAC perspective, feel free to fast forward to the day in the life section in this book and it will outline a few of the requirements from our perspective. To highlight the key areas:

- No commitment to your calendar without review
- Calendar Invites with Agenda
- No meeting less than 24 hours
- SEAC need to conduct a pre-call discovery before any meetings
- Demos do not win deals - thanks to YouTube - there's a ton of examples
- RFP's received with a less than two-week due date are column fodder
- Solutions, POV (Point of Views), Value discovery/mapping those to solutions
- Proof Offerings - Aka - Demos and Proof of Concepts need to be mutually agreed on
- Adherence to Sales Methodology, reporting, and compliance - BMANTR | MEDDPICC or XYZ

Recommended Books

To further understand the dynamics between AEs and SEs and to excel in the AE role, here are some recommended books with explanations on why they are relevant to this chapter:

1. "The Challenger Sale: Taking Control of the Customer Conversation" by Matthew Dixon and Brent Adamson
   - **Reason**: This book introduces the Challenger Sales model, which is highly effective for account executives to take control of sales conversations and drive customer value.
2. "SPIN Selling" by Neil Rackham
   - **Reason**: This book offers a classic methodology for understanding and addressing customer needs through a structured approach to questioning, which is crucial for AEs.
3. "The New Strategic Selling" by Robert B. Miller and Stephen E. Heiman
   - **Reason**: It provides insights into managing complex sales processes and building long-term customer relationships, aligning with the AE's responsibilities in coordinating teams and developing strategies.
4. "Sell with a Story: How to Capture Attention, Build Trust, and Close the Sale" by Paul Smith
   - **Reason**: This book highlights the power of storytelling in sales, helping AEs craft compelling narratives to engage clients and close deals effectively.
5. "New Sales. Simplified.: The Essential Handbook for Prospecting and New Business Development" by Mike Weinberg

- - **Reason**: A great resource for AEs focused on prospecting and developing new business, providing practical tips and strategies for success in these areas.

Quiz

To ensure understanding of the content covered in this chapter, here is a simple quiz:

1. What is one primary responsibility of an Account Executive?
   - a) Overseeing product development
   - b) Qualifying inbound leads and prospects
   - c) Managing customer support tickets
   - d) Conducting market research
2. Why is it important for SEAC to conduct a pre-call discovery before any meetings?
   - a) To impress the client with their knowledge
   - b) To ensure the meeting is productive and addresses the client's needs
   - c) To prepare a detailed technical demonstration
   - d) To fill out the CRM system accurately
3. What should an Account Executive do if they receive an RFP with a less than two-week due date?
   - a) Accept it and rush the preparation
   - b) Reject it as column fodder
   - c) Negotiate for more time
   - d) Ignore it
4. Which book introduces the Challenger Sales model?
   - a) "SPIN Selling"
   - b) "The New Strategic Selling"
   - c) "The Challenger Sale"
   - d) "Sell with a Story"

5. What is one key area that SEAC should adhere to in their responsibilities?
    - a) Developing new marketing strategies
    - b) Reporting and compliance with sales methodologies
    - c) Managing customer support tickets
    - d) Creating product roadmaps

Answers:

1. b) Qualifying inbound leads and prospects
2. b) To ensure the meeting is productive and addresses the client's needs
3. b) Reject it as column fodder
4. c) "The Challenger Sale"
5. b) Reporting and compliance with sales methodologies

Part 4 Day in the Life (DIL)

Chapter 4: Typical Work Breakdown

Transitioning from the previous chapter on AE expectations, let's delve into a typical work breakdown for a Solutions Engineer (SE), Solutions Architect (SA), or Solutions Consultant (SC). Understanding how time is allocated across various responsibilities will help manage expectations and improve efficiency.

"Success is not the key to happiness. Happiness is the key to success. If you love what you are doing, you will be successful." - Albert Schweitzer

Operation Commitments

When you look at a field S.E.A.C. , a typical work week is divided between sales activity, business operations, training, customer support, marketing support, and in some cases post-sales activity. This does not leave much room in the week to focus on sales disciplines. The typical breakdown for a 50-hour work week, okay, don't laugh—it will be longer than a 50-hour work week here in the States. We all could take a lesson from the Europeans on balancing work and life.

In my experience, your breakdown of the week will depend on what quarter you are in and what week of that quarter you are in.

So before we break into a quarterly breakdown, what is the baseline for an average week? You can expect that each week you will spend about 10 hours on weekly conference calls, which can be just listening or participating. Depending on whether you are traveling, you will have about 5 hours on expenses. Even if you are not traveling, you can spend about 2 hours a week on expenses. You will spend about 2 hours a week on enablement efforts and should block time for more investments. So we are up to 14 hours out of the gate on basics.

Marketing Team Commitments

You will have some commitments from the marketing team to conduct webinars, workshops, and meetups. I remember one week at Elastic, we had three open-source meetups late at night off-site. This required travel, preparation for presentations, practice, delivery of material, and follow-up with any questions not answered at the event. Before COVID, you had a quarterly marketing booth event; some of these could be fun, though some are very long days on your feet, and if not part of a major brand, your booth would be in the basement near the bathrooms.

I remember one time being invited to Orlando for a partner event. I showed up in the evening and greeted the ground team to find out about my booth assignment. To my surprise, the expectation was that I would be the keynote speaker for the morning event. I almost threw up on the person who told me this. I practiced all night and crushed the event. I had over a thousand people in the room, and many came up to me after to ask questions or tell me they loved my presentation. I found that marketing events could consume, on average, about 5 hours a week spread over time. Now we are up to 19 hours out of 50 to get to selling.

But wait, there's more, which can be customer support or follow-ups. Remember, today, you are dealing with SaaS customers, and you have to take care of them to get a renewal. I would average 5 hours of customer support and service calls every week. So we are now at 24 hours before we spend any time on an account.

Account Rep Commitments

Remember you will typically have about two reps aligned to you in the States, and in some EMEA/ASIA PAC regions, you may have a three-to-one ratio. Much of these European relationships are due to language situations and cultural boundaries. You may be the only SEAC in an emerging marketplace like São Paulo or Eastern Europe. You may have a 4 to 1 ratio in Asia PAC since this tends to be a later investment for most emerging technologies. You could have 40 to 60 accounts per rep with each rep you are aligned to. The rep will pull out the top leaders and give the others to the inside sales teams to run down.

Think about the magnitude of potential accounts you will participate in. On average, you will need to have, in the best case, thirty customers to keep spinning in the air. In the worst case, you could have up to eighty accounts. Also, remember that each rep will not care about the other reps' commitments. The rep will consider your time as all of their time and not be divided. More on that later on, how to work with your rep.

So you have 26 hours to work on accounts and plan for meetings. This is why you need to have some roles, rules, and responsibilities outlined with your account manager. Unfortunately, a rep will set up a meeting nine out of ten times without fully qualifying the meeting, thus wasting your time. As you can see, you do not have the time to waste. We will discuss how to work with the account manager and have a mutual relationship that respects the requirements outlined.

Recommended Books

To further understand and excel in the roles of SE, SA, or SC, here are some recommended books with explanations on why they are relevant to this chapter:

1. "The Effortless Experience: Conquering the New Battleground for Customer Loyalty" by Matthew Dixon, Nick Toman, and Rick DeLisi
    - **Reason**: This book provides insights into customer support and service, essential for maintaining SaaS customer relationships and ensuring renewals.
2. "The Trusted Advisor" by David H. Maister, Charles H. Green, and Robert M. Galford
    - **Reason**: Understanding how to build trust with clients is crucial for SEs, SAs, and SCs who are often seen as trusted advisors to their clients.
3. "Presentation Zen: Simple Ideas on Presentation Design and Delivery" by Garr Reynolds
    - **Reason**: This book offers practical tips on creating and delivering engaging presentations, which is a key part of the role for SEs, SAs, and SCs.
4. "SPIN Selling" by Neil Rackham
    - **Reason**: It provides a structured approach to sales conversations and is particularly useful for understanding customer needs and positioning solutions effectively.
5. "The Sales Acceleration Formula: Using Data, Technology, and Inbound Selling to go from $0 to $100 Million" by Mark Roberge

- **Reason**: This book offers strategies for leveraging data and technology in sales, which can help SEs, SAs, and SCs work more efficiently and effectively.

Quiz

To ensure understanding of the content covered in this chapter, here is a simple quiz:

1. How many hours a week, on average, do SEs, SAs, and SCs spend on weekly conference calls?
   - a) 5 hours
   - b) 10 hours
   - c) 15 hours
   - d) 20 hours
2. What is one of the key roles of marketing team commitments for SEs, SAs, and SCs?
   - a) Conducting quarterly financial audits
   - b) Conducting webinars, workshops, and meetups
   - c) Developing new product features
   - d) Managing customer support tickets
3. How many accounts, on average, does an SE, SA, or SC need to keep active in the best-case scenario?
   - a) 10 accounts
   - b) 20 accounts
   - c) 30 accounts
   - d) 40 accounts
4. Why is it important to outline roles, rules, and responsibilities with your account manager?
   - a) To ensure clear communication and efficient use of time
   - b) To prepare for performance reviews

- c) To manage personal finances
- d) To develop new marketing strategies
5. Which book provides practical tips on creating and delivering engaging presentations?
   - a) "The Effortless Experience"
   - b) "The Trusted Advisor"
   - c) "Presentation Zen"
   - d) "SPIN Selling"

Answers:

1. b) 10 hours
2. b) Conducting webinars, workshops, and meetups
3. c) 30 accounts
4. a) To ensure clear communication and efficient use of time
5. c) "Presentation Zen"

The Other 26 Hours

Having understood the critical importance of Q4 and the demanding workload it entails, we now turn our attention to how best to utilize the remaining hours in your week to meet and exceed your sales objectives.

"Success is not the key to happiness. Happiness is the key to success. If you love what you are doing, you will be successful." – Albert Schweitzer

So what is left?

Now that you have a basic understanding of what it takes to get through certain quarters and the baseline of hourly consumption per week, let's explore how to effectively use the remaining 26 hours to achieve your weekly requirements and ultimately overachieve your quarterly objectives.

Optimizing Time Management:

1. Customer Meetings and Follow-ups (10 hours):
    - Schedule regular check-ins with your top accounts to ensure their needs are met and to identify any potential issues early.
    - Use this time to conduct deeper discovery sessions and build stronger relationships with key stakeholders.
2. Strategic Planning and Deal Review (5 hours):
    - Allocate time each week for strategic planning and deal reviews with your account team.

- o This includes assessing the health of your pipeline, reviewing account plans, and strategizing on how to advance each deal to the next stage.
3. Product and Industry Knowledge Development (3 hours):
    - o Stay up-to-date with the latest developments in your industry and advancements in your company's products.
    - o Participate in online courses, webinars, or read industry publications to continuously improve your knowledge base.
4. Internal Collaboration and Training (3 hours):
    - o Work closely with your internal teams, such as marketing, product management, and customer support, to ensure alignment and leverage their expertise.
    - o Engage in ongoing training sessions to refine your skills and stay current with best practices.
5. Administrative Tasks and CRM Updates (2 hours):
    - o Keep your CRM system updated with the latest information on your accounts and deals.
    - o Ensure all administrative tasks, such as expense reports and compliance training, are completed in a timely manner.
6. Prospecting and Networking (3 hours):
    - o Dedicate time to prospecting new leads and expanding your professional network.
    - o Attend industry events, participate in online forums, and leverage social media to connect with potential customers and partners.

Recommended Books:

1. "Deep Work: Rules for Focused Success in a Distracted World" by Cal Newport
   - **Reason:** This book provides strategies for achieving deep focus, which is crucial for making the most of your available hours and boosting productivity.
2. "Essentialism: The Disciplined Pursuit of Less" by Greg McKeown
   - **Reason:** Essentialism teaches you to prioritize what truly matters, helping you manage your time more effectively and eliminate non-essential tasks.
3. "Atomic Habits: An Easy & Proven Way to Build Good Habits & Break Bad Ones" by James Clear
   - **Reason:** Building good habits and breaking bad ones can significantly impact your efficiency and effectiveness, especially when working within tight time constraints.
4. "The 7 Habits of Highly Effective People" by Stephen R. Covey
   - **Reason:** Covey's classic book offers timeless principles for personal and professional effectiveness, which are invaluable for maximizing your productivity.
5. "First Things First" by Stephen R. Covey
   - **Reason:** This book emphasizes the importance of time management and prioritization, crucial skills for making the most of your 26 hours.

Quiz:

1. How many hours per week should you allocate to customer meetings and follow-ups?
    - a) 5 hours
    - b) 10 hours
    - c) 15 hours
    - d) 20 hours
2. What should be the primary focus during your strategic planning and deal review sessions?
    - a) Reviewing administrative tasks
    - b) Assessing the health of your pipeline
    - c) Conducting product training
    - d) Scheduling vacations
3. How often should you update your CRM system?
    - a) Monthly
    - b) Weekly
    - c) Daily
    - d) Quarterly
4. Why is it important to stay up-to-date with industry and product knowledge?
    - a) To impress your colleagues
    - b) To ensure you can effectively meet customer needs
    - c) To pass time during slow periods
    - d) To fulfill company training requirements
5. What is a key benefit of engaging in ongoing training sessions?
    - a) Receiving certificates
    - b) Refining your skills and staying current with best practices
    - c) Networking with peers

- d) Reducing your workload

Answers:

1. b) 10 hours
2. b) Assessing the health of your pipeline
3. b) Weekly
4. b) To ensure you can effectively meet customer needs
5. b) Refining your skills and staying current with best practices

Chapter 5 : Time is the Dreaded Enemy

Q1 Kickoff

Transitioning from understanding the typical work breakdown of SEs, SAs, and SCs, let's dive into the first quarter of the year (Q1), a period marked by intensive planning and reflection. This chapter will guide you through the excitement and challenges of Q1 kickoff events.

"The beginning is the most important part of the work." - Plato

The first quarter of the year is typically the busiest time, filled with planning sessions for the new year and reflections on the past year. Expect the first two weeks of every quarter to be spent in rooms or virtually with your sales counterparts. Q1 often includes the yearly sales kickoff meeting. Before COVID, companies would host these events offsite near their HQs, such as in San Jose or San Francisco, CA.

At Adobe, my first Q1 kickoff was at the Fairmont Hotel in San Jose. Staying locally, just a mile from the main HQ office, was fantastic. The event was a chance to meet corporate employees, see the office, and walk the hallways. The main hall, with huge screens and about a thousand chairs, was buzzing with excitement. The internal conference coordination teams always put on a great show, starting their planning two weeks after the last event. Kudos to those unseen heroes!

Sales kickoff is the best time of the year, especially if you exceeded your targets the previous year. You'll hear from product and department leaders, usually revolving around a common theme. Marketing efforts are in full swing, and the end-of-day bar events are fantastic. The best part is meeting colleagues from all over the world face-to-face—people you've texted, chatted with, and emailed but never met. Back then, we didn't have Zoom, only profile pictures in our HRM system.

The week is packed, so don't expect to take any calls during the day. You'll be busy every minute. Stay alert during these events because you're always interviewing for your next position or maintaining your current one. As mentioned in my journey section, this week can be the best of the year if you keep your wits. There's zero tolerance for misbehavior, and you will be fired on the spot if you misbehave.

Personal Anecdotes

I remember an Adobe event in Vegas—on the surface, it sounded fantastic. But mix alcohol, gambling, and all-night parties, and you're bound to have issues. One time, an SE got drunk and verbally abused a sales rep. After a call from my boss, I went to human resources and met in the green room to discuss what would happen. Within an hour, we booked plane tickets, notified hotel security, and terminated the individual on the spot. They had one hour to get their belongings and be escorted out.

This isn't just a Vegas issue; it happened in Dallas, Texas, with Oracle. We had social media companies of 20-year-olds who didn't understand corporate America. Incidents included a fire alarm pulled on one floor, a fire extinguisher thrown through a glass window, and a team member doing drugs—all dealt with calmly and legally. DO NOT BE ONE OF THOSE PEOPLE!

On a lighter note, enjoy Q1 and understand that the first full month will be filled with a sales conference and localized Quarterly Business Reviews (QBRs). Avoid booking family vacations during Q1. The QBR alone may involve an offsite event aside from the big kickoff. In some cases, you may be asked to stay a week longer to leverage investment discounts for local QBRs.

Recommended Books

To better prepare for Q1 kickoffs and understand the dynamics of such events, here are some recommended books with explanations on why they are relevant to this chapter:

1. "Drive: The Surprising Truth About What Motivates Us" by Daniel H. Pink
    - **Reason:** This book provides insights into motivation, which is crucial for maintaining high energy and focus during intensive Q1 kickoff events.
2. "The First 90 Days: Proven Strategies for Getting Up to Speed Faster and Smarter" by Michael D. Watkins
    - **Reason:** It offers strategies for making a strong start in a new year, aligning well with the planning and reflection activities in Q1.
3. "Quiet: The Power of Introverts in a World That Can't Stop Talking" by Susan Cain
    - **Reason:** This book can help you navigate large, bustling events by understanding how to leverage introverted strengths in extroverted environments like Q1 kickoffs.
4. "Extreme Ownership: How U.S. Navy SEALs Lead and Win" by Jocko Willink and Leif Babin

- **Reason:** It emphasizes the importance of discipline and responsibility, which are key during Q1 planning and execution.
5. "Getting Things Done: The Art of Stress-Free Productivity" by David Allen
    - **Reason:** It provides productivity techniques that are invaluable during the busy and often overwhelming Q1 period.

Quiz

To ensure understanding of the Q1 kickoff content, here is a simple quiz:

1. What is a typical activity during the first two weeks of every quarter?
    - a) Family vacations
    - b) Planning sessions with sales counterparts
    - c) Product launches
    - d) Customer support reviews
2. Why is the Q1 kickoff meeting significant?
    - a) It's a time to launch new products
    - b) It's an opportunity to meet colleagues from all over the world
    - c) It's when financial audits are conducted
    - d) It's a time for marketing teams to take a break
3. What is the key to success during Q1 kickoff events?
    - a) Taking as many calls as possible
    - b) Staying alert and maintaining professionalism
    - c) Focusing solely on customer support
    - d) Avoiding all social interactions
4. Why should you avoid booking family vacations during Q1?
    - a) It's the best time to take a break

- b) The Q1 kickoff and QBR events require full attention and presence
- c) It's when product development happens
- d) It's a slow period with little activity
5. What book is recommended for understanding motivation during Q1 kickoffs?
   - a) "Drive" by Daniel H. Pink
   - b) "The First 90 Days" by Michael D. Watkins
   - c) "Quiet" by Susan Cain
   - d) "Extreme Ownership" by Jocko Willink and Leif Babin

Answers:

1. b) Planning sessions with sales counterparts
2. b) It's an opportunity to meet colleagues from all over the world
3. b) Staying alert and maintaining professionalism
4. b) The Q1 kickoff and QBR events require full attention and presence
5. a) "Drive" by Daniel H. Pink

Most Important Week - Week 6

As we transition from understanding the quarterly business reviews, it's essential to recognize the critical periods within each quarter that can significantly influence the overall success of your sales strategy. One such crucial period is Week 6, a time that demands heightened focus and precision.

"Success is the sum of small efforts, repeated day in and day out." – Robert Collier

Importance of Week 6

The key week in any quarter is Week 6. This is the middle of the quarter, and as such, your regional vice president needs to provide forecast accuracy to the executive team. This becomes very critical post-IPO, especially for public companies. Many do not realize that the Sales VP has to report some accuracy at Week 6 so that a public company can assess whether or not they need to adjust the news to the market before the end of the quarter.

Forecast Accuracy: The accuracy of the forecast during this week can determine strategic decisions and market communications for the remainder of the quarter. As a system engineer, your role is pivotal in providing the most accurate information to your sales peer to properly target your number.

Achieving a Technical Win: Understand that your job is to get the customer to a technical win. As outlined before, a technical win is where the client has agreed that you are the selected vendor and no other vendors are being considered. In addition, your contacts will sponsor your vendor at executive meetings.

Challenges Post-Tech Win: All of this sounds great, and you would think that if you had a tech win, you would win the deal. Unfortunately, several sales prevention teams on both sides can ruin a good technical win. On average, I have experienced best case you will have a purchase order eight weeks after a Tech Win. Too often, I have seen technical win aging reports that see three to four months. The reality is if a technical win is aged more than thirty days, you may or will have to re-evaluate the technical win.

Case Study: Elastic and the Boston Client At Elastic, we had a technical win with a big Boston client. The deal didn't close as the legal department was going back and forth for weeks in redlines. We did not check in with the client as we thought we had the technical win. In reality, the line of business was not going to wait for both legal departments to figure it out and as such, they were evaluating other software solutions. We lost that deal, and lots of finger-pointing occurred back to the SEAC organization. I agree we as an SEAC org should continue to keep the account warm with additional care and feeding, but in the end, we ended up being a difficult company to legally do business with.

Q2 and Q3 - The Best Quarters

I find the best quarters are Q2 and Q3 as you will find your sales motion starts to connect. You have weeded out the accounts you know are not going to perform or have pushed a few off to the partner organization to work their relationships. Note the best time to take a vacation is the last two weeks of Q2, Q3 and maybe Q4. Q4 vacations can be very touchy as a sales team may want to give your time away as a give/get effort for accelerating a deal. In my experience, if an SEAC is needed in the last two weeks of a quarter, you will not win that deal for that quarter.

Housekeeping and Compliance

Remember to get all your quarterly requirements completed before the end of the quarter. I would always have a list of people that did not complete their expense reports before the end of the quarter, or those who did not finish compliance requirements like video training or HR training. Please, please, please - get this done. Make sure at the end of any given week you clean up your house. Get your SEAC tracking updated regularly, have your expenses up to date and all special projects in good order. If not, I can promise you that you will be ranked as the lowest person in the group! And yes, companies silently stack rank people - never documented but it is done! Do not be naive!

Workshop: Prioritizing Tasks & Managing Week 6

Objective: Help sales professionals prioritize tasks effectively and manage their responsibilities during the critical Week 6 period.

Materials Needed:

- Post-it notes
- Voting dots
- Whiteboard or large paper sheets
- Markers

Duration: 2 hours

Step-by-Step Instructions:

1. Introduction (10 minutes):
    - Brief participants on the importance of Week 6.
    - Outline the workshop's objectives and process.
2. Brainstorming Tasks (20 minutes):
    - Ask participants to write down all tasks they typically handle during Week 6 on Post-it notes.
    - Encourage them to include every possible task, from forecasting to follow-ups.
3. Categorizing Tasks (20 minutes):
    - Have participants place their Post-it notes on a whiteboard or large paper sheets.
    - Work together to categorize tasks into groups such as "High Priority," "Medium Priority," and "Low Priority."
4. Identifying Key Tasks (20 minutes):
    - Distribute voting dots to participants.

- Ask them to place dots on the tasks they believe are the most critical for Week 6.
- Discuss the results and identify the top tasks that need the most focus.
5. Creating a Week 6 Plan (30 minutes):
   - Divide participants into small groups.
   - Each group creates a detailed plan for managing the identified key tasks.
   - Plans should include timelines, resource allocation, and contingency strategies.
6. Presentation and Feedback (20 minutes):
   - Groups present their plans to the larger group.
   - Provide constructive feedback and discuss potential improvements.
7. Conclusion (10 minutes):
   - Summarize the key takeaways from the workshop.
   - Encourage participants to apply these strategies in their upcoming Week 6.

Recommended Books

"The Challenger Sale" by Matthew Dixon and Brent Adamson

- **Reason:** This book provides insights into how to effectively challenge and push customers to think differently, which is crucial for securing technical wins and managing Week 6 strategies.

"Predictable Revenue" by Aaron Ross and Marylou Tyler

- **Reason:** Offers a deep dive into building a consistent and predictable sales process, essential for maintaining accuracy and efficiency during critical weeks.

"SPIN Selling" by Neil Rackham

- **Reason:** Focuses on the SPIN (Situation, Problem, Implication, Need-payoff) technique, which can help in structuring effective sales conversations and closing deals efficiently.

Quiz

1. What is the primary focus of Week 6 in a sales quarter?
    - a) Reviewing past performances
    - b) Planning for the next quarter
    - c) Forecast accuracy and securing technical wins
    - d) Conducting training sessions
2. Why is it critical to maintain regular contact with a client even after a technical win?
    - a) To negotiate pricing
    - b) To ensure legal teams are aligned
    - c) To keep the account warm and address any arising issues
    - d) To finalize the marketing strategy
3. What should you do if a technical win is aged more than thirty days?
    - a) Celebrate the win
    - b) Re-evaluate the technical win
    - c) Move on to other clients
    - d) Negotiate the terms again
4. When is the best time to take a vacation, according to the text?
    - a) The first two weeks of each quarter
    - b) The last two weeks of Q2, Q3, and Q4
    - c) The middle of Q1

- d) At the beginning of each quarter
5. Why is it important to complete all quarterly requirements and updates regularly?
    - a) To avoid penalties
    - b) To ensure you are ranked higher in performance evaluations
    - c) To impress clients
    - d) To increase your salary

Answers:

1. c) Forecast accuracy and securing technical wins
2. c) To keep the account warm and address any arising issues
3. b) Re-evaluate the technical win
4. b) The last two weeks of Q2, Q3, and Q4
5. b) To ensure you are ranked higher in performance evaluations

Q4 Game Time

As we grasp the importance of Week 6 in any quarter, it's crucial to shift our attention to the dynamics of the year's final quarter. Q4 is a pivotal period requiring strategic time management and an unwavering focus on closing deals.

"The difference between winning and losing is most often not quitting." – Walt Disney

Q4 Game Time

Q4 is game time. During this period, you will clearly see which deals are real and which are not. Most of your time will and should be concentrated on the best and biggest opportunities. This quarter requires making tough choices on your time investments. Remember, your quota is a combined AE number, and your commitment is to drive as much business as possible to overachieve your quota.

Prioritizing High-Impact Deals:

In Q4, it is crucial to support the rep who will overachieve your number. This can be a delicate discussion, but at the end of the day, the compensation plan is designed to drive behavior. Your behavior should aim to overachieve. Do not hesitate to make the hard choice of focusing your efforts where you maximize your revenue. Most RVPs will agree with this approach, and if not, you should question your leadership.

Shift from Prospecting to Closing:

Another significant shift in Q4 is moving from prospecting to full-on closing deals. It is surprising that sales operations and leadership do not provide hold accounts going into the new year. Representatives are unlikely to build a pipeline for a future rep's territory. Typically, all pipeline development begins to dwindle at the end of Q3 and throughout Q4. This explains why Q1 is often a tough quarter due to a lack of pipeline development.

Time Management:

To recap, you have a 50-hour work week, with almost half of that week filled with non-direct sales-related activities. This leaves you with about 1000 hours per year to overachieve your number. Considering you lose at least four full months focusing on sales meetings and events, you have eight months to hit your target.

Reflection on Time Management:

I had a business partner who always emphasized, "TIME IS THE DREADED ENEMY!" Ironically, he also put, "WE WILL WIN" in the same email. This guy was solid. Greg Petraitis, a sales leader animal, used to always ask, "What are the three things you can negotiate with? - 1) Price 2) Resources 3) Information." Thanks, Greg. As an SE, you cover number two and three!

Recommended Books:

1. "The Challenger Sale" by Matthew Dixon and Brent Adamson
    - **Reason:** This book provides insights into how sales professionals can take control of the sales process and drive customer decisions, crucial for success in Q4.
2. "SPIN Selling" by Neil Rackham
    - **Reason:** Understanding the SPIN selling technique can help you ask the right questions and close deals effectively, especially in the critical final quarter.
3. "Sales EQ" by Jeb Blount
    - **Reason:** This book explores the emotional intelligence aspects of sales, helping you manage the stress and pressure of Q4 while maintaining strong relationships with clients.
4. "New Sales. Simplified." by Mike Weinberg
    - **Reason:** This book offers practical advice on building and maintaining a strong sales pipeline, essential for preparing for Q4 and beyond.
5. "Sell with a Story" by Paul Smith
    - **Reason:** Learn how to leverage storytelling to make your sales pitches more compelling and memorable, an effective technique for closing deals in Q4.

Quiz:

1. What is the primary focus of Q4 for a sales professional?
    - a) Prospecting new clients
    - b) Closing the best and biggest opportunities
    - c) Attending sales training sessions
    - d) Building a sales pipeline for next year
2. Why is it important to support the rep who will overachieve your number in Q4?
    - a) To ensure a balanced workload
    - b) To maximize your revenue and meet your quota
    - c) To focus on building long-term relationships
    - d) To reduce time spent on administrative tasks
3. What typically happens to pipeline development at the end of Q3 and throughout Q4?
    - a) It increases significantly
    - b) It remains stable
    - c) It dwindles
    - d) It shifts to inside sales teams
4. How many hours per year, on average, do you have to overachieve your number after accounting for non-direct sales-related activities?
    - a) 500 hours
    - b) 1000 hours
    - c) 1500 hours
    - d) 2000 hours
5. What are the three things you can negotiate with in sales, according to Greg Petraitis?
    - a) Price, Resources, Information
    - b) Time, Money, Effort
    - c) Knowledge, Skills, Attitude
    - d) Products, Services, Support

Answers:

1. b) Closing the best and biggest opportunities
2. b) To maximize your revenue and meet your quota
3. c) It dwindles
4. b) 1000 hours
5. a) Price, Resources, Information

QBR: Quarterly Business Review

In the journey of understanding the various facets of sales engineering, it's essential to delve into the structured processes that drive performance and continuous improvement. One such critical process is the Quarterly Business Review (QBR). These reviews not only reflect on the past but also set the course for future success, ensuring alignment and focus across teams.

"Success is not final; failure is not fatal: It is the courage to continue that counts." - Winston Churchill

Quarterly Business Reviews (QBRs) are a cornerstone of sales organizations, providing a structured opportunity to reflect on past performance and plan for future success. Each quarter, the sales team gathers either remotely or locally to review what worked in the previous quarter, celebrate achievements, and strategize for the coming months.

What to Expect at a QBR

- **Team Involvement**: Typically, leaders from major business units such as Partner Teams, Training, Marketing, Professional Services, Legal, and Finance attend the QBR.
- **Customer Insights**: Some of the most impactful QBRs include presentations from actual customers who discuss their experiences with the sales cycle and team.
- **Product Roadmap**: Product management might present the roadmap, including future product demonstrations, providing insights into upcoming features and capabilities.
- **Sales Templates**: Sales leadership often sends out templates to gather data about two weeks before the event. This

preparation helps ensure that the presentations are focused and relevant.

In my experience, attending and participating in QBRs has been a mix of preparation and on-the-spot adjustments. For instance, during my tenure at Adobe, our QBRs often featured unprepared sales teams scrambling to update their slides just minutes before presenting. This chaotic environment taught me the importance of thorough preparation and collaboration with account executives.

Working closely with your account executives for QBR presentations is crucial. It's an opportunity to showcase your skills and define your brand in front of leadership. Your expertise in presenting can be a significant advantage, and investing time in these preparations will strengthen your long-term relationships and professional reputation.

Workshop: Preparing for a QBR

Objective: Equip SEs with the skills to prepare and deliver compelling QBR presentations.

Materials Needed:

- Laptop
- Presentation Software (e.g., PowerPoint)
- Sales Data and Metrics
- Template for QBR Presentations

Duration: 2 hours

Steps:

1. **Introduction (10 minutes)**: Explain the purpose of QBRs and their importance.
2. **Presentation Skills (30 minutes)**: Provide tips on creating engaging slides and delivering impactful presentations.
3. **Data Analysis (30 minutes)**: Teach how to analyze sales data and extract meaningful insights.
4. **Collaboration (30 minutes)**: Work in pairs to draft a sample QBR presentation.
5. **Practice (20 minutes)**: Practice delivering the presentation and provide feedback.

Recommended Books

1. "The Challenger Sale" by Matthew Dixon and Brent Adamson:
    - **Reason**: This book offers insights into effective sales strategies that can be crucial when preparing for

QBRs, especially in articulating the value proposition and handling objections.
2. "SPIN Selling" by Neil Rackham:
    - **Reason**: Understanding the SPIN (Situation, Problem, Implication, Need-payoff) technique can help in structuring your QBR presentations and discussions effectively.
3. "Cracking the Sales Management Code" by Jason Jordan and Michelle Vazzana:
    - **Reason**: This book provides a framework for sales management that can be beneficial in understanding the metrics and KPIs discussed during QBRs.

Quiz

1. What is the primary purpose of a QBR?
    - a) To celebrate sales team achievements
    - b) To review past performance and plan for future success
    - c) To introduce new products
    - d) To conduct sales training
2. Who typically attends a QBR?
    - a) Only the sales team
    - b) Leaders from major business units
    - c) Customers
    - d) Both b and c
3. Why is it important to work closely with account executives for QBR presentations?
    - a) To ensure alignment and focus
    - b) To improve presentation skills
    - c) To strengthen long-term relationships
    - d) All of the above

4. What is a common issue faced during QBR presentations?
    - a) Lack of preparation
    - b) Over-preparation
    - c) Too many customers attending
    - d) None of the above
5. Which book offers insights into effective sales strategies for QBRs?
    - a) "The Challenger Sale"
    - b) "To Sell Is Human"
    - c) "The Lean Startup"
    - d) "Thinking, Fast and Slow"

Quiz Answers

b) To review past performance and plan for future success

d) Both b and c (Leaders from major business units and Customers)

d) All of the above (To ensure alignment and focus, To improve presentation skills, To strengthen long-term relationships)

a) Lack of preparation

a) "The Challenger Sale"

Part 5 : Remember You are a Sales Person!

Chapter 6: Sales Methodologies

I know I mentioned sales processes earlier and what BMANTR and MEDDPIC are, but in this chapter, we will go into an extensive overview and even include some cheat sheets to help you master these methodologies.

"The best way to predict the future is to create it." – Peter Drucker

What is BANT and BMANTR

BANT (Budget, Authority, Need, and Timing):

BANT is a well-known sales qualification framework, extended to include Method and Risk, forming BMANTR. From a pre-sales perspective, BMANTR and MEDDPIC are equally valuable to learn. Although some sales organizations emphasize these steps, they often fail to enforce the discipline required to implement them effectively. Throughout this book, you'll notice various points in the sales timeline where it is appropriate to ask specific BMANTR questions. It's crucial to maintain a good relationship with your account manager and know when you can ask these questions if they are not. Remember, as an SE, you have a unique ability to ask questions without bias. Customers trust you more than the sales rep, providing you an opportunity to gather crucial information.

BMANTR Overview:

BMANTR does not supersede or circumvent a sales methodology; it complements the sales process. BMANTR enhances the customer/opportunity qualification process and can be introduced between the education and qualification stages of the sales cycle, serving as a necessary sanity check throughout the sales cycle.

Benefits of BMANTR:

- Provides a qualification method to address the six key deal criteria necessary for any qualified deal.
- Offers criteria to measure and manage investment against based on how many or how completely questions are answered.
- Provides criteria to judge the level of detail, quality, and consistency of information received throughout the sales cycle.
- Offers a baseline for give-gets when negotiating with information before spending resources and discussing price.
- Provides a "vernacular" that can regulate conversations between salespeople and sales management to drive fact-based conversations, reduce emotion, eliminate filibustering, and increase efficiency.
- Helps win deals, forecast more effectively, manage investment, pull out from deals that will be lost, and preserve value.
- Value is predicated on the quality of executing the BMANTR exercise, not just going through the motions. Garbage information in equals garbage out.

Examples of BMANTR Questioning:

Budget:

- Is this purchase Capex or Opex driven?
- Is license, maintenance, training, and services funded from the same line or separate lines? Are they the same color of money or different?
- Has the budget been identified and expressly earmarked for this purchase, or is this a part of a broader category buy (e.g., infrastructure)? What are the dependencies?
- Who owns this budget? Is this different from the individual given permission to exercise this budget?
- Is this one-year money or multiple-year monies? What is the customer's budgeting cycle?
- Are there any special requirements around the money, aka, is there a trigger to approve and release funds?
- Are there any international currency implications that need to be addressed?

Method:

- What are the evaluation criteria for determining if these capabilities are required?
- What are the evaluation criteria for technology selection?
- How do we measure success? Who determines success? Do we need to have this documented and agreed upon with the customer (e.g., POC Plan)?
- Who determines that the work that has been done maps to needs on the program and deems it meritorious for funding?
- How are you going to configure this, deploy this, evaluate this, decide on this?

- What is our role in this process? How do we assist? How do we support? What are the resource requirements? Other investments?
- What is the decision method? Email, meeting, with whom? When is this scheduled for? Has this expectation been set?
- Is a business case required to get this signed off on? What constitutes this? Do you have an example?

Authority:

- Who, at the end of the day, needs to say yes to this (not just IT, the LOB Stakeholder, or Executive Sponsor)?
- Who can say no?
- Have we met these people and confirmed that it is their intent to procure these capabilities?
- Who are the technical decision-makers, and the business decision-makers?
- Is the decision maker the same person that owns the budget with P&L?
- How is approval granted? Are there multiple approvers?
- Even if this is a departmental decision, does someone from the larger business have to brief and sign off?

Need:

- Why do they need this solution? What is the business, operational value, or GAP or CBI that this addresses?
- Can the need be quantified in TCO or ROI? Do we know the business case? Have we participated in its development?
- Is this an expressed explicit need (part of a reqs document for the program that the customer needs to meet), or an implicit need?

- How does this need map to the success of the company (401 level answer required here)?
- Is the decision-maker tied into this need?
- What is the cost of doing nothing? What are the risks?

Timing:

- If we understand why, and why us, then why now?
- What is the timeframe communicated for selection, decision, procurement? Has this expectation been set? How are we managing to this date? Do we have an agreed-upon Evaluation Plan or Reverse Calendar exercise confirmed with the Champion and Executive Sponsor?
- If this slips by the June timeframe, what other than our communicated discounts is affected? What is driving this timeframe for this to get procured, deployed? Funding availability, program schedule, need.
- Have we driven a compelling event to reinforce the customers? Do we have a strict before/after proposal in place that we have discussed and confirmed with the customer?

Risk:

- Direct and indirect (variable) risk… What is the risk of this not getting done…what could make this not happen?
- Competitive? Competing initiatives? Political? Etc.
- PESTLE: Political, Economic, Social, Technological, Environmental, and Legal Factors

MEDDPICC

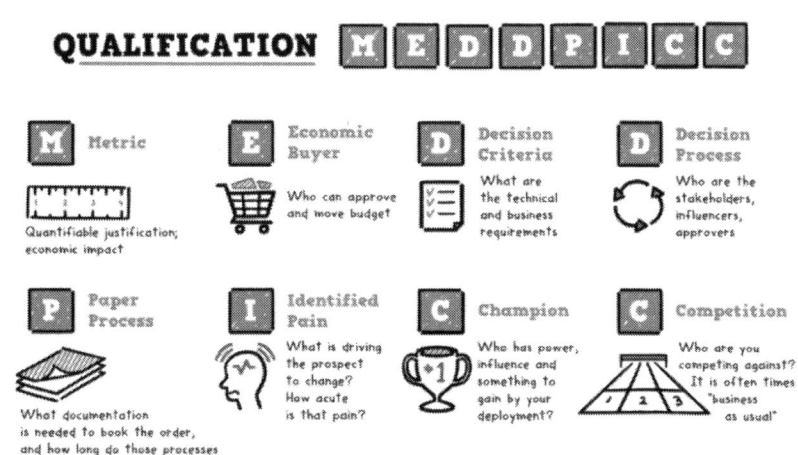

MEDDPICC has grown in popularity over the last few years. It is essentially BMANTR with a few tweaks. Both methodologies provide guardrails for the sales process and order to conversations with customers. It is crucial to quickly qualify out a contact or customer who is not worth the investment.

Definitions:

- **M (Metrics):** Quantifiable justification economic impacts. Define metrics to support purchase decisions.
- **E (Economic Buyer):** The person holding the keys to the dollars.
- **D (Decision Criteria):** Criteria for technology selection and evaluation.
- **D (Decision Process):** Understanding the internal purchasing process.

- **P (Paper Process):** Steps required to formalize the purchase.
- **I (Identify Pain):** The critical need driving the purchase.
- **C (Champion):** Individuals within the customer organization supporting the solution.
- **C (Competition):** Understanding the competitive landscape and internal obstacles.

Examples of MEDDPICC Questioning:

Metrics | Budget:

- Is this project budgeted/funded? If so, how much? Does that budget expire?
- Is it Capex or Opex?
- What is your annual budget cycle? Are your calendar/fiscal?
- Are there any other projects you can leverage funding/sponsorship/impact/benefit from to help fund?
- Where does this project rank in your fiscal priorities for this year?
- Is there an executive sponsor for this project's budget, and if so, who?
- How are you basing success metrics on? What are the success criteria?

Decision Criteria | Decision Process | Paper Process | Method | Timing:

- How are they measuring success, and what does success look like?
- How are they solving this challenge/issue/problem today?

- How do they purchase software/solutions? How do you evaluate software?
- How is this process aligned with their corporate initiatives?
- What does the desired future state look like?
- What's the impact of this not happening (aka do-nothing)?
- Are they going to be directly involved in the process/evaluation?
- Can we align our executive to yours to sponsor, enable, and provide an escalation path?

Decision Criteria:

- How is the decision made? By committee, team, business, or individual?
- What does the person stand to gain by success? What do they stand to lose if they are wrong?
- Who makes the decision?
- Can we set up a weekly cadence upon "technical win" for the remainder of the process to ensure alignment?

Paper Process:

- Assuming you have the technical win and they want your product, how do they procure your solution?
- Can they do e-sign/DocuSign, or is it wet signature only?
- Do they know the steps, approvals, and people all the way to the signatory and their schedule to do so?
- Do they require a PO? Do they use procurement software like SAP Ariba or Oracle Procurement Cloud?

Time:

- Have you outlined a transition plan when you migrate vendors?
- How far out do you need to provide notice of intent not to renew?
- How long should we allow for your internal process once we have technical/commercial alignment?
- What happens if it is late? What's the impact?
- What have you communicated to your leadership about the timing and impact of this decision?
- When does this solution need to be in place? When is the existing agreement due for renewal?

Economic Buyer | Champion | Authority:

- Do they or can they sign via DocuSign or wet signature?
- Do you know who is signing? Is it a decision by the committee?
- Is the signor's authority tied to how much the solution is?
- When does the board get together to review projects?
- Who can say no? Who can say yes?
- Who is going to be your sponsor for the project? Who has "skin in the game" ownership of the project's success?

Identify Pain | Need:

- Is there a risk or concern with the existing vendor?
- What happens if they don't execute on time? What is the impact on the business?
- What is lacking with your current solution that's forcing a change or reevaluation?

- What is the business driver for making this decision?
- What are the most important criteria for making a change (risk/cost/political)?

Competition | Risk:

- How does this solution/problem reduce their risk?
- How long have you been using the current solution?
- Is your champion aligned to change or risk-averse?
- What is the competitive landscape within your evaluation?
- What is the cost of switching (tangible and intangible)?
- Who is the incumbent? Why would you stay? Why would you switch?

Recommended Books:

1. "SPIN Selling" by Neil Rackham
   - **Reason:** This book offers an in-depth look at a consultative selling process, which complements both MEDDPICC and BMANTR methodologies by focusing on asking the right questions.
2. "The Challenger Sale: Taking Control of the Customer Conversation" by Matthew Dixon and Brent Adamson
   - **Reason:** It provides insights on how to teach, tailor, and take control of customer conversations, crucial for any sales professional.
3. "New Sales. Simplified.: The Essential Handbook for Prospecting and New Business Development" by Mike Weinberg
   - **Reason:** A comprehensive guide to developing new business, which is fundamental for the early stages of the sales process.

4. "The Sales Acceleration Formula: Using Data, Technology, and Inbound Selling to go from $0 to $100 Million" by Mark Roberge
   - **Reason:** This book highlights the use of data and technology in scaling sales, which aligns well with structured methodologies like MEDDPICC and BMANTR.
5. "Solution Selling: Creating Buyers in Difficult Selling Markets" by Michael T. Bosworth
   - **Reason:** It provides a detailed approach to solution selling, aligning with the need to understand and solve customer problems effectively.

Quiz:

1. What does BMANTR stand for?
   - a) Budget, Authority, Need, Time, Method, Risk
   - b) Budget, Authority, Need, Timing, Method, Results
   - c) Budget, Authority, Network, Time, Method, Risk
   - d) Budget, Authority, Need, Timing, Metrics, Risk
2. Which element in MEDDPICC is focused on identifying economic impacts?
   - a) Decision Process
   - b) Metrics
   - c) Champion
   - d) Identify Pain
3. In BMANTR, what is the importance of understanding the customer's budgeting cycle?
   - a) To impress the customer
   - b) To align your sales efforts with their fiscal schedule
   - c) To determine their organizational structure

- d) To understand their marketing strategy
4. What should you do if you discover that your contact cannot answer the decision process questions in MEDDPICC?
    - a) Move on to another contact
    - b) Ask for an introduction to someone who knows
    - c) End the sales engagement
    - d) Skip the decision process questions
5. Why is it crucial to have multiple champions within the customer's organization?
    - a) To increase your network
    - b) To have different points of contact
    - c) To ensure broader support and insight
    - d) To avoid reliance on one individual

Answers:

1. a) Budget, Authority, Need, Time, Method, Risk
2. b) Metrics
3. b) To align your sales efforts with their fiscal schedule
4. b) Ask for an introduction to someone who knows
5. c) To ensure broader support and insight

Chapter 7: The Sales Journey - Step by Step

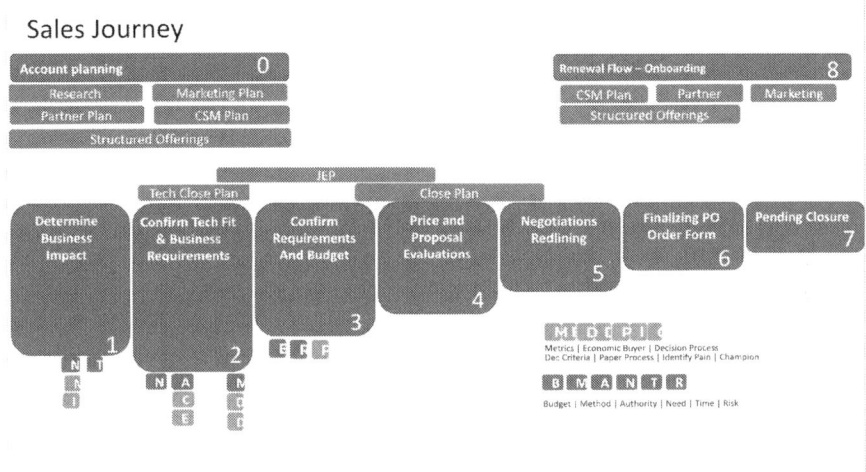

Previously, we delved into the intricacies of different sales methodologies, particularly focusing on BMANTR and MEDDPICC. In this chapter, we'll provide a step-by-step overview of the sales journey, detailing each stage and incorporating relevant industry practices and best strategies. Additionally, we'll include cheat sheets and practical tips to help you navigate each phase effectively.

"Success in sales starts with the customer, not with the sales process." – Steve Jobs

The sales journey is a complex process involving several stages, each requiring specific actions and strategies. Below is an in-depth look at each step, from the initial account planning to the final closure of the deal.

1 Determine Business Impact

Stage Detail: The Inside Sales team has pushed this opportunity to the account team. The Account Executive (AE) reviews the lead, conducts a series of calls to qualify the opportunity, and tries to identify the Critical Business Issues (CBIs).

Level: No Commit

Age: 1 - 5 Weeks

Industry Insight:

At this stage, it's crucial to identify the key pain points of the business and align them with your solution. Effective questioning and active listening are essential skills here.

2 Confirm Tech Fit & Business Requirements

Stage Detail: This stage can last a very long time depending on the number of people involved and the requirements to prove out. The goal here is to achieve a Technical Win. More on that later.

Level: Upside / Forecast

Age: 1 - 9 Months*

Industry Insight: Building a solid technical case involves thorough testing and validation of your solution against the customer's needs. Engage with technical stakeholders early and often.

3 Confirm Requirements - Budget

Stage Detail: This can be a continuation of stage 2. The SEAC will spend a large amount of time here to close out the requirements. This information is usually teased out earlier in the process. In reality, no money or budget means less likely you will have a deal. Unless you are trying to pull latent pain or unaware issues to the surface, which can take a lot of value discovery requirements.

Level: Forecast

Age: 1 - 2 Months

Industry Insight: Understanding the customer's budget cycle and financial constraints is critical. Use this information to align your proposal with their fiscal realities.

4 Price & Proposal

Stage Detail: Proposals are fairly easy to construct. The challenge comes with price changes, discounts, or legal term discussions.

Level: Commit

Age: 1 - 5 Weeks

Industry Insight: Ensure your proposal clearly articulates the value of your solution. Be prepared to justify pricing and address any concerns about costs or terms.

5. Negotiations & Redlining

Stage Detail: Negotiations on price can be impactful. Deals can be lost if the Finance team does not approve discount levels.

Additionally, the legal team can delay a deal significantly. Deals may also be lost due to legal complications on either side.

Level: Commit

Age: 1 - 8 Weeks

Industry Insight: Effective negotiation skills are crucial. Understand the customer's priorities and be willing to find mutually beneficial solutions. Always involve legal and finance teams early to anticipate and mitigate potential roadblocks.

6. Finalize PO / Order Form

Stage Detail: Typically straightforward. A Purchase Order (PO) or Order form can usually be approved through the customer workflow in about a week.

Level: Commit

Age: 1 - 10 Weeks

Industry Insight: Ensure all terms are clear and agreed upon. Follow up regularly to keep the process moving and address any last-minute issues promptly.

7. Pending Closure

Stage Detail: Just waiting for the order form to be faxed, emailed, or signed via DocuSign.

Level: Win

Age: 1 - 3 Weeks

Industry Insight: Maintain communication and provide any needed support to finalize the deal. Celebrate the win but also prepare for the next steps in implementation and customer success.

Recommended Books:

1. "SPIN Selling" by Neil Rackham
    - **Reason:** Offers an in-depth look at consultative selling, helping you to ask the right questions at each stage of the sales journey.
2. "The Challenger Sale: Taking Control of the Customer Conversation" by Matthew Dixon and Brent Adamson
    - **Reason:** Provides insights on how to teach, tailor, and take control of customer conversations, crucial for navigating complex sales cycles.
3. "New Sales. Simplified.: The Essential Handbook for Prospecting and New Business Development" by Mike Weinberg
    - **Reason:** A comprehensive guide to developing new business, fundamental for early stages of the sales process.
4. "The Sales Acceleration Formula: Using Data, Technology, and Inbound Selling to go from $0 to $100 Million" by Mark Roberge
    - **Reason:** Highlights the use of data and technology in scaling sales, aligning well with structured methodologies.
5. "Solution Selling: Creating Buyers in Difficult Selling Markets" by Michael T. Bosworth

- **Reason:** Offers a detailed approach to solution selling, crucial for understanding and solving customer problems effectively.

Quiz:

1. What is the primary goal of Stage 2 in the sales journey?
    - a) To identify budget constraints
    - b) To achieve a Technical Win
    - c) To finalize the purchase order
    - d) To begin negotiations
2. How long does Stage 3 (Confirm Requirements - Budget) typically last?
    - a) 1 - 5 Weeks
    - b) 1 - 2 Months
    - c) 1 - 9 Months
    - d) 1 - 10 Weeks
3. What are the main challenges in Stage 5 (Negotiations & Redlining)?
    - a) Technical validation
    - b) Identifying budget
    - c) Price changes and legal term discussions
    - d) Finalizing the order form
4. Why is it important to engage with technical stakeholders early in Stage 2?
    - a) To understand their budget cycle
    - b) To validate the technical fit of your solution
    - c) To begin price negotiations
    - d) To finalize the purchase order
5. What should you do during the Pending Closure stage?
    - a) Begin a new sales process
    - b) Wait for the order form passively

- c) Maintain communication and provide needed support
- d) Negotiate price changes

Answers:

1. b) To achieve a Technical Win
2. b) 1 - 2 Months
3. c) Price changes and legal term discussions
4. b) To validate the technical fit of your solution
5. c) Maintain communication and provide needed support

Chapter 8: Sales Stages In Detail

Step Zero

As we dive deeper into the sales process, it's essential to remember that a significant amount of groundwork is laid before we reach the later stages of a deal. In this chapter, we'll explore Step Zero, the critical initial phase where the foundation for successful sales engagements is established.

"The secret of getting ahead is getting started." – Mark Twain

In Step Zero of any sales cycle, the account manager, the SDR (Sales Development Representative), and in some cases, the SE (Sales Engineer) review the account list. They will decide which accounts to focus their sales efforts on. There's a tremendous amount of groundwork that happens before we get to steps one or two in the sales cycle that solution engineers are not typically involved in outlining.

The salesperson invests countless hours sitting with their SDR, selecting those accounts. The SDR, inside the sales team, will essentially "dial for dollars," spending all week dialing accounts, trying to entice them to have a conversation. Their ultimate goal is to achieve a meeting with the account manager. Some SDRs excel at qualifying in and qualifying out an account. Unfortunately, there are a few who qualify too many in, resulting in the need to qualify them out as soon as possible. This comes down to managing those 26 hours within the week and focusing your time on accounts with the highest probability of success.

I strongly recommend building a tight relationship with your SDR and/or inside sales team, for they can benefit from your experience. Hopefully, you can learn from how they approach a customer through Discovery. In many companies I worked at, one of my requirements was for a new hire to shadow or team up with an SDR. Since the SDR was good at conducting a quick elevator pitch and probing the account to identify critical business and technical issues, the new hire SEAC would quickly begin formulating their talk track.

Over 80% of our time in the first stages of a customer relationship will essentially be spent being a therapist, lying the customer on a couch and asking them about their challenges and needs. If the company you get hired into doesn't practice this, feel free to take the initiative. Remember, your job is to close business, and do that as expeditiously as possible.

Workshop: Account Planning and SDR Collaboration

Objective: Help participants understand the importance of Step Zero in the sales cycle and develop strategies to collaborate effectively with SDRs.

Materials Needed:

- Whiteboard and markers
- Account lists
- Laptops/tablets
- SDR call scripts
- Post-it notes
- Voting Dots

Duration: 2 hours

Step-by-Step Instructions:

1. Introduction (10 minutes):
   - Brief overview of Step Zero and its importance in the sales cycle.
   - Discuss the roles of the account manager, SDR, and SE in this phase.
2. Breakout Session 1: Account List Review (30 minutes):
   - Divide participants into small groups.
   - Each group reviews a sample account list and selects key accounts to focus on.
   - Groups present their chosen accounts and rationale to the rest of the participants.
3. Breakout Session 2: SDR Call Script Development (30 minutes):
   - In the same groups, develop call scripts for SDRs to use when reaching out to selected accounts.
   - Discuss the key elements of a successful call script and the importance of qualifying accounts early.
4. Breakout Session 3: Role-Playing (30 minutes):
   - Groups conduct role-playing exercises where participants take turns being the SDR, account manager, and SE.
   - Practice making calls, qualifying accounts, and setting up meetings.
5. Review and Voting (10 minutes):
   - Post all account plans and call scripts on the wall.
   - Participants use voting dots to indicate which plans and scripts they find most effective.
6. Debrief and Q&A (10 minutes):

- Discuss the results and feedback from the voting session.
- Address any questions and provide additional tips on effective account planning and SDR collaboration.

Recommended Books

1. "Predictable Revenue: Turn Your Business Into a Sales Machine with the $100 Million Best Practices of Salesforce.com" by Aaron Ross and Marylou Tyler
   - **Reason:** This book provides insights into building a scalable sales development team and the importance of effective SDRs in generating predictable revenue.
2. "Fanatical Prospecting: The Ultimate Guide to Opening Sales Conversations and Filling the Pipeline by Leveraging Social Selling, Telephone, Email, Text, and Cold Calling" by Jeb Blount
   - **Reason:** It covers various prospecting techniques, which are crucial for SDRs in Step Zero of the sales process.
3. "The Sales Development Playbook: Build Repeatable Pipeline and Accelerate Growth with Inside Sales" by Trish Bertuzzi
   - **Reason:** This book offers strategies for building and managing an effective sales development team, emphasizing the role of SDRs in the initial stages of the sales cycle.
4. "New Sales. Simplified.: The Essential Handbook for Prospecting and New Business Development" by Mike Weinberg

- **Reason:** It provides practical advice on prospecting and new business development, which are critical for success in Step Zero.
5. "SPIN Selling" by Neil Rackham
    - **Reason:** Focuses on the importance of asking the right questions and understanding customer needs, which is essential for SDRs when qualifying accounts.

Quiz

1. What is the primary goal of an SDR in Step Zero?
    - a) To close deals
    - b) To qualify accounts and set up meetings with the account manager
    - c) To handle customer support requests
    - d) To manage account renewals
2. Why is it important to build a relationship with your SDR?
    - a) To delegate all your work
    - b) To benefit from their experience and improve customer approach strategies
    - c) To avoid making sales calls yourself
    - d) To monitor their performance
3. What should you do if an SDR qualifies too many accounts in?
    - a) Focus on the accounts with the highest probability of success
    - b) Ignore the extra accounts
    - c) Ask the SDR to requalify all accounts
    - d) Schedule meetings with all accounts
4. Why is it beneficial for a new hire SE to team up with an SDR?

- a) To handle administrative tasks
- b) To learn quick elevator pitches and probing techniques
- c) To manage the SDR's workload
- d) To avoid customer interactions

5. What is a common activity in the first stages of a customer relationship?
    - a) Negotiating contracts
    - b) Being a therapist and understanding customer needs
    - c) Handling technical support issues
    - d) Finalizing purchase orders

Answers:

1. b) To qualify accounts and set up meetings with the account manager
2. b) To benefit from their experience and improve customer approach strategies
3. a) Focus on the accounts with the highest probability of success
4. b) To learn quick elevator pitches and probing techniques
5. b) Being a therapist and understanding customer needs

The First Stage

In the previous chapter, we discussed the foundational elements that set the stage for successful sales engagements. Now, let's delve into the intricacies of the sales journey, starting with the critical first stage. Here, we'll explore how to uncover customer needs, identify timing, and pinpoint the pain points that drive purchasing decisions. Understanding this stage is vital, as it lays the groundwork for all subsequent interactions and strategies.

"Discovery consists not in seeking new lands but in seeing with new eyes." – Marcel Proust

Discovery

You will notice that at sales stage 1 is where you're going to find answers to needs and timing and identify the pain. This is the critical stage of getting to the root cause of those challenges for the customer to solve. Typically as a SEAC, you will not get engaged until sales stage 2 and possibly sales stage 3, but the bulk of your time will be spent determining the business impact, confirming the technical fit, and business requirements.

This stage could be stalled for up to a full year. I would run aging reports at all the companies I've worked at and see a deal move from no commit to upside to forecast and back to no commit. When investigating why the movement occurred, it was typically because we did not do enough discovery of the fundamental nature of our client's issues. We did not do the work; we were "hoping" the deal would happen.

As you move through the sales timeline, you can appreciate the amount of work your account manager has to complete to finalize the purchase. Much of your time will be spent in the early sales stages, but your account manager has to confirm requirements, budget price proposals, negotiate the red lines, which can be death to an account opportunity, finalize the order form, and then close the deal. You will find that too often, the sales prevention teams—legal and finance—will cause the termination of a deal that you may have spent 18 months developing. Those teams are there to protect the organization both legally and financially. The work required can be overbearing for an account manager during these phases of a deal committed to sales leadership.

A few things you'll notice above the sales stages are the gray boxes that showcase a technical close plan, a joint execution plan, and a close plan. These are all specialized tools to help guide those critical steps with the customer's involvement, forcing commitment and equal partnership in a successful purchase or technical win. I'll provide more insight into this later in the book but certainly, take a look at technical close plans and joint execution plans.

Research

Diving into account planning and research, you will find that all successful pre-sales engineers do a great job at research before walking into a customer meeting. Here are a few key things to consider when doing research:

1. Annual Reports and 10-Ks:
    - It's amazing how often the account management team overlooks the annual reports of public companies. The 10-K is an excellent resource for specific details surrounding risks and headwinds that

your solution could solve. Use PDF search tools to find keywords like "search" or "security." You'll be surprised at how often these terms come up.
2. Social Media and Business Tools:
    o Utilize LinkedIn and other social tools to understand who your Champion is and how they operate. Personal interests shared on platforms like Facebook and Instagram can help you build a more personal connection.
3. DISC Profiling:
    o Understanding the interpersonal dynamics and emotional reactions of your target individuals can be crucial. DISC profiling helps you tailor your approach to suit the individual's personality.
4. Investing in Customer and Competitor Stock:
    o Investing in shares of a customer or their competitor can provide valuable insights. As a stockholder, you can attend quarterly or annual presentations, gaining deeper insights into the company.
5. Job Boards and Career Pages:
    o Monitor your customer's career page and job boards. This can provide insights into their current needs and future plans. For example, if a company is hiring for skills that your solution supports, it can indicate a strong potential for your product.

Workshop: Customer Research and Discovery

Objective: Help participants understand the importance of thorough research and discovery in the first stage of the sales process.

Materials Needed:

- Laptops/tablets
- Access to the internet
- Copies of annual reports and 10-Ks
- Social media profiles
- DISC profiling tools

Duration: 2 hours

Step-by-Step Instructions:

1. Introduction (10 minutes):
   - Overview of the importance of research and discovery in the first stage of the sales process.
2. Breakout Session 1: Annual Report Analysis (30 minutes):
   - Divide participants into small groups.
   - Each group reviews a sample annual report and 10-K, searching for key terms and identifying potential business challenges.
3. Breakout Session 2: Social Media Research (30 minutes):
   - Groups use LinkedIn and other social tools to gather information about a sample customer's key stakeholders.
   - Discuss how this information can be used to build a relationship.
4. Breakout Session 3: DISC Profiling (30 minutes):

- Participants use DISC profiling tools to analyze the personalities of sample stakeholders.
- Develop tailored communication strategies based on DISC profiles.
5. Review and Discussion (20 minutes):
    - Groups present their findings and strategies.
    - Discuss the importance of each research tool and how it contributes to a successful sales process.

Recommended Books

1. "SPIN Selling" by Neil Rackham
    - **Reason:** This book provides a framework for asking questions that uncover the needs and pain points of customers, essential for the first stage of the sales journey.
2. "The Challenger Sale: Taking Control of the Customer Conversation" by Matthew Dixon and Brent Adamson
    - **Reason:** It introduces a sales approach that challenges customers' thinking, helping to uncover deeper insights and drive the sales process forward.
3. "Insight Selling: Surprising Research on What Sales Winners Do Differently" by Mike Schultz and John E. Doerr
    - **Reason:** This book highlights the importance of bringing valuable insights to the customer, aligning with the discovery and research focus of the first stage.
4. "Customer Centric Selling: The Message Driven Sales Process" by Michael T. Bosworth and John R. Holland
    - **Reason:** It emphasizes the importance of aligning your sales approach with the customer's needs and challenges, which is critical in the first stage.

5. "New Sales. Simplified.: The Essential Handbook for Prospecting and New Business Development" by Mike Weinberg
   - **Reason:** It offers practical advice on prospecting and new business development, which are crucial activities in the early stages of the sales cycle.

Quiz

1. At which sales stage do you typically find answers to customer needs and timing?
   - a) Stage 1
   - b) Stage 3
   - c) Stage 5
   - d) Stage 7
2. Why is research important in the first stage of the sales process?
   - a) To close deals quickly
   - b) To understand the customer's challenges and needs
   - c) To prepare sales contracts
   - d) To manage internal reports
3. What is a valuable resource for understanding the risks and headwinds faced by a public company?
   - a) LinkedIn profiles
   - b) Facebook posts
   - c) Annual reports and 10-Ks
   - d) Job boards
4. How can DISC profiling help in the sales process?
   - a) By identifying the customer's budget
   - b) By tailoring your approach to suit the individual's personality

        - c) By preparing technical documents
        - d) By managing sales quotas
    5. Why might investing in a customer's stock be beneficial?
        - a) To increase personal wealth
        - b) To gain insights into the company and build rapport
        - c) To influence the company's decisions
        - d) To qualify for employee benefits

Answers:

1. a) Stage 1
2. b) To understand the customer's challenges and needs
3. c) Annual reports and 10-Ks
4. b) By tailoring your approach to suit the individual's personality
5. b) To gain insights into the company and build rapport

Sales Stages Two and Three - Your Breakdown

As we delve into the intricacies of sales stages, it's essential to recall the sales methodologies we previously discussed. In this chapter, we'll explore the critical stages two and three in the sales process, providing an extensive overview and cheat sheets to help navigate these stages effectively. Understanding these stages is pivotal as they are where you'll spend the majority of your time, identifying customer needs and ensuring a technical win.

"Plans are only good intentions unless they immediately degenerate into hard work." – Peter Drucker

The Account Manager has a huge meeting with a really important client! - LOL

These two stages are where you will spend the bulk of your time. They are crucial for identifying the customer's critical business and technical issues, confirming whether you're talking to the key players, and understanding how to achieve a technical win. A fantastic book, the gold standard, is "Demo to Win" by Robert D. Riefstahl. His book provides extensive information on how to work with your rep and deliver demonstrations that help close business. I have contracted with Rob at previous companies to provide training for teams and highly recommend his training for your organization.

Managing Your Time

As you work through the week, you realize that 26 hours is really not a lot of time to do your job effectively. You will need to work with your account managers to understand how to divide your time equally. Account managers often call you 24 hours before they want you to meet with a client, saying they have a huge opportunity. When you ask for details, you might get vague responses like, "Don't worry about it. I've already spoken to them and they want to see what we showed Nike last week." This indicates that the account manager might not have all the necessary information. If they're not willing to allow you to conduct Discovery, be skeptical about the success of that meeting.

14 Days Before Meeting

To ensure success in front of a customer, establish some level of agreement on what you need before the meeting:

- At least 14 days before the meeting, have a call.
- Conduct a discovery call with the account manager to understand the issues.
- Discuss calendars to book your time appropriately. Never let the account manager schedule your time without consulting you.
- The rep should set up calendar invites with internal and external hold dates. Internal invites are valuable for practice before the meeting.
- Meeting invites should have a clear agenda and links to Salesforce or the CRM solution used. If there's no internal calendar invite, there's no meeting.
- Set up internal pre-meeting and post-meeting discussions.
- Ideally, all of this should happen 14 days before the meeting.

9 Days Before Meeting

Nine days before the meeting, agree with your account manager on a pre-call Discovery with your business champion. Review the sales team's conversations and identify the MEDDPICC questions you want to ask. Revalidate the issues outlined with the account team and always check with the customer if anything has changed since the last discussion.

3 Days Before Meeting

Three days before the meeting, sit down with your coach, sales account manager, and any supporting personnel. Walk through the agenda and slides. Everyone should know their roles and responsibilities in the room. Review logistics, room setup, and security details. Ensure you have done your due diligence on the people attending the meeting, including names, titles, and LinkedIn references.

2 Days Before Meeting

Two days before the meeting, ensure everyone knows their roles, rules, and responsibilities. Role-play your presentation and meeting flow. Make sure everyone understands the tasks at the end of the meeting. Every meeting should have a call to action with mutual follow-ups for both you and the customer.

Post-Meeting Logistics

Plan where you will meet after the customer meeting. Avoid meeting in places like the lobby or a nearby Starbucks where your customer or competitors might be. Choose a location two to three blocks away. Set up a content folder on the internal network or Google Drive for the team to collaborate and place their notes.

Workshop: Effective Meeting Preparation

Objective: Help participants understand the importance of thorough preparation and effective collaboration in meeting success.

Materials Needed:

- Laptops/tablets
- Access to the internet
- Sample meeting agendas
- Calendar tools

Duration: 2 hours

Step-by-Step Instructions:

1. Introduction (10 minutes):
    - Overview of the importance of preparation and collaboration in meeting success.
2. Breakout Session 1: Calendar Coordination (30 minutes):
    - Divide participants into small groups.
    - Each group reviews sample meeting requests and coordinates their calendars for optimal scheduling.
3. Breakout Session 2: Discovery Calls (30 minutes):
    - Groups conduct mock discovery calls to gather information and identify critical issues.
4. Breakout Session 3: Role-Playing (30 minutes):
    - Participants role-play a meeting scenario, assigning roles and practicing their presentation and meeting flow.

5. Review and Discussion (20 minutes):
    - Groups present their meeting plans and discuss the importance of each preparation step.
    - Discuss how effective preparation can impact meeting success and customer relationships.

Recommended Books

1. "Demo to Win" by Robert D. Riefstahl
    - **Reason:** This book provides a comprehensive guide to delivering effective demonstrations that help close business, aligning with the focus on customer meetings in stages two and three.
2. "The Sales Development Playbook: Build Repeatable Pipeline and Accelerate Growth with Inside Sales" by Trish Bertuzzi
    - **Reason:** This book offers strategies for managing the early stages of the sales process, including working with SDRs and account managers, which is crucial for stages two and three.
3. "Selling to the C-Suite: What Every Executive Wants You to Know About Successfully Selling to the Top" by Nicholas A.C. Read and Stephen J. Bistritz
    - **Reason:** It provides insights into understanding and engaging with top executives, essential for securing technical wins and advancing through the sales stages.
4. "New Sales. Simplified.: The Essential Handbook for Prospecting and New Business Development" by Mike Weinberg

        - **Reason:** This book offers practical advice on prospecting and business development, critical activities in the early stages of the sales cycle.
    5. "Insight Selling: Surprising Research on What Sales Winners Do Differently" by Mike Schultz and John E. Doerr
        - **Reason:** It highlights the importance of bringing valuable insights to the customer, aligning with the discovery and research focus of stages two and three.

Quiz

1. At which sales stages will you spend the bulk of your time?
    - a) Stage 1
    - b) Stages 2 and 3
    - c) Stage 5
    - d) Stage 7
2. Why is it important to conduct a discovery call 14 days before a meeting?
    - a) To close deals quickly
    - b) To understand the customer's issues and book your time appropriately
    - c) To prepare sales contracts
    - d) To manage internal reports
3. What should you do 9 days before the meeting?
    - a) Finalize the order form
    - b) Conduct a pre-call discovery with your business champion
    - c) Send the proposal
    - d) Review the annual report
4. How should you handle post-meeting discussions?
    - a) Meet in the lobby immediately after the meeting
    - b) Walk across the street to a nearby Starbucks

- c) Choose a location two to three blocks away from the customer's office
- d) Discuss over email

5. Why is role-playing important 2 days before the meeting?
   - a) To finalize the budget
   - b) To ensure everyone understands their roles and the meeting flow
   - c) To conduct additional discovery calls
   - d) To prepare the technical close plan

Answers:

1. b) Stages 2 and 3
2. b) To understand the customer's issues and book your time appropriately
3. b) Conduct a pre-call discovery with your business champion
4. c) Choose a location two to three blocks away from the customer's office
5. b) To ensure everyone understands their roles and the meeting flow

Chapter 9 – Sales Methodology & Tools

As we've discussed the various stages of the sales journey and methodologies like BMANTR and MEDDPICC, it's crucial to have the right tools at your disposal to effectively navigate each stage. In this chapter, we'll delve into some essential sales tools that can significantly enhance your ability to plan, execute, and close deals successfully.

"Tools are only as good as the hands that wield them." – unknown

In the world of sales, having the right tools can make all the difference. Below are some of the key tools you should incorporate into your sales strategy, along with descriptions and their value propositions.

Account Plan

Description: Select a few accounts you see a large return on time investment and blueprint the annual sales design to penetrate that account and ultimately close that account.

Value: When done correctly, the plan is very helpful. Unfortunately, most organizations inspect Account plans quarterly and not weekly during forecast calls to verify the plan is in action. It becomes a check-in-the-box exercise.

See http://www.SEWorklife.com for Samples

Technical Close Plan

Description: "Mr. Customer, how do you purchase software and what are the steps necessary to achieve a technical win? A technical win in our opinion is where you have selected us as the only vendor of choice, you will sponsor us to the business and have discontinued future evaluations." This plan will outline all the necessary steps to achieve a technical win at your customer.

Value: If the customer is not willing to participate in this type of plan, you are either talking to the wrong person(s) or they are not serious about you winning this contract.

See http://www.SEWorklife.com for Samples

Joint Execution Plan

Description: "Mr. Customer, if you are planning to have a solution deployed by MONTH 20XX, then can we set up some time and work backwards from that date to outline what steps are necessary to achieve a technical win, include all approval parties, manage through legal, finance, establish necessary implementation teams, and identify their on-ramp for implementation, user acceptance, and user training before go-live?"

Value: If the customer is not willing or does not know how they purchase software, it would be good to get that out of the way earlier in the sales process. A great way to detect if the customer is a decision maker or someone who is looking for help.

See http://www.SEWorklife.com for Samples

Workshop: Utilizing Sales Tools Effectively

Objective: Help participants understand how to effectively use sales tools to enhance their sales strategy and improve deal closure rates.

Materials Needed:

- Whiteboard and markers
- Laptops/tablets
- Printed templates of Account Plans, Technical Close Plans, and Joint Execution Plans
- Post-it notes
- Voting Dots

Duration: 2 hours

Step-by-Step Instructions:

1. Introduction (10 minutes):
    - Brief overview of the sales tools.
    - Importance of integrating these tools into the sales process.
2. Breakout Session 1: Account Plan (30 minutes):
    - Divide participants into small groups.
    - Each group selects a target account and develops a basic Account Plan using the provided templates.
    - Groups present their plans to the rest of the participants.
3. Breakout Session 2: Technical Close Plan (30 minutes):
    - In the same groups, develop a Technical Close Plan for the selected account.

       - Discuss the challenges and strategies for achieving a technical win.
4. Breakout Session 3: Joint Execution Plan (30 minutes):
       - Groups work on creating a Joint Execution Plan.
       - Emphasize the importance of timeline management and involving all stakeholders.
5. Review and Voting (10 minutes):
       - Post all plans on the wall.
       - Participants use voting dots to indicate which plans they find most feasible and well-structured.
6. Debrief and Q&A (10 minutes):
       - Discuss the results and feedback from the voting session.
       - Address any questions and provide additional tips on using these tools effectively.

Recommended Books

1. "The New Strategic Selling" by Robert B. Miller and Stephen E. Heiman
     - **Reason:** Provides insights into strategic account planning and how to effectively manage and close complex sales.
2. "SPIN Selling" by Neil Rackham
     - **Reason:** Focuses on the importance of asking the right questions and understanding customer needs, which is critical for creating effective sales plans.
3. "The Challenger Sale: Taking Control of the Customer Conversation" by Matthew Dixon and Brent Adamson
     - **Reason:** Offers a unique approach to sales that emphasizes the importance of teaching and tailoring

customer interactions, aligning well with the use of sales tools.
4. "Solution Selling: Creating Buyers in Difficult Selling Markets" by Michael T. Bosworth
    - **Reason:** Provides a detailed methodology for understanding and solving customer problems, which is essential for developing Technical Close Plans.
5. "The Sales Acceleration Formula: Using Data, Technology, and Inbound Selling to go from $0 to $100 Million" by Mark Roberge
    - **Reason:** Highlights the use of data and technology in scaling sales, aligning with the structured approach of using sales tools.

Quiz

1. What is the primary purpose of an Account Plan?
    - a) To track sales quotas
    - b) To blueprint the annual sales design for key accounts
    - c) To list potential leads
    - d) To manage customer support requests
2. Why is a Technical Close Plan important?
    - a) It outlines steps to achieve a technical win
    - b) It helps in legal negotiations
    - c) It tracks sales performance
    - d) It identifies new markets
3. What should you do if a customer is not willing to participate in a Joint Execution Plan?
    - a) Ignore the customer

- b) Reevaluate if they are the right person or if they are serious about the contract
    - c) Continue with the sales process without it
    - d) Offer a discount
4. Which sales tool helps in managing timelines and involving all stakeholders?
    - a) Account Plan
    - b) Technical Close Plan
    - c) Joint Execution Plan
    - d) Sales Forecast
5. What is a key benefit of using BMANTR in the sales process?
    - a) It reduces the need for technical support
    - b) It augments customer/opportunity qualification
    - c) It simplifies legal documentation
    - d) It eliminates the need for negotiations

Answers:

1. b) To blueprint the annual sales design for key accounts
2. a) It outlines steps to achieve a technical win
3. b) Reevaluate if they are the right person or if they are serious about the contract
4. c) Joint Execution Plan
5. b) It augments customer/opportunity qualification

Chapter 10: Game Day

Earlier in this book, we touched upon the importance of preparation and methodologies like BMANTR and MEDDPICC. Now, it's game time. In this chapter, we will go into extensive detail about the day of the big meeting. From setting up the room to effectively engaging with the client, these steps will ensure that you make the most of this critical hour.

"Success is where preparation and opportunity meet." – Bobby Unser

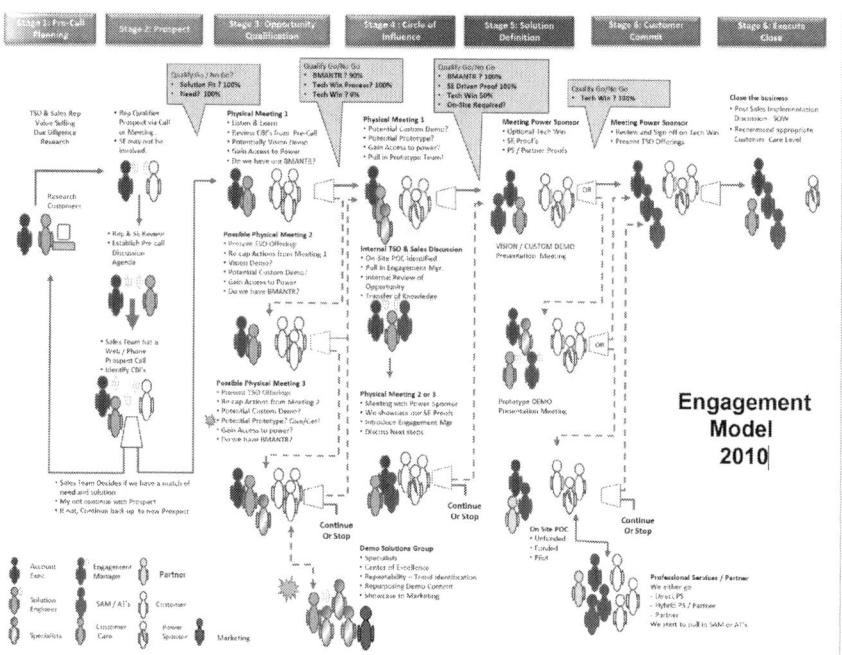

Illustration – My Old Process at Adobe

Okay, it's game time; meeting day has arrived.

You've done all your due diligence; you're ready for this event to take place. This will be one of the most important hours of time invested. Everyone is busy, and we only have 26 hours a week to actually do our job. Can you imagine what the customer has to go through during the week to get a vendor chosen and purchase approved through their process?

Be There Early

If you're on time, you're late. Be there early to gain entrance to the room so you can set up your laptop. Next, figure out where you're going to sit and where everyone else is going to sit in the room. Do not all sit on one side of the room. If you have more than three people, spread across the group. This way, you can make eye contact with your own people and see the room in its entirety. I like to use the analogy of actors on and off stage as we go through a meeting. Keep in mind that you as a pre-sales engineer are probably going to be on stage more often than your account manager. Make sure your account manager is taking notes while you're up talking to the audience, and you take notes if your account manager is up talking to the audience.

Sign-In Sheet

The first thing you should have ready to go is a sign-in sheet, with names, titles, emails, and mobile numbers. Have all of this listed and printed, ready to go. A best practice is to not put your logo on top. This is not about you; this is about the customer. Have the customer's logo on the sign-in sheet. That sign-in sheet should be passed around and collected at the end of the event.

Meeting Kick-Off

The account manager kicks off the call/meeting. They will conduct internal introductions, review the agenda, and have the opportunity to review the critical business and technical issues discovered during the one-on-one call with your champion. The account manager should now pivot to the customer for introductions, leaving the business and technical issues either on the whiteboard, sticky notes, or even on the screen. The account manager should ask everyone to introduce themselves by name, title, what they want to get out of today, and whether or not they agree with the list of issues outlined. This last piece is critical since there may be people who do not agree with the issues list. You want to know that information immediately.

On Stage

Now you're on stage. It is your time to take everything you've practiced and all the research you put into this meeting and display it as you move through your conversation. This will be a combination of slides, whiteboard skills, and demonstrations to showcase the technology as it meets the requirements. One of the best tips is to have the list of issues outlined during your discovery call on a poster board, the whiteboard, or on Post-It notes. As you walk through your solution and slides, get audible responses from your audience regarding the acceptance of your solution for each issue. When you get acceptance, physically walk up to the whiteboard and check that off with a giant blue check mark. Ideally, by the end of your presentation, the board should be fully checked off, indicating that you've addressed all issues.

Closing the Meeting

Now your sales rep gets up to close out the meeting. Next to them is the list of issues outlined at the beginning of the meeting, clearly checked off or not checked off as presented by the pre-sales solution engineer. A favorite question to ask, or for your account manager to ask, is, "What's preventing us from moving forward since it looks like we've checked off and identified solutions to many of your issues?" These check marks were validated by the individuals in the room. Depending on your relationship and the stage within the sales process, this is usually where you would ask for a joint execution plan to identify the next steps in order to move forward.

Post-Meeting Debrief

So, you've completed your first meeting, and all parties have met off-site as agreed. They already have the scheduled calendar invite, so those who were remote will dial in. They can't give you the excuse that they are double-booked because you booked this time well in advance. You head off-campus, away from the employees of the company you were just at, and discuss the "done well and do better" 15-minute debrief. The account team assigns responsibilities and deadlines for follow-ups, and a follow-up email thanking them is sent out. You've completed your first official meeting.

Understanding the Process

I hope this gives you a good understanding of what's involved in the prep and execution of a meeting with a customer. Remember, you may have five different customer meetings per week, each requiring this level of prep and understanding of the customer situation. This is why you need an agreed-upon relationship with your account manager regarding how you operate in the field together. Because you're not just helping this one account manager, you might be helping two or three others, turning those five customer meetings into fifteen.

Workshop: Effective Customer Meetings

Objective: Help participants master the preparation and execution of customer meetings to maximize success.

Materials Needed:

- Laptops/tablets
- Projector/whiteboard
- Sample sign-in sheets
- Meeting agenda templates

Duration: 3 hours

Step-by-Step Instructions:

1. Introduction (15 minutes):
    - Overview of the importance of preparation and execution in customer meetings.
2. Breakout Session 1: Setting Up the Room (30 minutes):
    - Divide participants into small groups.
    - Each group practices setting up a meeting room, including laptop setup and seating arrangements.
3. Breakout Session 2: Role-Playing the Meeting Kick-Off (45 minutes):
    - Groups role-play the meeting kick-off, including internal and customer introductions.
4. Breakout Session 3: Presentation and Whiteboarding (45 minutes):
    - Participants practice presenting solutions and using the whiteboard to check off issues.
5. Review and Discussion (30 minutes):

- Groups present their meeting plans and discuss the importance of each preparation step.
- Discuss strategies for effective meeting execution and follow-up.

Recommended Books

1. "Demo to Win" by Robert D. Riefstahl
    - **Reason:** This book provides a comprehensive guide to delivering effective demonstrations, a critical skill for game day presentations. I absolutely love this book and the author has started a very successful consulting practice.
2. "SPIN Selling" by Neil Rackham
    - **Reason:** Offers valuable insights into the questioning and probing techniques essential for understanding customer needs during meetings.
3. "The Challenger Sale: Taking Control of the Customer Conversation" by Matthew Dixon and Brent Adamson
    - **Reason:** Explains how to effectively engage with customers and challenge their thinking, aligning with the goals of game day meetings.
4. "Sales EQ: How Ultra High Performers Leverage Sales-Specific Emotional Intelligence to Close the Complex Deal" by Jeb Blount
    - **Reason:** Emphasizes the importance of emotional intelligence in sales, crucial for managing customer interactions during high-stakes meetings.
5. "Cracking the Sales Management Code: The Secrets to Measuring and Managing Sales Performance" by Jason Jordan and Michelle Vazzana

- **Reason:** Provides insights into managing sales processes and performance, which can help in planning and executing effective customer meetings.

Quiz

1. Why is it important to arrive early on the day of the meeting?
   - a) To avoid traffic
   - b) To set up the room and be prepared
   - c) To have breakfast with the team
   - d) To chat with the customer
2. What should be included in the sign-in sheet?
   - a) Names and titles only
   - b) Names, titles, emails, and mobile numbers
   - c) Only emails
   - d) Names and mobile numbers
3. Why should the customer's logo be on the sign-in sheet?
   - a) To make it look official
   - b) To show that the meeting is about the customer, not you
   - c) To impress the customer
   - d) To follow company policy
4. What is the purpose of the pre-meeting discussion?
   - a) To socialize with the team
   - b) To review the agenda and roles
   - c) To finalize the order form
   - d) To relax before the meeting
5. Where should the follow-up meeting with your team take place?
   - a) In the customer's lobby
   - b) At a nearby Starbucks

- c) At least two to three blocks away from the customer's office
- d) In the parking lot

Answers:

1. b) To set up the room and be prepared
2. b) Names, titles, emails, and mobile numbers
3. b) To show that the meeting is about the customer, not you
4. b) To review the agenda and roles
5. c) At least two to three blocks away from the customer's office

Part 8: Let's Get You a Job!

Chapter 11: Job Search and Interview Process

In the previous chapter, we covered essential strategies and best practices for engaging with customers and conducting successful meetings. Now, let's shift gears and focus on the crucial steps to securing a job in the presales field. This chapter will guide you through the job search process, from understanding corporate hiring cycles to optimizing your LinkedIn profile and preparing for interviews. Whether you're leaning towards corporate America or a startup, this guide will help you navigate the path to your next career move.

"The future depends on what you do today." – Mahatma Gandhi

By now, you are either really eager to venture down a presales career path, or I have completely scared you during the day in the life overview of your average week. I have to say all jobs have their challenges, but if you want to be freed from your desk, given the freedom to be that trusted customer technical advisor, and be viewed as a critical person in a sales process, this job is the best you will ever have!

Marketing 101

The Marketing Campaign for You

The first step in any marketing campaign is to understand the classic 4 P's of marketing: Product, Place, Promotion, and Price, with your Target Market at the center. Not to mention demographics and psychographics. True, this is to market a product, but guess what? You are the product, and you have a price, location requirements, and will need to promote yourself.

Define Your Target Market

What is your target market? Earlier, we discussed various roles available, from traditional FAB (Features, Advantages, Benefits) solutions to back-office bottom-up technical architectural solutions. What you decide here will limit or expand the target audience we will be looking to focus on. For example, if you want to be a solution architect, where you are 80% technical and 20% sales, then you will be looking at infrastructure and operations software brands. If you are more 60% technical and 40% sales, you may be looking for a mix of FAB-type solutions like ServiceNow or Veeva solutions. If you are more 60% sales and 40% technical, then you would be looking at shrink-wrap solutions like Microsoft Office, Adobe solutions, and others.

Corporate vs. Startup

Now that you have decided on the type of role and vendor solution you want to pursue, you need to determine if you are a startup person or a corporate person. As discussed, both have their pros and cons. Your interview style will be different depending on which type you choose, and we will discuss that in a second. If you feel you are a corporate America type and look for a massive number of people with a consistent work rhythm and a well-defined scope, then you will start in the Fortune 500 lists. If you are looking to have a voice at the table, be a part of a movement or innovation technology with fewer rules regarding roles, rules, and responsibilities, then startups are a great place for you.

In my career, I have worked for both, and depending on where you are in life, I found that corporate America provided some cover during uncertain economic times, especially having three very young kids. However, later in life, I found that my experience provided great value to startups in their efforts to build teams quickly, overachieve quotas, and participate in strategic planning.

Corporate Job Search

When deciding on a corporate job search, you have a number of things to consider in your plan. A corporation will typically not post a position unless it has budget approval. You need to understand how a position becomes available inside a large organization. Corporations are predictable when it comes to hiring practices. I would first look at when the company has its end of the year. Not all public companies end their year on December 31st. For example, Adobe had their end of year in November and Oracle at the end of May. Why this matters is understanding OPEX and budget cycles. Everything comes down to money and timing. At Adobe, our OPEX was in July before the end of the year, and as a Director, I knew what our headcount was going to look like before the end of that year. Select the companies you want to target, identify when their fiscal year ends and work backward about 4 to 5 months before the end of their year. An easy way to figure out their end of year is to look at the stock info or just look at their annual report. As a director, I would start my search immediately and well before the position was posted on the internet or any sites.

Understand that corporate America will not use headhunters and has heavily invested in HR teams to prospect for new talent. However, startups may use outside firms to augment their internal teams as a cost management way to ramp their teams. I have had some amazing talent acquisition teams work for me finding people, and actually, all of them were amazing! I plan on having an entire podcast on this topic interviewing those teams. They work mostly inside LinkedIn Recruiter. As a standard member in LinkedIn, you do not see LinkedIn Recruiter. LinkedIn Recruiter is a completely different interface from your consumer view; it allows the recruiter to filter, share, and collaborate on individuals available in the market. Remember, the big win for many of these recruiters is pulling a candidate from another company. So when you do finally enter the SEAC career path, remember recruiters will ping you every so often. I would recommend you keep a watchful eye on their names and connect with them in anticipation of a possible move out of your current company in two to three years.

Optimize Your LinkedIn Profile

Like many business applications you aspire to sell, everything comes down to data, how you access, search, and the impact of those search results. Recruiters will use LinkedIn search and filters to line up the perfect targeted candidate audience. Understanding in order for the best chance to be viewed by these recruiters will be determined on how your profile is set up. SEO (Search Engine Optimization) is not just for company websites, Amazon, or Google results. SEO can benefit you, provided you set up your profile page with the proper key terms. If you do this correctly, your profile will match the recruiter's filters and you will be at the top of the search result window. The good news is that there are plenty of optimization tools on the market to scan through your LinkedIn profile and give you an SEO score. Some may even provide insights into what you should change to improve that score. For example, Jobscan.co, Resumeworded.com, Inlytics.io, and Medium.com. Just do a search for LinkedIn Optimization in Google.

LinkedIn has a host of content to even help you manually adjust your profiles. There was a blog post back in 2017 that has recently been updated to January 2022 by Jane Deehan, Sr. Content Marketing Manager at LinkedIn, focusing on 20 core things to include in your profile edits. Many of these should be common sense, but she does a great job listing them out. I will include a copy in the back of the book or on a website to keep as an archive in case it goes to the internet black hole someday. Here is a sample of the 20 key things to do:

1. Choose the right profile picture
2. Add a background photo
3. Make your headline more than just a job title
4. Turn your summary into a story
5. Declare war on buzzwords
6. Grow your network
7. List your relevant skills
8. Spotlight the services you offer
9. Spread the endorsement love
10. Manage your endorsements
11. Take a skills assessment
12. Request recommendations
13. Showcase your passion for learning
14. Share media and marketing collateral
15. Get credit for your thought leadership with publications
16. Share relevant content from LinkedIn feed

17. Add comments
18. Follow relevant influencers for your industry
19. Become an employee advocate
20. Publish long-form content and use it to start conversations

Additional Research

I would recommend looking at a number of presales engineers' career paths already working at the target companies on your list. If you have a specific company you really want to work for, take a moment and mirror some of those who have had a successful tenure. Additionally, review that company's website and look at what their culture and mission are. This is usually in the "About Us" link at the bottom of any company's page. Just like DISC profiling, you want to profile the company you are targeting. It would be wise to first see if you line up with those culture and mission items. If not, DO NOT try to fake your way into that company; no job is worth not aligning with those missions. However, if you do line up with those missions, then start to post content on your LinkedIn page supporting those missions. Those companies' HR departments will notice those postings and it could give you the edge you need to be in the top ten list.

I won't go too much into how to optimize your LinkedIn profile, as mentioned earlier, there are many sites to help you with that. However, one area you cannot escape from is "Key Words." This is the foundation for any search engine to filter through. Just like when you search on YELP for a place to eat that is German, fresh, has outdoor seating, and is dog-friendly, your profile will need to match up with that type of search to be selected from the thousands out there. You need to think like the recruiter and identify the key words that best match the job profile they are looking for. Hint: take a look at the job description for key words and look at the people already hired there for additional key words.

Here is a great document provided by some of my HR friends on how internal departments work. This is a global sales engineering recruitment doc - thanks, Kunzie, for the insights!

Quiz

1. What are the classic 4 P's of marketing?
    - a) Product, Price, Place, Promotion
    - b) Product, People, Place, Promotion
    - c) Product, Profit, Place, Promotion
    - d) Product, Price, People, Promotion
2. What is the first step in a corporate job search?
    - a) Applying for jobs online
    - b) Identifying when the company's fiscal year ends
    - c) Networking with employees
    - d) Attending career fairs
3. Which LinkedIn tool is primarily used by recruiters to find candidates?
    - a) LinkedIn Jobs
    - b) LinkedIn Recruiter
    - c) LinkedIn Premium
    - d) LinkedIn Learning
4. Why is SEO important for your LinkedIn profile?
    - a) It helps you find jobs more easily
    - b) It improves your profile visibility to recruiters
    - c) It ensures your profile looks professional
    - d) It allows you to connect with more people
5. What should you include in your LinkedIn profile summary?
    - a) Job title and company name

- - b) List of skills and endorsements
  - c) A compelling story about your career journey
  - d) Contact information and social media links

Answers to the Quiz

1. a) Product, Price, Place, Promotion
2. b) Identifying when the company's fiscal year ends
3. b) LinkedIn Recruiter
4. b) It improves your profile visibility to recruiters
5. c) A compelling story about your career journey

Chapter 12: Leverage SEO

Global Sales Engineering Recruitment 101

In the previous chapter, we discussed how to tailor your LinkedIn profile to match how HR and recruiters use LinkedIn Recruiter. Now, let's delve into the specific techniques recruiters use, particularly Boolean search methods, to find candidates. Understanding this will help you optimize your profile effectively.

Boolean Search 101

Boolean search operators allow you to broaden or limit your search based on specific criteria. Here are the basics:

- **OR**: Results contain any of the words you enter. For example, ("sales engineer" OR pre OR "solution engineer" OR "solutions engineer" OR "solution consultant" OR "solutions consultant" OR "sales consultant" OR "pre sales" OR presales). This is good for job titles.
- **AND**: Results contain all of the words you enter. For example, "Data Warehouse" AND "Business Intelligence" AND Cloud. This is good for keyword searches and finding candidates who meet all requirements.
- **NOT**: Results will not contain the word. For example, "Sales Engineer" AND NOT Oracle. This is useful if trying to avoid certain large companies.
- **Quotation Marks**: Results will contain the exact phrase or job title. For example, "Sales Engineer" vs. Sales Engineer. This will bring up anyone with "sales engineer" in their title.

Boolean Examples

Here are some practical examples of how Boolean search can be used for job titles, keywords, and company names:

- Job Titles:
    - "sales engineer" OR "sales engineering" OR "pre-sales" OR Presales OR "pre sales" OR "solution sales" OR "solutions sales" OR "solution consultant" OR "solutions consultant" OR "solution Architect" OR "solutions Architect" OR "systems Engineer" OR "Field Enablement" OR "Sales consultant" OR presales OR "Technical sales"
    - "Sales Engineering Manager" OR "Solution Consulting" OR "Sales Consulting" OR "Presales Manager" OR "pre sales director" OR "solutions engineering" OR "customer Engineer" OR "technical specialist"
    - "Data Scientist" OR "Data Science Consultant" OR "Data Science Architect"
- Keywords:
    - "Data warehouse" AND "business intelligence" AND SQL AND Cloud
    - "Data warehouse" AND "business intelligence" AND Teradata OR Redshift OR Netezza OR Greenplum
- Companies:
    - Cloudera OR Hortonworks OR MapR OR Pivotal OR IBM OR bluedata OR Jethro OR AWS OR Microsoft OR Google OR "treasure Data" OR Cazena OR Altiscale OR Qubole OR CenturyLink OR Databricks OR striim OR confluent OR

Dataartisans OR Gridgain OR terracotta OR Fastdata

Messaging Tips

When reaching out to potential candidates, recruiters follow certain best practices:

- **Ask for introductions** through mutual connections.
- **Keep it short**: The average reader spends 15-20 seconds scanning your message.
- **Explain why you are reaching out**: Be specific about their background and why it makes them a great fit.
- **Follow up**: Send a LinkedIn connection request.
- **Be selective**: Ensure you are only messaging and speaking with the very best talent.
- InMail response rate: Averages 30-50%.

Attracting Passive Talent

To attract passive talent, recruiters leverage their entire team to find the right candidates. Here are some strategies:

- **Start the conversation right**: Be targeted and personal. Emphasize impact over skill-laden job descriptions. Passive talent is 120% more likely to want to make an impact.
- **Mention culture**: 56% are more likely to be seeking an improved corporate culture.
- **Build long-term relationships**: Avoid making it seem like a sales interaction.
- **Keep projects up to date**: Archive candidates who are not a fit.

- **Listen**: Start your conversation by understanding the candidate's needs and motivations.

Message Examples

Here are two examples of messages that recruiters might use to reach out to potential candidates:

Example 1

css

Copy code

Name,

I oversee the X team at ABC and we are actively seeking a senior level sales engineer with X experience. Based on your X, Y, Z experience, I thought you'd be an excellent fit.

Please let me know if you would be open to a quick chat to learn more.

Best Regards,

Name

Example 2

vbnet

Copy code

Name,

I came across your profile and was impressed with your _____ and _____ experience. Based on this, I believe you would make a great fit for my team's Sales Engineer opening.

This role will offer you the ability to make _____ impact and gain experience with ____.

Please let me know if you are open to an informal chat to learn more.

To learn more about ABC, check out our new podcast episodes here!

Sales Engineering Boolean Cheat Sheet

Here's a quick reference for Boolean searches specifically tailored for sales engineering positions:

- Titles:
    - "sales engineer" OR "sales engineering" OR "pre-sales" OR Presales OR "pre sales" OR "solution sales" OR "solutions sales" OR "solution consultant" OR "solutions consultant" OR "solution Architect" OR "solutions Architect" OR "systems Engineer" OR "Field Enablement" OR "Sales consultant" OR "Sales Engineering" OR "solutions Engineering" OR "solution architecture"
- Former Employers:
    - MapR OR "MapR Technologies" OR Tableau OR "Tableau Software" OR Jethro OR SAP OR Pentaho OR "Hitachi Vantara" OR Sisense OR Lotame OR Cloudera OR Mesosphere OR Hortonworks OR Informatica OR Teradata OR "Hewlett Packard

Enterprise" OR Splunk OR NuoDB OR Atscale OR Qlik OR Appdynamics OR Slalom OR Tibco OR Pivotal OR Greenplum OR Netezza OR Marklogic OR Thoughtspot OR Microstrategy OR "HP VERTICA" OR Zoomdata OR Datameer OR Platfora OR Qbase OR Microsoft OR Birst OR "Pivotal Software" OR Delphix OR IBM OR "amazon web services"

- Industry Related Companies:
  - "Amazon Web Services" OR Google OR Cloudera OR Microsoft OR Oracle OR Teradata OR Cognos OR Netezza OR MemSQL OR MapR OR SAP OR 1010data OR "Treasure Data" OR MariaDB OR Neo4J OR Actian OR "Alibaba cloud" OR MarkLogic OR Pivotal OR Greenplum OR Cazena OR Pentaho OR Panoply OR Qubole OR Numetric OR Databricks OR Looker OR Dataiku OR Tableau OR QLIK OR Alteryx OR Cohesity OR "Cockroach Labs" OR Talend OR Gridoc OR Informatica OR "information Builders" OR Delphix OR "Rapid insight" OR Tealium OR Striim OR Alooma OR Actifio OR Hortonworks OR "domino data lab" OR Sisense OR EnterpriseDB OR Splunk OR MongoDB OR Datastax OR Mesosphere OR NuoDB OR Atscale OR Thoughtspot OR Microstrategy OR Zoomdata OR Datameer OR Platfora OR Bluedata OR Confluent OR Elastic OR Interana OR ArangoDB OR StreamSets OR Couchbase OR InfluxData OR Dremio OR Trifacta OR Attunity OR Mulesoft OR Infoworks OR "waterline data" OR "New Relic" OR Datadog OR "pure storage" OR Pepperdata OR "Arcadia data"

OR Gooddata OR H2o.ai OR algolia OR Manna OR VMware OR Tibco OR Yellowfin OR Segment OR CloverETL OR Heap OR "periscope data" OR DataTorrent OR Jethro OR Hazelcast OR WallarooLabs OR Fastdata OR Clustrix OR VOltBD OR Paradigm4 OR ORientDB OR TamR OR Paxata OR Unifi OR Snaplogic OR Xplenty OR Matillion OR Import.IO OR Alation OR Okera OR Manta OR SignalFX OR Datadog OR Unravel OR Anodot OR Alluxio OR Qumulo OR SQREAM OR Incorta OR Kyligence OR Semarchy OR "Stibo Systems" OR Reltio OR SAS
- Technology Partners:
    o AWS OR BMC OR Fivetran OR Google OR Informatica OR Looker OR Matillion OR Microsoft OR Sigma OR Tableau OR Talend OR Alteryx OR Attunity OR Chartio OR Dataguise OR Datarobot OR Domo OR Microstrategy OR Qubole OR Segment OR Stitch OR Wherescape OR Zelp OR "ab Initio" OR Agnity OR Alation OR Ascend OR Atscale OR Avora OR Birst OR Bryteflow OR Cdata OR CloverETL OR Collibra OR Databricks OR Dataiku OR Denodo OR "Dimensional Michanics" OR Diyotta OR "Domino Data Lab" OR ETLEAP OR GoodData OR h2o.ai OR "heap analytics" OR "HEVO DATA" OR Hunters.AI OR Immuta OR "information builders" OR Keboola OR Lacework OR Loome OR Lyftron OR Mparticle OR Paxata OR "Periscope Data" OR Sisense OR "Pyramid Analytics" OR Rivery OR SECUPI OR Snaplogic OR SQLSTREAM OR STREAMSETS OR Striim OR TamR OR Thoughtspot OR Vision.Bi OR

wandisco OR Winnow OR Workato OR Xplenty OR Zetaris OR Zoomdata
- EMEA Related Companies:
  - MapR OR Tableau OR SAP OR Pentaho OR "Hitachi Vantara" OR Sisense OR Cloudera OR Mesosphere OR Hortonworks OR Informatica OR Teradata OR Splunk OR Qlik OR Tibco OR Pivotal OR Marklogic OR Thoughtspot OR Microstrategy OR Datameer OR Platfora OR Microsoft OR Birst OR "Pivotal Software" OR Delphix OR Databricks OR confluent OR Pentaho OR Alteryx OR Datameer OR Rapidminer OR Datawatch OR MongoDB OR sprinklr OR Dataiku OR "Domino Labs" OR Couchbase OR Datastax OR kognitio OR Exasol OR Talend OR Trifacta OR Streamsets OR Mulesoft OR snaplogic OR Tealium OR actifio OR Datadog OR Splunk OR Unravel OR pagerduty OR "Pure storage" OR d2iq OR Kinetica OR Elastic OR Domo OR Atscale OR "Arcadia Data" OR Microstrategy OR Birst OR Sisense OR "information builders" OR "h2o.ai" OR datarobot OR Sumologic OR VMware OR Tibco OR Teradata OR Syncsort OR Looker OR Fivetran OR Matillion OR servicenow OR nutanix OR hashicorp OR zscaler OR dataminr OR unpatch OR outsystems OR gitlab

Understanding these methods and using them to tailor your LinkedIn profile and resume will significantly increase your chances of being noticed by recruiters. This chapter should give you a good foundation on how HR functions and the importance of optimizing your profile for better search results.

Chapter 13 Hiring Process

In the previous chapter, we delved into the intricacies of job searching and optimizing your LinkedIn profile to stand out to recruiters. Now, it's time to take a closer look at the interview process itself. Understanding how companies evaluate candidates can significantly improve your chances of landing your dream job.

"Success is where preparation and opportunity meet." — Bobby Unser

Adobe Interviewing circa 2011

I remember the early years at Adobe when the HR Department did not have a standardized hiring guide. Depending on whom you spoke to, you would receive different guidance on what to say, what not to say, and how to say it. To address this inconsistency, I constructed an SC Hire workflow to help my managers and others through a consistent process. This image is from April 2011; I am sure they have guidelines by now. I am not sure what the guides are today at Adobe, but I don't believe it could be too far off this one.

Just as a good salesperson should have a joint execution plan or an agreed-on close plan with a customer, you too should have the opportunity to ask, "So what is the process end-to-end for XYZ brand to hire someone?" I love asking this. Unfortunately, many hiring managers do not know the end-to-end process, and it's best to understand if they know the process. Remember, they will be the ones having to fight for you and ensure you are moving through the process correctly. Just like any sale, there are lots of people involved after the decision to hire you has been made.

Adobe's unique element at the time was not focused on architecture but more on how you could tell a story, ask questions, and think creatively. Our enterprise SOA solutions required a 100-foot infrastructure depth to ensure the implementation teams felt comfortable with deployments. This was way before Cloud, Virtual Machine, and Kubernetes level deployments. You kids have no idea about the challenges we had back in the day to implement enterprise software. SAP then required a team of people to be on-site for no less than nine months to get things operational.

Adobe has a religious relationship with its market and its employees. I enjoyed my early years working for Adobe. As we grew, we buttoned up our process to ensure hiring the best of the best. The key to all these interview guides, stories, and examples are to be prepared. You need to think on your feet. Remember, you will always be interviewing from the front desk clerk to the individual standing next to you.

In preparing for your presentation day, understand that some organizations will either request you to learn their solution and present it to them or they may have you look to introduce a technology that you are familiar with or possibly positioned before. I do not believe in forcing candidates to learn your brand's technology for a presentation. I always viewed this stage as an opportunity to see them at their best. If they presented something they had just learned, I could not tell if it was that the candidate could not understand it in two weeks or if they were just awful presenters. The best way to test this is to remove the uncertainty of the product and pitch to focus on their delivery, question handling, and overall style.

The interview team will have to become familiar with the technology they are selling to better understand what type of questions to ask. It will allow the interview team to tell if they are bullshitting their way through the presentation. Thanks to the internet, a quick search on the pros and cons of any brand will give you a good baseline, not to mention a short YouTube video review before the meeting is advisable. I remember one session where I think I knew more about the tech this person was positioning than they did. When I probed during the interview, the candidate struggled with getting to a point where they would say, "I don't know and need to get back to you." Remember, it's OK to say I don't know, and in fact, I would always try to get a candidate to get to that point.

How to Prepare for a Role-Play Interview

This is easy, I outlined the typical Day in the life of an SE earlier in the book, and you should follow these best practices:

1. I would encourage you to have a pre-call with your primary interviewer to conduct a discovery like any other session.
2. I would encourage you to dry run your presentation with the "customer," i.e., the interviewer, before the meeting.
3. Understand what you typically do with face-to-face meetings, location, security, Wi-Fi, and presentation devices.

Will the room have a whiteboard or a flipchart? Go through that checklist; who else will be at the meeting? Could you provide their emails before the meeting so I can follow up immediately? These are the basics for your regular job. You would be surprised how often an SC candidate would not take me up on my offer to review content. The same holds for any Zoom session; ensure you can access the meeting earlier than the rest to set up and verify that chat will be available in the tool. As a hiring manager, these types of preliminary checks were gold.

I would focus on understanding to what degree the candidate had a profound "Curse of Knowledge." A "Curse of Knowledge" is all the things you have experienced that have impacted or influenced your next Day's journey in all that you do. For example, in the early 2000s, I purchased a BMW for my wife, which had a heated steering wheel. Living in NJ in the winter, this was a fantastic innovation. From that point forward and still, to this day, every time I look to purchase a car, I ask, "does it have a heated steering wheel?" This example is the curse of knowledge. The same can be true with candidates like yourself, who may not have years of experience. For example, at Adobe, during the demo phase where the candidate would come into the office and present to the team, I would always have a broken projector in the room, pull all the markers off the whiteboard, leave a dry marker for fun, and have a whiteboard and flip chart. This will truly test the natural abilities of the candidate.

Each candidate that Day would come in and typically on time, which is late in my book, and plug their laptop into the projector. It would never fail; they would try to manage the room while they spun up the projector, and nope. The projector would try to spin up with nothing but the fan in the background. Some may say this is cruel but think about it. What I am testing here is being prepared for the worst-case scenario. Some candidates would pivot to the whiteboard, which is excellent up to the point when they would pull the dry marker off to use it. Then, sure enough, they would ask, could we get another projector or some markers and I would say sorry, no, this is what we have. They would then try to have us huddle around the 13" screen and have a presentation.

At the end of the second day of interviews, a candidate showed up ten minutes early. He asked if he could check the equipment before starting. I welcomed him into the room, and he spun up the projector, and it failed. He pulls out a mini Pico Projector from 2011, sets it up, and is ready for the meeting. He instinctively pulls out his three markers to put his name, date, and the issues discovered over the phone. I was blown away. I hired him on the spot. He was my best hire and used the "Curse of Knowledge" to his advantage. He had battle scars and was prepared for that meeting. A few lessons learned for all of you—on time is late, so ask for permission to come in early, verify equipment and Wi-Fi, and always have a backup and then have backup for that backup. Here is an idea—print out the presentation; paper is still a valuable tool in a pinch.

Oracle Interview Guide

I sharpened the saw at Oracle, where Tim Loomis emphasized the importance of a well-tested, structured hiring process. This process became my gold standard, regardless of whether the product was profoundly architectural or simply business feature-driven. At Oracle, before engaging in any business or sales discussions, candidates had to pass a technical review. If a candidate couldn't pass the technical screening, there was no sense in progressing further and wasting other people's time.

The Process

1. **Technical Review:** The first step was a thorough technical screening. This ensured that only candidates with the necessary technical expertise moved forward in the process. It was a critical step, especially for roles that required deep technical knowledge.
2. **Leadership Interviews:** After passing the technical part, the candidate would face a series of interviews conducted by future leaders within the company. These interviews served dual purposes: allowing the candidate to understand the job better and enabling future leaders to develop their interview skills.
3. **Field SC Interviews:** The next stage involved interviews with account executives (AEs) from the field, who might or might not work directly with the candidate. This step was crucial as it allowed the AEs to have a stake in the hiring decision, fostering accountability and ensuring a good fit.

Chapter 14: The Interview Day

After several rounds of phone and web-level interviews, we would invest in bringing the candidates to Dallas, Texas. The reason for choosing Dallas was its proximity to the airport, making travel convenient and cost-effective for both Oracle and the candidates.

The Night Before

Tim was a master at organizing these events. He would host a dinner the evening before the game day, allowing us to observe the candidates in a relaxed, social setting. It was enlightening to see candidates who had impressive resumes and interviewed well, but lacked table manners or drank too much. I recall one evening where a candidate's overindulgence led me to escort them back to their room and, the next morning, hand them an updated flight ticket. This pre-interview dinner was a real-life test to ensure candidates met the company's standards even outside a formal setting.

The Game Day Structure

During the game day, we had a well-organized schedule involving various people and rooms. We always included a few future SC leaders to manage the Green Room, which was the waiting area for all candidates.

The Green Room Dynamics

The Green Room was crucial as it allowed candidates to interact freely. Future SC leaders would observe these interactions, noting how candidates engaged with each other. Some were protective of information, while others were open and helpful. The SCs in the Green Room provided valuable feedback during the debrief, sometimes swaying the interview team's decisions based on their observations.

Lunch Meetings

The hiring manager would take each candidate out to lunch, offering another opportunity to understand the candidate better and observe them in a different setting. This was a time for candidates to ask questions, provide feedback, and demonstrate their social skills. I remember one candidate who felt comfortable enough to order a beer during lunch, which, while surprising, gave us insight into their comfort level and decision-making process.

Conclusion

The comprehensive interview process at Oracle ensured that we hired the best candidates who not only had the technical expertise but also fit well within the company culture. The process was rigorous but necessary to maintain high standards and ensure long-term success for both the candidate and the company.

Areas of Focus

In our hiring process, we focused on specific attributes to evaluate candidates comprehensively. Each interviewer would take a few of these areas to investigate during their individual interviews. These attributes are relevant for any level of interview, and preparing answers to these questions can significantly enhance your chances of success.

1. Professional Acumen

- Observe the candidate's choice of words, attire, eye contact, grooming, and overall polish.
- Evaluate where you can see this person in 3-5 years in their career at Oracle.
- Assess the highest level they can present to within an organization, especially the "C" level.
- Determine the levels they have previously presented to within an organization.

2. Personal Drive
    - Ask for examples of where they have driven change.
    - Understand what motivates them to get up each day and go to work.
    - Inquire why they work and how they define success.
    - For previous SCs, request examples of their revenue contributions.
    - Discuss the objectives they were given and how they met or exceeded them.

3. Presentation Skills
    - Look for examples of their presentation skills.
    - Determine if they use Zen principles, props, or other engaging methods.
    - Assess how they engage the audience and differentiate from other presenters.
    - Request examples of results achieved through their presentations.

4. Communication Skills
    - Evaluate their verbal communication abilities.
    - Review their writing skills if any materials other than a resume were provided.
    - Ensure they are clear and articulate in their communication.

5. Industry Expertise

- Ask for examples of industries in which they have worked.
- Inquire about their efforts to broaden their knowledge in those industries.
- Rate their level of expertise on a scale of 1-10.
- Investigate any formal training they have received in those industries.

6. Software Experience
   - Determine what software applications they have worked with.
   - Understand how they learned the software and any training they achieved.
   - Discuss how they used the application.
   - Assess their ability to learn new products and technologies.

End-of-Day Review Process

At the end of each interview day, the interview team would gather to compare notes and score each candidate on a large whiteboard. We listed all criteria and used post-it notes to represent each candidate. We would move the post-it notes up or down based on mutual agreement. This collaborative process, although time-consuming, ensured a comprehensive evaluation. After reaching a conclusion, we updated all notes in Oracle's HRM tool and completed the necessary forms to move the candidate forward or decline.

Key Elements of Adobe and Oracle Interview Styles

Adobe Interview Process

- **Flexibility in the Process**: Initially, there wasn't a structured hiring guide, and much depended on the interviewer.
- **Focus on Storytelling and Creativity**: Adobe emphasized candidates' ability to tell a story, ask insightful questions, and think creatively.
- **Role Play and Presentation**: Candidates were evaluated on their ability to present, handle questions, and engage the audience.
- **Testing Under Pressure**: Situational tests, such as dealing with a broken projector or using dry markers, were used to assess candidates' problem-solving skills under pressure.
- **Attention to Details**: From punctuality to technical preparedness, every small detail was evaluated.

Oracle Interview Process

- **Technical Screening First**: Oracle prioritized a technical review before proceeding with business and sales discussions.
- **Structured Multi-Stage Process**: The process included interviews with future leaders and account executives, fostering a sense of accountability.
- **Centralized Interview Location**: Candidates were flown to Dallas for in-person interviews, including a pre-interview dinner to observe candidates' social behaviors.

- **Green Room Dynamics**: Observing candidates in a waiting room environment provided insights into their interpersonal skills and collaboration.
- **Matrix Evaluation**: A comprehensive end-of-day review involved scoring each candidate on various attributes, with collective decision-making.

Key Elements of Both Styles

- **Preparation and Professionalism**: Both Adobe and Oracle valued thorough preparation and professionalism.
- **Adaptability and Problem-Solving**: Candidates' ability to adapt and solve problems under pressure was crucial.
- **Technical and Presentation Skills**: Both companies evaluated technical knowledge and the ability to present and communicate effectively.
- **Interpersonal Skills**: Observing candidates in social settings (dinners, green rooms) provided additional insights into their suitability.
- **Detailed Evaluation**: A structured and detailed evaluation process ensured a comprehensive assessment of each candidate.

Quiz for Adobe and Oracle Interview Processes

Adobe Interview Quiz

1. What was the main focus of Adobe's interview process?
    - A) Technical skills
    - B) Storytelling and creativity
    - C) Financial acumen
    - D) Physical endurance
2. How did Adobe test candidates' ability to handle pressure during the interview?
    - A) By asking technical questions
    - B) By giving them a challenging coding task
    - C) By creating situational tests like a broken projector
    - D) By making them run a marathon
3. What is an important preparation tip for an Adobe interview?
    - A) Learning Adobe's technology thoroughly
    - B) Preparing a comprehensive business plan
    - C) Arriving early and verifying equipment and Wi-Fi
    - D) Bringing a gift for the interviewers
4. What was emphasized during the role-play interview at Adobe?
    - A) Product knowledge
    - B) Customer engagement and presentation style
    - C) Financial analysis
    - D) Coding skills
5. What unique element did Adobe include in its evaluation process?
    - A) Technical tests
    - B) Storytelling and creativity

- C) Financial modeling
- D) Physical fitness tests

Oracle Interview Quiz

1. What was the first stage of Oracle's interview process?
   - A) Presentation skills assessment
   - B) Technical screening
   - C) Behavioral interview
   - D) Social dinner
2. Why did Oracle conduct interviews in Dallas, Texas?
   - A) To leverage central location for inexpensive travel
   - B) Because of Oracle's headquarters
   - C) Due to availability of better facilities
   - D) To impress candidates with a luxurious setting
3. What was the purpose of the green room at Oracle interviews?
   - A) To relax candidates before the interview
   - B) To observe candidates' interactions and behaviors
   - C) To provide technical tests
   - D) To give candidates a break
4. How did Oracle's interview process ensure accountability from the sales team?
   - A) By making them attend a technical test
   - B) By involving them in the interview process
   - C) By having them create the interview questions
   - D) By giving them final decision-making authority
5. What was a key factor in Oracle's decision-making process after interviews?
   - A) Individual interviewer's opinion
   - B) Collective scoring and discussion
   - C) Candidate's salary expectations

- D) Candidate's academic qualifications

Answers to the Quiz

Adobe Interview Quiz

1. B) Storytelling and creativity
2. C) By creating situational tests like a broken projector
3. C) Arriving early and verifying equipment and Wi-Fi
4. B) Customer engagement and presentation style
5. B) Storytelling and creativity

Oracle Interview Quiz

1. B) Technical screening
2. A) To leverage central location for inexpensive travel
3. B) To observe candidates' interactions and behaviors
4. B) By involving them in the interview process
5. B) Collective scoring and discussion

Snowflake Interview Guide

Thanks, Neal Wadhwani, for making this process better! - [Neal Wadhwani on LinkedIn](#)

At Snowflake, we took the best practices from the last thirty years and crafted what I believe is the best interview process. Bill Van Hout and Ben Green collaborated to construct a role-play exercise encapsulating everything we had hoped to look for. Like with other brands, we always started with the technical review. Here is a good example of a technical review; note this will be typically outlined in the HRM system greenhouse or workday as an example. You have to pass this assessment before being moved to the next Level.

As you can see from the above chart, you are looking at well over three months to get to a potential offer out. This timeline will be critical for your search; as mentioned earlier, you need to understand how the target company operates from budgeting to Q1 new year launches. The earlier you are in the pipeline, the better chance you have of being selected. As a hiring manager, that Q1 sales conference was a key target date to have people in seats. The quickest way to ramp an individual is to get them at that conference, and it typically only happens the second to the third week of Q1. Some organizations have Mid-year SC summits like Adobe, Oracle, and Elastic, and you can bet that this will be the last two weeks of Q2 or the first two weeks in Q3. You must know the target company's financial cycles to best position your prospecting timing.

Technical Review Example

- **Pros**: Candidate fits the profile required for a solution engineer role:

- - He has experience with the DW stack: ETL, BI, DW, Hadoop Cloudera
  - He has some experience in presales being in this role since 2016.
  - He checks all the boxes for the technical attitude for a presales role at Snowflake
- **Cons**: I have personally competed in the field with candidates in the past (Hortonworks vs. Cloudera), and he didn't strike me as an aggressive seller, but looking back at his resume, it was his first role as an SEAC . He had time to learn in between.
- **Conclusion**: He checks all the boxes for technical aptitude Candidates have exposure and experience with the traditional DW stack (ETL, BI, DW) but also the Cloudera Big Data stack. His past experience can make him successful in a Snowflake pre-sales role, as he shouldn't have any issues with positioning Snowflake with the six workloads. For all intents and purposes, he passed the technical interview & requirements.
  - One point to follow up on and needs to be put to a stress test is his ability as a seller during the next phase of the interview.

Technical Questions for Interview

1. Explain Data Stacks
2. What does Snowflake do in 30 seconds?
3. Have you worked with an MPP database?
4. In 30 seconds, explain to me what <insert complex technology> does in terms a business person would understand.
5. Explain to me what an MPP system is.

6. Explain to me what a cost-based optimizer is.
7. Does Datastax (Cassandra) have a cost-based optimizer?
8. What is a data frame in Spark?
9. Are you familiar with and have used the following SQL functions?
10. Can you tell me about some of the BI tools in the space?
11. Talk to me about ETL vs. ELT.
12. How does data lineage play a role in this?
13. Which Cloud are you most familiar with?
14. What is an OUTER JOIN?
15. How would you remove duplicates from a table?
16. Let's say I have a sales table with three columns (INVOICE_NUM, CUSTOMER_NUM, TOTAL_INVOICE_AMT). What's the SQL to get me the top 10 customers by Revenue?
17. What's a STAR schema?
18. What is OLTP vs. OLAP?
19. What does ACID stand for?
20. What is an RPO RTO? What is it used for?
21. What's a Lambda Architecture?
22. What is a SQL Windowing Function?

Database Specific

- Describe your expertise with Databases from 1 to 10
- Describe your expertise with SQL from 1 to 10
- Describe one database performance problem you hit during a POC and how you fixed it.
- Describe your exposure to the database ecosystem.

Job Interview Setup

The last team did a great job outlining the interview setup. We used a brand: Inspired Brands. Note that this is not a public company, making it difficult for the candidate to find information. However, this brand had great socialized content on the web and its home page. Everything started with an email:

John, Congratulations! You have been accepted as a finalist for the Sales Engineer role. One of the final steps we would like to complete is to see your Discovery, presentation, and demonstration skills in action. To do this, we have created a role-play exercise utilizing a scenario from a real customer. We ask that you pick a product or solution that you would like to "sell" to our customers. This should be a product that you know well enough to be able to present the value of the solution and demonstrate its value through a demo. The role play will consist of two phases - a 30-45 minute mock discovery call allowing you to uncover whatever you can that will help you in the second phase - a presentation and demonstration. The presentation interview will be a 90-minute interview. We will give you 60 minutes to present and demonstrate to us your chosen product or solution. The last 30 minutes will be time - out of character - for any of the Snowflake participants to ask you questions. What I need from you: Please reply back to this email with the product or solution you plan on representing. After that, I will provide you with a list of names, email addresses, and the fictitious role they will be playing for a few people that will be present at the mock Discovery call. It will be up to you to coordinate an appropriate time for the discovery call - keeping in mind we will limit it to 45 minutes maximum. Once you have completed the discovery call, we will then schedule the final presentation and demonstration. Keep in mind that there may be additional "actors" present in the final presentation that were not in attendance for the discovery call. Finally, what you need from me: The customer we have chosen to role-play with is Inspire Brands. I have attached a presentation that lays out just a few "first meeting" notes to get you started. I will make myself available to you for any questions, advice, etc., as needed. Good luck!

Note the last line - I will make myself available to you for any questions, advice, etc., as needed. This was a baiting statement to see how the candidate would take us up on our offer. Again, always surprised at how many did not!

The Rules

The SEAC Candidate has been invited to a 90-minute interview comprised of two parts:

- ~30-45 minute Presentation/Demonstration of a solution/presentation of a technology product they are comfortable with (e.g., Tableau, StreamSet, Elastic, etc.)
- The remainder of the 90 minutes will be an out-of-character Panel interview with AE(s), DM, and SEAC director.

Prior to this interview, the SEAC candidate has been asked to run a 45-minute discovery session based on the role-play scenario with me and possibly Kevin Kunz. The goal of this discovery exercise is to see if the candidate:

- Does appropriate research on the customer in advance
- Can effectively run a discovery session
- Presents their solution taking into account the things they learned during Discovery

Each Snowflake attendee (AE, DM) will be asked to read through the scenario in advance, choose a role, and stay in character as much as possible. After the role-play, everyone is welcome to pepper the candidate with questions about their background, business, technical acumen, etc.

Role Play Scenario

45-Minute Discovery Call - Shared with Candidate For this role-play, we will be using a real customer. We will assume that prior to this business/technical Discovery, we've had a first meeting where the customer has shared some basic information with you or your sales rep and has requested a demonstration of your solution. Your sales rep asked for a discovery session in advance of the presentation/demonstration to learn more about the customer and their needs. This call is your opportunity to ask what you need to prepare for that presentation/demonstration.

First Meeting Notes:

- Inspire Brands is a holding company for several retail restaurant brands, including Arby's, Baskin Robbins, Dunkin Donuts, Buffalo Wild Wing Cafe, Jimmy John's, and Sonic.
- Inspire is always in a state of M&A activities, looking to add brands that fit their corporate vision- To Invigorate Great Brands and Supercharge their long-term growth.
- Inspire corporate is looking to develop a stronger analytic capability to provide cross-brand performance, assist M&A, etc.

The Discovery call will be tailored to the product/solution you choose to present. For instance, if you decide to present a BI/Visualization tool like Tableau, then we will tailor our answers to what our needs are around this type of tool. If you are presenting a database solution to us, we will tailor our answers to that.

There will be one or more individuals participating in the discovery call. I will definitely be there in the role of Director of Analytics However, there may be additional individuals attending. We will share their role with you on the discovery call.

Keep in mind that there will be additional actors that will participate in your presentation/demonstration that were not on the discovery call. We will provide them with background and what we share with you during Discovery so that they can stay in character.

Scenario Background - Internal

We are expecting the candidate to uncover this information, so don't offer up everything if they don't ask for it. However, keep in mind that we are only scheduling Discovery for 45 minutes.

Background: IRB Holdings (Inspire Brands) is in a constant state of M&A to add brands to its portfolio. Currently, their brands include Buffalo Wild Wings, Dunkin Donuts, Baskin Robbins, Arby's, Jimmy John's, and Sonic.

Purpose of the Project: As a holding company of mostly independently run brands, IRB is working to build an enterprise analytic capability to do things like:

- Cross-brand performance
- Cross-brand affinity (e.g., can we determine what customers dine at which brands and how much overlap?)
- Enable better, more seamless onboarding of new brands
- Share benchmarked data back to brands

- Cross-Brand Digital Media, Marketing, and Loyalty Brand Analytics for customer spending and outreach optimizations
- Restaurant Tech (IoT) and ERP System Analytics for FP&A, Supply Chain Optimization, and Product Analysis

Keep in mind that, depending on what the candidate is going to present, we may need to modify this to align with what they are presenting.

Scenario Challenges - Internal

We are expecting the candidate to uncover this information, so don't offer up everything if they don't ask for it. However, keep in mind that we are only scheduling Discovery for 45 minutes.

Business/Technical Challenges:

1. The goal is to add three new brands per year.
2. The goal is to increase sales by > 16.2% within three years of the brand coming into the Inspire family. How do you do that if you can only store three months' data?
3. The Director of Marketing wants to create an affinity/reward program to increase cross-brand dining. Only Buffalo Wild Wings currently captures customer data to-date.
4. Obviously, IRB's brands are increasing the number of products they are selling through delivery services. They would like to do a better job understanding the impact of these services (which services, how much $$ are they losing to them, can they get affinity data from these services?)
5. A new CTO who came from Arby's has declared that within the next two years, ALL on-premise solutions MUST be moved to Cloud.

6. IRB has chosen Azure for their Cloud, but as they acquire brands, they may bring in their own CSP, so IRB must have both a multi-cloud strategy and the ability to easily migrate a brand to the IRB environment if they so choose. Remember, CIO came from Arby's, so we can decide if he/she is a Google bigot or not.
7. Not all brands share all data with corporations.
8. Each brand shares its data in different ways - some through files via SFTP, some through database links.
9. Each brand shares data at a different pace (some nightly, some weekly).
10. No standard data model across brands (makes cross-brand benchmarking performance difficult).
11. Each brand has its own analytic solution ranging from Oracle to SQL Server to BigQuery.
12. IRB built an Azure Data Lake solution prior to selecting Snowflake.

Role Play Actors

Depending upon the technology solution the SEAC chooses to present, we may need to modify/add additional roles:

- Dir of Analytics for IRB: How do I get data faster, standardize the data and provide the analytics that the business wants.
- CTO: How do I support the business initiatives while reducing cost, providing scale.
- VP of Marketing
- ETL Developer
- BI Analyst
- Marketing Analyst

Chapter 15: What Should We Be Looking For?

Meeting Start:

- Does he/she have an agenda slide up on the screen or a Title slide (ideally No Slide – focus should be on the presenter and not the background)?
- Before they begin – do they go around the room and ask to introduce yourself, your role, and what you want to get out of today's meeting – or why are you here today?
- Does the candidate record the who's who in the room and where they are located – plus note what is important to them to be used later in the present?
- Do they review the key learnings collected from the Discovery?
- Do they ask those who were not on the call to validate the list and add any additional items?
- Do they present our scenario or generally present their solution? Is it obvious that they listened to our Discovery and customized their presentation to address our?

Keep an Eye on the Presentation:

- TST (Do they practice Tell / Show / Tell)
    - Tell them what you are going to show them.
    - Show them.
    - Tell them the value.
- Storytelling

- o Do they tell stories, or is it a regurgitation of a slide?
- o Does the story have a Beginning / Middle / End (Is there a villain and a hero)?
- o Do we have conflict/drama/and solutions?
- Tie it Back to the Discovery
  - o Do they bring back what is important to the room?
  - o Are they engaging relevant individuals in conversation based on Discovery?

PowerPoint:

- How many slides?
- Do the slides support the conversation?
- Does the candidate read the slide?
- Rule of Three's – or do we have more than three bullets – max should be 5?
- Do they practice – Touch / Turn and Talk?
  - o Touch what you will present.
  - o Turn and talk to the audience.
  - o Clear the slide.

Rat Holes & Observations:

- Do they go into grave details when asked a question?
- Are they talking about pricing Offer POC?
- Filler words.
- BEGS (Body Language, Eye Contact, Gestures, Speaking Voice).
- Confidence, Command of the room, Coachability.

Demonstration:

- Did they set the stage – preview/trailer of what the candidate will walkthrough - Demo Agenda?
- Tell / Show / Tell.
- Did they revisit the key CBI, and did he have a printout of those?
- So when going through the demo – does the Candidate stop to get accepted after each CBI is checked off during the demonstration?
- Does the Candidate do FAB – Feature Advantage and Benefit – This is a feature dump, and hoping for something to stick?
- Did the candidate tie value / Revenue to the discussion?
- Did the candidate call out the audience member by name when answering/addressing a business concern? – person's name is the most valuable word.
- Did they pause to keep the audience engaged?
- When asked a question that the candidate did not know the answer to – actually write it down – You need to write it down so we can check at the end of the role-play – did they use the whiteboard to write down the CBI and the Parking Lot area for follow-up?
- Did we take them down any rat holes?
- Did they take the bait on Pricing – SCs are never to discuss price.
- Did the candidate – walk the room or stay behind the podium? – we want walkers – it keeps people awake, and you can follow the audience's head follow you, so you know they are engaged.

Closing:

- Closing – painting the customer into a corner – for the rep to close.
- Did the candidate review the checklist if provided or revisit the first slide on CBIs to check with the room if we met their demands? If so, this is the chance for the rep to ask, if we met the requirements, what would prevent us from moving forward?
- Did the candidate review the follow-ups written down?
- Above all, was the candidate memorable? Did they set the bar high for our competitors to try to climb?
- Remember, we are in sales. Did the SEAC paint us into a decision box and ask that hard question, "Is anything preventing us from moving forward? And if so, what and why?"
- Never leave a meeting without action items and agreeing on the next meeting timelines. As they say, this is a game of inches. Every encounter gets you closer to the goal line. Those who know me will laugh since I know nothing about sports.

Chapter 16: The Things I Always Looked For and Why

Agenda

For the love of God, have an agenda at the beginning of your presentation. Ensure that the agenda was reviewed by the sponsor after the discovery call. It's crazy how often I don't see an agenda. An agenda is not only a roadmap; it can also tell the audience about the timing and structure of the presentation.

Challenges Outlined

Did you put the CBI's (Critical Business Issues) on the board that were discovered by the one person you spoke to? Showing these challenges at the beginning and referencing them at the end demonstrates thoroughness and attention to detail.

Room Introductions

Did you go around the room during introductions to verify the expectations of the new people involved? Remember, they may not know why they are there, or you may find out who the real power sponsor is.

Tell, Show, Tell

Tell me what you will show me, show me what you told me, and then reiterate the value. This structure helps ensure clarity and reinforcement of key points.

So What and Why Do I Care

When the candidate makes a statement or mentions a feature, they should back it up with why the audience should care about it. This shows the ability to connect technical details to business value.

Admitting "I Don't Know"

Humility is crucial. We cannot know everything, and in fact, I would likely not trust you if you did know everything. It's okay to say, "I do not know!"

Value Selling

Tie everything back to money. People do not buy stuff unless they can justify it. ROI means two things: Return on Investment or Return on Influence. Some decision-makers base their decisions on how it will impact their promotions or bonuses.

Zoom Features

You are in an interview - dress for the part, show respect, and my God, have pants on! Do not move too much in Zoom - the lag in refresh makes you look like a zombie.

Filler Words

Classic. I remember my old boss used to have a tin can in the back of the room with a few rolls of nickels. Every time I said "Umm" - CLANG in the tin. CLANG, CLANG... It was so annoying, but not as much as the number of UMs. It did break me; therapy cured a lot!

Taking Action Items

I can get that candidates are nervous as they present in an interview - but write stuff down. Take a pause and let the audience know. "Let me write that down." I would carry post-it notes with me, write down the question, put it up on the wall or glass window. So at the end of the meeting, I could reference those issues or questions. The customer emotionally connects to that post-it. Humans typically care more about their needs than others. So play to that emotion in a meeting!

Talking Pricing

As an SC, you should NEVER talk about price - this is always the Sales Team's responsibility. I am amazed at how I can get some candidates to offer a price or even a discount because we are a big company.

Offering Free POC

This is one of my biggest pet peeves - did they offer up a free POC? Remember, POCs do not win deals and in many cases, can delay a deal if not properly constructed. Never give anything away.

Give Gets

Give/Get - Never give anything away unless you get at least equal value or more in return.

Tech Rat Hole

Did they lose the business people in the room, you know, the people who have the money to buy this solution? If it doesn't solve their issues, we will not sell anything. Showing how technically advanced you are will not close business.

Timing

Did we go over time? Did the candidate try to shove 10lbs of content into a 5lb bag? Did they pivot and adjust on the fly?

Closing

Did they paint us into a corner and try to close us? Based on what I see, is there anything preventing us from moving forward?

Candidate Feedback

This is another aspect I picked up from Tim at Oracle; we would always provide feedback to the candidate. This initially was surprising to me, but when you put yourself in the candidate's shoes, they would welcome this feedback and give them a chance to internalize or gauge how they did. At the time, I was in the customer experience architecture team, and this transcends to candidate experience as well. We would always go around the room to provide feedback on both pros and cons that we all took notes on during the event.

Workshop

To apply the concepts learned, you can create a workshop using Post-it notes and Voting Dots. Here's a step-by-step guide:

Materials Needed

- Post-it notes
- Voting Dots
- Whiteboard or large paper sheets
- Markers

Duration

- 60 minutes

Instructions

1. Preparation (10 minutes):
    o Divide the participants into small groups.
    o Give each group Post-it notes and markers.
2. Identifying Key Points (20 minutes):
    o Ask each group to identify the key attributes of a successful interview based on the chapter.
    o Have them write each attribute on a Post-it note and place it on a whiteboard or large paper sheet.
3. Voting (10 minutes):
    o Give each participant Voting Dots.
    o Ask them to vote on the attributes they believe are most important by placing dots on the Post-it notes.
4. Discussion (20 minutes):
    o Review the attributes with the most votes.

- Discuss why these attributes are critical and how to apply them in real-life interview scenarios.

Quiz

1. Why is having an agenda important in a presentation?

    - A) It shows the audience you are organized.
    - B) It provides a roadmap and helps manage time.
    - C) It gives the audience a sense of structure.
    - D) All of the above.

2. What should you do if you don't know the answer to a question during an interview?

    - A) Make up an answer.
    - B) Ignore the question.
    - C) Admit you don't know and offer to follow up.
    - D) Change the subject.

3. Why should SCs avoid discussing pricing?

    - A) It's always the responsibility of the Sales Team.
    - B) SCs might not have accurate pricing information.
    - C) Discussing pricing can complicate the sales process.
    - D) All of the above.

4. What is the benefit of using post-it notes to track questions during a meeting?

    - A) It shows you are attentive and organized.
    - B) It helps you remember to address all points.
    - C) It makes the customer feel their concerns are important.
    - D) All of the above.

Book Recommendations

1. "Demo to Win!" by Robert D. Riefstahl

This book offers practical techniques for presenting software solutions. It provides valuable insights into how to conduct effective demonstrations that close deals.

2. "The Challenger Sale" by Matthew Dixon and Brent Adamson

This book introduces the concept of challenging customers' thinking to provide solutions that can genuinely benefit them, rather than just selling them a product.

3. "SPIN Selling" by Neil Rackham

SPIN Selling is based on a 12-year, one million dollar research study into effective sales performance. The SPIN (Situation, Problem, Implication, Need-payoff) technique can be applied to interviews to uncover deeper insights into a candidate's thought process and problem-solving abilities.

Quiz Answers

1. All of the above
2. Tell/Show/Tell
3. ROI
4. Never give anything away

Part 10: You are Accepted

Chapter 17: Compensation Plans

After mastering the art of the interview process and securing your dream role, the next step is to understand how you will be compensated for your hard work and dedication. In this chapter, we will delve into the intricacies of compensation plans, focusing on the vital aspects of personal commission rates (PCR) and how they influence your overall earnings.

"Success is not the key to happiness. Happiness is the key to success. If you love what you are doing, you will be successful." – Albert Schweitzer

Just a side note, this is not a non-profit job; we are here to overachieve our quotas. The best part of this job is winning, and the effort you put into this role will payout in a large commission check. Some variables are out of your control, but the one thing you will always focus on is your PCR, or personal commission rate. It has amazed me how so many SEAC and SE leaders do not understand the formula for a PCR.

Let's say you have an "OTE" On Target Earnings of $200,000. Typically, an SEAC will have a 70/30 split - 70% base salary and 30% commission. So for this example, we would have a base of $140K and a commission of $60K. Essentially, you are risking $60K of your OTE for the year, and this is paid out quarterly. Though some organizations will do commission payouts monthly. If you achieve 100% of your Quota and no more than that, you will have achieved $60K in commission checks.

OTE - $200,000
Base 70% - $140K
Comm 30% - $60K

Now let's assume you have a combined quota of $1,000,000. You need to achieve 100% of a million dollars to get paid out $60K.

What is my PCR?
Your personal commission rate is based off of your agreed OTE, which is different from your peers, unless they negotiated the same OTE as yours.

PCR = Variable / Quota
$60,000 / $1,000,000 = 6% for you
If a peer was paid $180,000:
Var at 30% = $54,000
Quota $1,000,000
PCR = 5.40%

Hence the "Personal" part of PCR. Here is a typical SaaS compensation plan to review. I will include a collection of compensation plans for you to look at that will cover a number of versions. Of course, I will delete the company names so I won't get sued.

Performance Commission Plan
Sales Engineer
Name: Crazy Eddie (1990's reference)
Total Annualized 2018 Sales Quota: $43,065,012
Base Salary: $180,000

Annualized Commission at 100% of Quota: $75,379
Annualized On Target Earnings (OTE): $255,379

Sales Quota

For 2018, the total annual bookings quota for 2018 is $43,065,012, and breaks down as follows:

- SaaS and Guaranteed Data Bookings (ACV) = $14,046,608
- Managed Service, Non-Guaranteed Data and Professional Services Bookings (Contract Value) = $29,018,404

Quota Retirement

a. SaaS and Guaranteed Data – Quota retirement will be based on (ACV). Additionally, if the deal has a time-specific exit option (e.g., one-time option to cancel after 90 days), then initial quota retirement will be based only on the guaranteed period with the balance retired after the right to cancel has passed and not been exercised. Contracts are subject to extension of time for review and approval by the Company's executive management. All deals sold in the fiscal year will retire quota for that plan period.
b. Managed Services, Non-Guaranteed Data, and Professional Services – Contracted bookings retire quota. All deals booked in the fiscal year will retire quota for that plan period. Each $1 of Managed Services, Non-Guaranteed Data and Professional Service sales counts as $1 of quota retired.

Commission Rates

Commissions are based on attainment of bookings targets, as outlined below:

SaaS and Guaranteed Data Bookings
(85% of potential on-target commission)

- For each % of attainment, 1% of total SaaS and guaranteed data on-target commissions payout will be earned.
- If you exceed the target on an annual basis you will receive a 50% kicker on your annualized commission rate. You can achieve this in total or on a per component basis. For clarity, the SaaS rate (including accelerator) for all bookings over 100% attainment equals 0.454% of bookings.
- Attainment will be calculated quarterly on a YTD basis, measured against full-year quota that is pro-rated at 25% per quarter.
- If YTD attainment exceeds prorated quota, then earned commissions for that period will be paid at the non-accelerated rate unless full-year quota has been exceeded, in which case the payment made will include accelerators.

Managed Services (MS), Non-Guaranteed Data and Professional Services Bookings
(15% of potential on-target commission)

- Managed Services, Non-Guaranteed Data and Professional Services bookings attainment will be calculated in aggregate and will be paid based on the following table:
    - < 50% attainment = 0% payout
    - For each % of attainment above 50% and up to 100%, 2% of total MS on-target commissions payout will be earned.
    - If you exceed the target on an annual basis you will receive a 50% kicker on your annualized commission

rate. You can achieve this in total or on a per component basis. For clarity, the managed services rate (including accelerator) for all bookings over 100% attainment equals 0.04%.
- Attainment will be calculated quarterly on a YTD basis, measured against full-year quota that is pro-rated at 25% per quarter.
- If YTD attainment exceeds prorated quota, then earned commissions for that period will be paid at the non-accelerated rate unless full-year quota has been exceeded, in which case the payment made will include accelerators.

Sample Payment Calculation
Q1 SaaS attainment = 100%
100 points x 1% = 100% of YTD SS commission potential
Q1 MS attainment = 90%
40 points (90% attainment - 50% cliff) x 2 = 80% of YTD MS commission potential

Payment Calculation
SaaS (85% weight) = 100% x 85% = 85%
MS (15% weight) = 80% x 15% = 12%
Total = 85% + 12% = 97% of Total YTD commission potential

Any negative bookings adjustments in future periods related to this plan year that cause a negative adjustment to previously-paid commissions can be recaptured against future commission payments. For example, a negative bookings adjustment made in March 2018 for a 2017 deal will reduce the Q1 2018 payment scheduled to be paid in April 2018.

Plan Terms & Conditions

1. **TERM.** This Sales Compensation Plan ("The Plan") is effective on April 3, 2018 and continues through December 31, 2018 (the "Term"). This Plan supersedes and replaces all prior compensatory plans, offers or arrangements of any kind, oral and written.
2. **BASE COMPENSATION.** Your base salary during the term is payable twice a month, twenty-four pay periods per year.
3. **COMMISSIONS.** The commission incentive portion of the plan is intended to reward eligible staff for meeting their assigned sales quota. All payout calculations are located in plan details above.
4. **DEFINITIONS.** The following definitions apply to terms used in this Plan.
    - **Sales Quota** – the quota assigned to the sales organization for the sales and delivery of any and all ABC Co product Sales.
    - **Guaranteed Quota** – the quota associated with any non-recoverable draw payments. Quota retirement will be calculated based on your on target commission payout rate.
    - **Company** – ABC Co
    - **Contract** – an enforceable written agreement signed by the customer and an authorized representative of the Company (or a group of agreements signed contemporaneously by a single customer and an authorized representative of Company) that is not subject to any material contingencies.
    - **Bookings** – Total value of all eligible products sold on a contract

- **Annual Contract Value (ACV)** - is the total value of renewable SaaS divided by the contract's length (in years).
- **Pass-Through** – services that may be delivered by ABC Co Networks for the convenience or benefit of a client. The recognized revenue from a pass through is not paid commission and will not count towards quota.
- **Guaranteed Data** – data sales where customers will pay the entire contract amount regardless of product usage. In order to qualify as guaranteed, payment terms must be no longer than monthly in arrears. Additionally, any guaranteed data sale with payment terms longer than monthly in arrears shall be considered non-guaranteed and paid as such.
- **Non-Guaranteed Data** – data sales where customers are not liable for full contract amount if they do not use the product.
- **Earned Commissions** – based on attainment of each bookings component through the last complete quarter of your employment. For example, except as defined in your offer letter (if applicable) or employment contract (if applicable), if your employment is terminated for any reason and your last day of employment is November 15th, your earned commissions will be based on bookings through September 30th.

Plan Payments

Commission payments on sales will be paid quarterly based on YTD bookings attainment as detailed above. Contracts are subject to extension of time for review and approval by the Company's executive management.

5. UN-CAPPED PLAN.

    The commission plan is uncapped, meaning that there is no limit to the amount of commissions that can be earned for business booked in a fiscal year.

6. CHARGEBACKS.

    The company has the right to charge back commissions based on the following scenarios.
    - **Customer Non-Payment** – If a customer invoice is not paid within 90 days of the invoice date, this non-payment by the customer will result in the contract value being debited, after a 60 day grace period, to the CRO. Any previously paid commissions or other incentives, associated with a "non-payment contract" will be owed by the CRO and will be recovered against the CRO's future commission earnings.
    - **Customer Cancellation** – There may be a 100% charge-back of incentive compensation and quota on services/bookings that are canceled by a customer.

7. **NO EMPLOYMENT CONTRACT.** This Plan is merely a guideline for sales commissions or bonuses, which you may be eligible to receive. It is not an employment agreement, nor does it guarantee employment for any period of time, or otherwise affect your status as an at-will employee.

8. **FISCAL YEAR PAYMENTS.** Payouts will be based on the terms of the Plan in effect when the actual contract was signed. The timing of payments is per item (5) above, and may therefore fall into a subsequent fiscal year. For example, bookings/contracts signed in Q4 of FY18 will have an associated payout in FY19.

9. **PLAN ADMINISTRATION**. This Plan shall be administered and interpreted solely by the Company and may be changed, amended or terminated at the sole discretion of the Company at any time without prior notice. All decisions by the Company related to this Plan shall be final.
10. **ABC Co CHANNEL**. Quota and commissions will be paid out on Partner/Channel opportunities which are managed by the CRO's team. Commissions will be paid out commensurate with selling directly to a direct buyer after deducting and Partner and Channel fee.
11. **TERMINATION OR TRANSFER**. If your employment with the Company terminates for any reason prior to the date of payment of any commission, bonus or other compensation identified in the Plan, regardless of the date of any Contract execution, you will only be entitled to earned commissions as defined above. Contracts need to be signed in order for payout to occur.
12. **DEATH OR DISABILITY**. If you die or become disabled during the Term, you or your estate will be paid any commissions or bonuses earned before your death or disability.
13. **CONFIDENTIALITY**. This Plan, including all of its terms, is confidential to you and the Company. You recognize and agree that you shall not discuss the contents of this Plan with any other employee of the Company, except as authorized by the CEO or CFO of ABC Co. Any discussions of the contents of this Plan with others may be grounds for termination.
14. **MODIFICATIONS**. This Plan may not be modified except in writing by the Company's executive management.

15. **SPIF's**. Special Incentive Features (SPIF's) are published by the Compensation Review Board and are intended to provide incentives to employees. If any SPIF's become effective during the fiscal year this will be communicated via email to plan participants.
16. **COMPENSATION ISSUES**. Any issue regarding your commission payment needs to be brought to the CEO or CFO of ABC Co Networks.

Workshop

Objective: Understand how to calculate and optimize your personal commission rate (PCR) based on different sales scenarios.

Materials Needed: Calculator, pen, paper, sample commission plans

Duration: 1 hour

Steps:

1. **Introduction (10 minutes)**: Briefly explain the concept of OTE, base salary, commission, and PCR.
2. **Case Study (20 minutes)**: Provide a sample compensation plan similar to the one outlined above. Have participants calculate the PCR based on different OTEs and quotas.
3. **Group Discussion (15 minutes)**: Discuss how different factors like exceeding quotas, cliff structures, and accelerators affect the final commission payout.
4. **Q&A (15 minutes)**: Open the floor for any questions regarding the calculation and implications of PCR.

Quiz

1. What does OTE stand for?
   - A) On Time Earnings
   - B) On Target Earnings
   - C) Optimal Target Earnings
   - D) On Time Efficiency
2. If an SE has an OTE of $200,000 with a 70/30 split, what is their base salary?
   - A) $140,000
   - B) $60,000
   - C) $100,000
   - D) $200,000
3. How is the Personal Commission Rate (PCR) calculated?
   - A) Base Salary / Quota
   - B) OTE / Quota
   - C) Variable / Quota
   - D) Commission / Quota
4. In a SaaS compensation plan, what is typically the weight of SaaS and Guaranteed Data Bookings in the commission calculation?
   - A) 70%
   - B) 85%
   - C) 50%
   - D) 15%
5. What does ACV stand for in a sales commission plan?
   - A) Annual Customer Value
   - B) Average Contract Value
   - C) Annual Contract Value
   - D) Adjusted Commission Value

Answers

1. B) On Target Earnings
2. A) $140,000
3. C) Variable / Quota
4. B) 85%
5. C) Annual Contract Value

Books Recommended

1. "Compensating the Sales Force" by David J. Cichelli
    - **Reason:** This book provides a comprehensive guide on how to design, implement, and manage sales compensation plans that drive performance.
2. "Sales Compensation Essentials" by Jerry Colletti and Mary S. Fiss
    - **Reason:** It offers insights into the fundamentals of sales compensation, making it a great resource for those new to understanding commission structures.
3. "The Sales Compensation Handbook" by Stockton B. Colt
    - **Reason:** A practical handbook that covers a wide range of topics related to sales compensation, from plan design to administration and communication.

Chapter 18: Sales Incentive Options

Transitioning from understanding how compensation plans work, we move into the exciting realm of additional incentives and stock compensation. These elements can significantly boost your overall earnings and are essential to consider when negotiating a job offer. Let's dive into the specifics of SPIFs and stock options, and how they can impact your financial future.

"Success is not just about making money. It's about making a difference." – Unknown

SPIFs (Sales Performance Incentive Funds)

SPIFs are additional incentives designed to motivate sales teams to achieve specific goals or milestones outside the standard compensation plan. These can be highly motivating and rewarding, especially when aligned with strategic company objectives.

1. Types of SPIFs:
    - **Cash Bonuses:** Immediate financial rewards for achieving specific targets.
    - **Non-Cash Rewards:** Items like gadgets, vacations, or gift cards.
    - **Experiences:** Events or activities such as team outings or exclusive trips.
2. Importance for SEAC Teams:
    - SE (Sales Engineer), SA (Solution Architect), and SC (Solution Consultant) teams should also benefit from SPIFs, as they play a crucial role in closing deals and driving sales success.
3. Negotiating SPIFs:

- During your interview or negotiation process, ask about SPIFs and how they are distributed among the team. This can provide insight into how the company values and rewards its employees.

Stock Compensation

Stock compensation can be a game-changer, providing significant financial benefits if the company's stock performs well. However, it's essential to understand the different types of stock compensation and their implications.

IPO Shares vs. RSU Stocks

1. IPO Shares (Initial Public Offering):
    - Provide the holder the right to buy company stock at a future date at a price established at the time of issue.
    - Example: If offered pre-IPO shares at a strike price of $75 and the company goes public at $180, you can buy and potentially sell at a profit.
2. RSU Stocks (Restricted Stock Units):
    - Give the holder a commitment to receive the value of a certain number of shares in the future without paying upfront.
    - Typically have a vesting schedule, such as a one-year cliff followed by quarterly vesting.

Tax Considerations

1. RSUs:
    - Taxed as income when they vest and become liquid.

- Companies may withhold some RSUs to cover taxes or offer options to pay taxes with cash.
2. Stock Options:
    - Not taxed until exercised.
    - If held for at least a year post-exercise, they are taxed at the capital gains rate, which is generally lower than income tax rates.

Acceleration Upon Acquisition

If a startup is acquired, acceleration clauses can significantly impact your financial outcome by speeding up the vesting of your stock options. This can be a crucial element in your employment contract.

Workshop

Objective: Understand and negotiate SPIFs and stock compensation effectively.

Materials Needed:

- Whiteboard and markers
- Sample employment contracts
- Calculators

Duration: 1 hour

Instructions:

1. Introduction (10 minutes):
    - Discuss the importance of SPIFs and stock compensation.
    - Explain different types of SPIFs and stock options.
2. Group Activity (30 minutes):
    - Split into small groups and review sample employment contracts.
    - Identify SPIFs and stock compensation clauses.
    - Calculate potential earnings from stock options and RSUs under different scenarios.
3. Discussion (20 minutes):
    - Each group presents their findings.
    - Discuss strategies for negotiating SPIFs and stock compensation.

Quiz

1. What does SPIF stand for?
   - a) Sales Performance Incentive Funds
   - b) Sales Personnel Incentive Funds
   - c) Sales Performance Internal Funds
2. What are RSUs?
   - a) Restricted Stock Units
   - b) Revenue Stock Units
   - c) Retained Stock Units
3. How are RSUs taxed?
   - a) When they vest
   - b) When they are sold
   - c) When they are granted
4. What is the benefit of a non-recoverable draw?
   - a) It does not need to be paid back if you leave the company.
   - b) It is only given as a bonus.
   - c) It has a higher tax rate.
5. What is an IPO share?
   - a) A share that can be bought at the public offering price.
   - b) A share given as a bonus.
   - c) A share with no vesting period.

Quiz Answers

1. a) Sales Performance Incentive Funds
2. a) Restricted Stock Units
3. a) When they vest
4. a) It does not need to be paid back if you leave the company.
5. a) A share that can be bought at the public offering price

Chapter 19: How Much Are You Worth

It's important to understand the various elements that contribute to your overall earnings. From understanding compensation matrices and negotiation strategies to leveraging stock options and SPIFFs, this chapter will equip you with the knowledge to maximize your financial rewards and career growth. Let's dive into the details and ensure you are well-prepared to negotiate the best possible compensation package.

"Your focus determines your reality." - Qui-Gon Jinn, Star Wars

Compensation Matrix (LOW | MID | HIGH)

Level	Low	Mid	High	RSU (New Hire)
IC3	$168,000	$210,000	$252,000	150,000
IC4	$184,000	$230,000	$276,000	200,000
IC5	$216,000	$270,000	$324,000	300,000

Illustration 10.2.2021

In this illustration, you will find what we call a compensation matrix. "IC" stands for Individual Contributor, and the number represents the title. IC3 is a standard Sales Engineer (SE, SA, SC), an IC4 is a Senior Sales Engineer (SE, SA, SC), and an IC5 is a Principal Sales

Engineer (SE, SA, SC). Some companies, like Oracle, have a Master Principal title, which would be an IC6. The hiring manager is bound by this matrix, and it is crucial that negotiations stay within these guidelines. Typically, if you are an entry-level SC IC2 with about two years of experience, you may qualify for an IC3 position. Let's say you had a Mid salary at your previous company of $190,000 OTE, and you feel you should have about a 10% increase for an IC3 role when moving to a new company. Thus, you are really looking for at least $200,000. This is good news since the midpoint for an IC3 is $210,000. The manager will have no problem negotiating below the midpoint for your offer. Unfortunately, this means you left money on the table. Here is where negotiations and knowledge are power to secure the best offer. Remember, changing jobs is the best time to maximize your earnings. Once you are within a company, expect at most a 2 to 5% increase year over year. It can take a long time to achieve the raise you're seeking! So, practice your negotiation skills before you even interview!

When you started the interview process, I can guarantee that the hiring manager or even the recruiter wanted to know your salary requirements. This is a tough question to ask and even tougher to answer. In some jurisdictions, it can be considered illegal to request this information. The challenge with providing this information upfront is that you could undermine your own negotiation leverage. Your number could be beyond the midpoint that the hiring manager has to work with, and you could be disqualified. Or, you could state a base number well below the midpoint, thus leaving money on the table.

I have spoken extensively about the midpoint, but let me explain why this matters. If a high point option exists, why not aim for the maximum, right? Wrong. Here's Reason: Human Resources tends to keep offers below the midpoint for several good reasons. The first is growth within the organization. If, after nine months, the organization wants to reward your efforts with a pay increase but not a title change, they have room for mid-year or end-of-year monetary promotions. If you are too far over the midpoint, you may be passed over for another year until you meet the requirements for a title promotion.

The second reason relates to corporate OPEX, or operating budgets. Remember, you are a sales resource that costs the company a lot of money. With every dollar invested in the solution engineering team, the sales team's quotas have to increase to keep things profitable. When I was a young manager at Adobe, I was naive about this. However, thanks to Josee Murray in sales ops, it was clarified for me. Thanks, Josee, for that lightbulb moment. Too often, individuals view their job as just that: a job that pays. However, in sales, you have a base salary, and you can exceed by risking a portion of your earnings against this quota. It's the quota that sales ops must balance correctly, or the company ends up losing money by paying out too much to the sales team. Or worse, the ops team pays out too little, and you start to lose salespeople who are incentivized to go elsewhere so they can earn more. It's a challenging role to have and try to please everyone involved.

The last point comes down to acquiring and retaining talent for the organization. I have been in situations where legacy team members have been paid up to $60,000 less than new hires. Of course, "no one" is supposed to know another person's salary, but with sites like Glassdoor and word of mouth, it will get out. So, consider a person who has been with the company from the start and is being paid below the midpoint. They find out a new hire is making thirty thousand more than they are. As a manager, you have a tough situation on your hands. Outside of trying to push for a promotion, your only recourse is the stock side of the equation. Remind the individual that they have a better stock package than the new hire, or at least you hope so. Too often, people forget about the stock packages, the stock purchase program, or the matching they have received on 401Ks. As a manager, you must look at the entire financial picture and not just balance the business outside.

What does all this mean for you at this stage? I recommend during that first intro call, if the human resources person asks you your salary requirements, DO NOT answer the question. Take a chapter out of Sales 101. Let's role-play that a bit. "Hi Kevin, so tell me what your salary requirements will be before we get too far down the line." "Oh, thanks, Karen, for asking that question. I understand that compensation is a big combination of factors. Before I answer that, can you provide me with the Low, Mid, and High budget for this position?" Initially, you may just get a, "well, I cannot provide that answer," and I would follow with, "Okay, that is fair. Could you provide me with what the midpoint could be?" You still may get no answer, or you may just get lucky. A great technique in objection handling is Match, Understand, Resolve. Match: Demonstrate a complete willingness and fearlessness to address the concern. Empathy, not agreement. You are slowing down for the yellow light. Understand: Identify the true nature of resistance and what the resolution would be. Find out what would have to happen to resolve this concern to the customer's satisfaction or, in this case, the hiring manager's middle ground. Resolve: work towards a mutual resolution to genuine issues. I have a complete workshop on this methodology and will post on the website.

Chapter 20: Let's make a deal

Offer Negotiation Stage

Congratulations, you've made it past the interviews and have been selected for a position. This is a fantastic time in your life and typically only happens about a dozen times, so reward yourself—maybe not with a Mercedes or BMW M4 just yet. You do NOT have a job until you receive an official offer letter. DO NOT quit your current job until you've navigated through the negotiation phases and received that final offer. This conversation is merely a verbal offer, presenting an opportunity for you to ask questions or make requests.

If you've followed some of the hiring workflow discussions in this book, you already set the stage for this verbal discussion a few weeks back during your initial conversation. Reflect on that conversation because I can assure you that the hiring manager noted your salary and benefit requirements at the beginning. This is not the time to deviate significantly from what was discussed early on. Behind the scenes, the manager has been working with their director, VP, HR, and finance to justify the numbers you presented earlier. The back office process can be daunting, akin to trying to close a deal with a customer. Be very clear and upfront with the hiring manager early on. If you make significant changes now, it can sour the relationship and potentially pull you out of candidacy. I have been involved in several situations where the SE thought they had knocked it out of the park or believed we were desperate to hire someone, thus feeling they had leverage. I don't know many managers who would be intimidated by this, as it sets the wrong tone for future relationships.

I have terminated all negotiations with candidates because of these last-minute asks.

You should be prepared with all things discussed from the beginning regarding compensation and benefits requirements on paper or in the cloud Google doc. Remember that you may have about three to five opportunities in the running; keeping them all straight in your head will be a challenge. Do not forget to say thank you, then sit back and listen to what the individual has to say. Take notes as you go through your mental checklist; in the end, the hiring manager will want to close you; I recommend a soft yes, allowing you the chance to review the terms discussed over the phone. I would not wait too long, as the paper process for approval is moving through the system, and the last thing the hiring manager wants to do is resubmit through the workflows. At Adobe, the CEO would be involved in workflow approvals, and at Oracle, the executive council would approve all senior-level positions. So there is a lot of work on the hiring manager's part in the background. Respect that they have worked hard to get here, but also understand you have some leverage.

Whether this call is a phone call or more typically a Zoom call to visually see you at this stage, be prepared. When I make a verbal offer to a candidate, I always look to do that over the web to see the reaction as I outline the offer to them. Be prepared, and ensure you react enthusiastically to the phone or web call. Your body language will be evident over the web and can be sensed over the phone. Typically, I will review what the candidate presented as an ask earlier in the workflow. I will always reference my approval for X dollars On Target Earnings with a 70/30 variable commission outlined. I typically do not have any quota details as, most often, assignments are made after onboarding. I will mention the number of stock options if they are available in the offer. I will discuss what I had to negotiate internally so the candidate realizes my work to get this offer together. After that first positioning, I will pause, look for a reaction, and give the candidate a chance to make a statement. The first question will tell me if we have accepted the numbers or not. If the candidate starts with - "Thank you so much, that is a great offer and in line with what we discussed, can you let me know if we have room in stocks?" - I know I have the candidate on the hook and will not have to return for more money on salary. Many managers will reserve stocks from what was accepted internally as a negotiation option. If we need to negotiate, I always have a few shares ready to go. Having those stocks in reserve prevented me from wasting time going back for approvals. If the candidate accepted the compensation and stock at face value, I would sweeten the final offer with those reserve stocks to provide goodwill. If the candidate asked questions about benefits and not stocks, the same situation, I knew we had a signed candidate as benefits are not likely to change and are baked into the Full-Time Employee costs. As for vacation days, companies have figured out in the states to give their employees "unlimited vacation," Unlimited vacation is another way of saying they don't owe you any accrued vacation payout if you decide to leave the company. You should push for another week or two if they do not have unlimited vacation. As a manager, it can be easy to obtain approvals from the back office.

If you recall, we discussed the Low | Med | High OTE matrix earlier in the book, and if you conducted your Discovery well, you would know where you fall in this matrix. In addition, you should be concerned with the title you offer; this is directly tied to IC levels - Individual Contributor Level 1,2,3,4. Each level provides a different overlapping Low | Med | High OTE matrix. Unless you are getting paid significantly for a principal SEAC level, I would not want to enter any new company at the Principal or Master Principal levels.

The principal level means you have no room for growth and monetary payout. Your goal is negotiating an OTE level between MED and HIGH, giving you space for growth. Your hiring manager may have you just over the Midpoint, but their job is to get you below the Midpoint, and HR will look to enforce that level.

You may find that the hiring manager is looking to get an acceptance over the phone so they can move forward to close out the requisition. As mentioned, it's OK to say yes with the caveat of reviewing the benefits book and final numbers. This can be a ticking time bomb, especially with any global economic issues that could cause the req to become frozen. If you get that verbal, you should be prepared to say yes and get that official offer letter as quickly as possible. I remember at Adobe and Oracle, both during some global economic issues impacting hiring for the company, and in less than 24hrs they froze my headcount. All offers were frozen or terminated, and thus no hires.

You will be asked when to start the new position during this conversation. Most hiring managers want you to start immediately, but understand that you want to do right by your current company and give them at least two weeks. However, depending on when you get this offer, the company could be at the beginning of its new year. It would be best for you to be at the annual kickoff meeting or the semi-annual SE summit at the end of their Q2. But, since you have been reading this book, you already know those key dates, as you have done your research before engaging the company. So it would be best if you were prepared not to miss those events. If your hiring manager plays good chess, they have hired you well before the end of the new year so you can get productive quickly. When asked about your timing, you may want to confirm what might be driving the date sooner than two weeks. I recommend you take at least a whole week off between jobs. This is the best time to leave the world a bit, as you will not have a company email or be pressured to take a meeting until you start. If you can afford to take a whole week, do it!

Compensation Negotiation Checklist

Before the Meeting:

1. Research Compensation Matrix:
    - Understand the IC levels (IC3, IC4, IC5) and their corresponding salary ranges (Low, Mid, High).
    - Know the RSU (Restricted Stock Units) allocation for each level.
2. Assess Your Current Position:
    - Evaluate your current salary and determine your desired increase.
    - Ensure your desired salary aligns with the new company's midpoint or slightly above.
3. Prepare Your Salary Requirement Strategy:
    - Do not disclose your salary requirements upfront.
    - Instead, ask for the Low, Mid, and High Budget for the position.
    - Use objection handling techniques: Match, Understand, Resolve.

During the Meeting:

1. Initial Salary Discussion:
    - When asked for your salary requirements, respond with questions about the budget ranges for the position.

- Demonstrate a willingness to address concerns empathetically and work towards a mutual resolution.
2. Verbal Offer:
    - Listen carefully to the verbal offer.
    - Ensure all aspects of the offer are covered: base salary, variable commission, stock options, benefits, and vacation days.
    - Show enthusiasm and appreciation for the offer.
3. Negotiate for Better Terms:
    - If the offer is close to your expectation, ask if there is room for more stock options.
    - Ensure you understand the total compensation package, including benefits and potential for future raises.
4. Assess Stock Options:
    - Confirm the number of stock options or RSUs.
    - Understand the vesting schedule and any conditions tied to the stocks.
5. Vacation and Benefits:
    - Clarify the vacation policy, especially if it's "unlimited vacation."
    - Push for additional vacation time if necessary.

Post-Meeting:

1. Review Offer:
    - Take a moment to review the offer carefully.
    - Consider consulting a financial advisor if stock options are a significant part of the package.
2. Respond Promptly:
    - Don't delay your response to the offer; aim to provide a soft yes quickly while you review the terms.
    - If needed, request clarification on any points that are not clear.
3. Finalizing the Offer:
    - Confirm the start date, keeping in mind any strategic company events like annual kickoffs or summits.
    - Ensure you take some time off between jobs if possible.
4. Get It in Writing:
    - Do not resign from your current position until you have received and signed the official offer letter.

Quick Tips:

- Practice your negotiation skills before the interview process begins.
- Always be prepared with a mental checklist during the offer discussion.
- Maintain a positive and professional demeanor throughout the negotiation.
- Remember that this is one of the few opportunities to significantly boost your compensation—make the most of it!

Summary of Key Points

1. **Understand the Compensation Matrix**: Know where you fit and aim for the Mid to High range.
2. **Negotiate Smartly**: Avoid giving away your salary requirements too early.
3. **Consider All Aspects**: Base salary, commission, stock options, and benefits are all important.
4. **Timing Matters**: Align your start date with key company events for maximum impact.

Workshop: Negotiating Your Compensation Package

Materials Needed:

- Notepad and Pen
- Calculator
- Internet Access (for research)
- Sample Compensation Plans (provided in the book)

Duration: 2 hours

Steps:

1. **Research**: Spend 30 minutes researching typical compensation packages for your role and industry.
2. **Self-Assessment**: Evaluate your skills and experience to determine your worth.
3. **Role-Play**: Partner with a friend or colleague to role-play the negotiation process.
4. **Mock Negotiation**: Use the sample compensation plans to practice negotiating different scenarios.

5. **Review**: Reflect on your performance and identify areas for improvement.

Recommended Books

1. "Negotiating Your Salary: How to Make $1,000 a Minute" by Jack Chapman
    - This book offers practical strategies for negotiating your salary and getting the best possible deal.
2. "The Art of Negotiation: How to Improvise Agreement in a Chaotic World" by Michael Wheeler
    - Wheeler provides insights into the dynamics of negotiation and how to effectively reach agreements.

Quiz

1. What is the primary purpose of a compensation matrix?
    - A. To limit salary increases
    - B. To provide a guideline for fair compensation
    - C. To determine stock option availability
2. Why should you avoid giving your salary requirements too early?
    - A. It can lead to disqualification
    - B. You might leave money on the table
    - C. Both A and B
3. What is a common reason for Human Resources to keep salaries below the midpoint?
    - A. To reduce company expenses
    - B. To allow room for growth and promotions
    - C. To avoid paying too much in commissions
4. When is the best time to negotiate your compensation package?
    - A. During the initial interview
    - B. After receiving a verbal offer
    - C. After starting the job
5. What should you always ensure before resigning from your current job?
    - A. That you have received a verbal offer
    - B. That you have a written offer letter
    - C. That you have discussed benefits

Answers:

1. B. To provide a guideline for fair compensation
2. C. Both A and B
3. B. To allow room for growth and promotions
4. B. After receiving a verbal offer
5. B. That you have a written offer letter

Part 9: You got the job – Now What

Chapter 21: Congrats Day 1 - Ready to Start

You've successfully navigated the job search and negotiation process. Now that you've accepted the offer and are ready to begin, it's time to focus on getting off to a strong start in your new role. Day 1 is more than just setting up your workstation; it's about laying the foundation for your success. Let's dive into the essentials that will set you up for a stellar beginning.

"In my experience, there's only one motivation, and that is desire. No reasons or principle contain it or stand against it." — Jane Smiley

Welcome back from your two or three-week vacation. Hopefully, you took my advice, relaxed, organized, and are ready for your next venture. You should have received your already configured laptop and possibly your remote office setup by now. In addition, I am sure marketing sent you a welcome box with all types of goodies, from thermoses to squeeze stress balls. The fun part comes for the next 30, 60, and 90 days of onboarding. I will provide a series of onboarding checklists, but I am confident your organization has some established lists.

The most critical thing to consider is that you will become extremely busy after your first account meeting. Therefore, between now and your first meeting, you need to take care of a list of prerequisites that will negatively impact you later if not done immediately. The big things to accomplish are:

- Write your Bio for the boss
- HRM Profile
- Email Filters
- Enablement Schedule
- Office Badge
- Slack or Communication Tools
- Tax Documents - W4 or Localized Government Docs
- Benefits Completed
- ESPP Documentation
- 401K Selections
- HR Enablement
- Demo Site Access
- Have a Sherpa

Bio for your Boss

If you want your Bio to represent you, take a moment and write the Bio for your boss. Your boss will appreciate the ghostwriting of this email. Keep it short, one thing personal, one thing business, and maybe a fun fact not found in the LinkedIn Profile.

HRM Profile

Human Resource Management systems drive several other systems inside an organization. So take the time and upload a professional photo, which will appear in all org charts. Update who you are, how many kids you have, and what you like to do. Fill out as much as you can in the profile. Leaders above you will use the HRM system every quarter to get an understanding of each person. You have a

LinkedIn profile; however, leaders always default to the HRM to build charts and presents.

Enablement Schedule

The HRM system should update your calendar with sales kickoffs and your scheduled boot camp at HQ. However, I would not trust that this system will manage this correctly. Find out when your trip will be so you can coordinate with your family, book travel early, and understand the prerequisites before arriving. I remember my first onboarding when we had less automation, and I had a wedding to attend during the already scheduled Bootcamp. Unfortunately, the next class filled up, and I had to wait for an entire quarter before attending.

Communication Systems

You will find that email is becoming less and less critical in work communications. The quicker you understand what your team uses to communicate, the faster you will get up to speed. The worst situation is when leadership works with a different communication tool than the field SC team and sales. I had this situation at Snowflake, where Sales used email, SC used Slack, and My leadership used Trello. As a leader, I had to manage all three communication methods. Not an ideal situation.

Email Filters

Most startups will contract with Gmail or maybe even an open-source email. Larger organizations might have Outlook or some other classic email hosting ability. As soon as your email becomes active, your boss will send a notification welcoming you to the company; your inbox will be full. In addition, the internal IT team that VM'd your machine included what the default groups in your email were. As a result, you will have a ton of emails from marketing, corporate announcements, product engineering, partners, you name it. You must learn their system and turn those filters on to clear the noise.

Tax Documents - W4 or Localized Government Docs

I know this sounds like a no-brainer, but you would be surprised how many SCs do not take the time to fill out their ADP or Payroll information correctly. And find out they owe a ton of taxes and penalties at the end of the year. Plus, you do not want the HR department to call your boss, who has to ride you to get that stuff done. So while at those sites, getting the 401K, benefits all out of the way.

Human Resource Required Enablement

If you are at a startup, you may not have many HR-required courses. However, if starting at a publicly traded company, HR is there to mitigate risks to the organization. You must take the time to complete the diversity, ethics, harassment, data protection, and Security enablement. These courses are the most painful ever! You cannot cheat through these; take the weekend, lock yourself in a room and get it DONE! You will thank me later for getting these done early. Take screenshots that prove you completed the courses, as many of these systems do not accurately record your results. The last thing you want to do is re-do these courses. As a director and a VP, I would get weekly reports from my team on who did and did not complete the courses. These are not optional; the last thing you want is for your boss to get called out on a leadership call for incomplete results. Do not do this to your boss!

Enablement Apps - Learning Management Systems

Learning management systems have come a long way since the early 2000's and there are so many to choose from. The good news for you is that the company that hires you, will probably have one already implemented. I would highly recommend that you figure out quickly which one they have landed on. Go to the app store and download the app to your phone. We used to use Mindtickle at a few companies and this app is fantastic. They have a full library and are typically broken down by mandatory and non-mandatory content. The LMS will keep track of your activity and in some cases you can build out your own learning path. The best part is that the application offers feedback to the management team and they can keep the information fresh, as well as see your progress. Insert Darth Vader music in the background. Depending on your leadership this can be a good thing or bad.

The best part of the application is that you can play the videos and audio as you work out in the morning, have a long drive to the office or a client. I used to travel to Boston from New Jersey, a five-hour drive or a five-hour air travel journey (1hr to airport | 1hr ahead of takeoff | 45 Min Flight | Logan Delay or EWR Delay 45 min | 1hr lost on the ground to get to the final destination). I would clear through the mandatory content within a few weeks of onboarding. Though I would always create a plan for me to continue to pick up product enhancements, board meeting replays etc.

One word of caution with these systems will be content aging and expiration. Depending on the team managing this content, some of the information will be stale. I recommend reviewing all the dates associated with the content details. In addition, you may find that Product Marketing is providing an elevator pitch that may not have been tested in the field. This is not a dig on Marketing teams, just the simple fact that they are not in the field and the content coming from the SEAC organization will be battle tested.

Workshop

Title: Onboarding Essentials Workshop

Objective: To ensure new hires understand and complete all essential onboarding tasks.

Materials Needed:

- Laptop
- Internet Access
- HR Documents
- Learning Management System Access
- Calendar

Duration: 2 hours

Step-by-Step Instructions:

1. Introduction (10 mins):
    - Overview of the workshop objectives.
    - Importance of completing onboarding tasks early.
2. Bio Writing (20 mins):
    - Guide on how to write a professional bio.
    - Participants write their bios and share with the group.
3. HRM Profile Setup (20 mins):
    - Instructions on updating HRM profile.
    - Participants update their profiles live.

4. Email Filters Setup (20 mins):
    - Demonstrate setting up email filters.
    - Participants set up their filters.
5. Enablement Schedule Overview (20 mins):
    - Discuss the importance of the enablement schedule.
    - Participants review their schedules and mark important dates.
6. Communication Tools Setup (20 mins):
    - Overview of communication tools used by the company.
    - Participants set up and familiarize themselves with these tools.
7. Tax Documents and Benefits Enrollment (20 mins):
    - Guide on filling out tax documents and enrolling in benefits.
    - Participants complete these tasks.
8. Q&A and Wrap-Up (10 mins):
    - Open floor for any questions.
    - Summary of the workshop and final reminders.

Book Recommendations

1. "The First 90 Days" by Michael Watkins

   - **Reason:** This book offers strategies and tools for new leaders to make a strong start in their new roles. It provides a roadmap for successfully transitioning into a new job.

2. "The New One Minute Manager" by Ken Blanchard and Spencer Johnson

   - **Reason:** This book emphasizes the importance of setting clear goals, providing immediate feedback, and recognizing achievements, which are crucial during the onboarding period.

3. "Radical Candor" by Kim Scott

   - **Reason:** Effective communication and feedback are vital from day one. This book teaches you how to be a kick-ass boss without losing your humanity, which is valuable in building early relationships.

4. "The Lean Startup" by Eric Ries

   - **Reason:** Understanding the startup mentality and how to navigate it can be incredibly beneficial for new hires, especially in tech environments.

5. "Crucial Conversations" by Kerry Patterson, Joseph Grenny, Ron McMillan, and Al Switzler

- **Reason:** This book provides tools for handling difficult conversations, a skill that can be particularly useful as you integrate into a new team and culture.

Quiz

1. What is the first thing you should write when starting your new job?

- A. Your resume
- B. Your Bio for the boss
- C. Your LinkedIn profile
- D. Your first sales report

2. Why is it important to update your HRM profile?

- A. It helps with payroll
- B. Leaders use it to understand their team
- C. It's required by law
- D. It improves your LinkedIn visibility

3. What should you do if your HR asks for your salary requirements?

- A. Provide an exact number
- B. Refuse to answer
- C. Ask for the Low, Mid, and High budget for the position
- D. Tell them your current salary

4. Why is it crucial to complete HR-required enablement courses early?

- A. To avoid penalties
- B. To ensure compliance and avoid redoing them later
- C. To get a bonus
- D. To impress your boss

5. What should you do with your Learning Management System app?

- A. Delete it after onboarding
- B. Use it to complete mandatory content and track progress
- C. Share it with friends
- D. Only use it during work hours

Answers:

1. B. Your Bio for the boss
2. B. Leaders use it to understand their team
3. C. Ask for the Low, Mid, and High budget for the position
4. B. To ensure compliance and avoid redoing them later
5. B. Use it to complete mandatory content and track progress

Chapter 22: Having a Sherpa Program

Stepping into a sales engineering role in a dynamic and rapidly changing market can be a challenge, even for experienced professionals. To navigate this landscape effectively, having a structured mentorship and shadowing program can make all the difference. Enter the Walkabout Program—an initiative designed to bridge the gap between technical expertise and sales excellence by leveraging the knowledge and experience of seasoned professionals.

"In my experience, there is no such thing as luck." — Obi-Wan Kenobi, Star Wars

The Walkabout Program (TWC)

By Ben Greene..

Program Overview/Summary

The sales engineering organization has historically consisted of profoundly technical and specialized sales engineers who, in some cases, have never had any sales or sales engineering experience. The complexity of the technology necessitated this hiring profile, along with its ecosystem and the competitive landscape, which was very favorable due to our first-mover status. However, the data cloud/platform market is changing rapidly, as are the competitive dynamics within the sales process. As a result, competition is evolving and catching up. It is no longer enough to educate customers on your platform. As sales engineers, we need to sell alongside the account executives to win and continue the company's growth trajectory. This is not simply an observation but an ongoing commentary from senior sales executives I have worked with.

Some sales engineers at our company have always done this. Still, a good majority have never practiced some of the basic fundamental selling techniques of any sound technical seller. A good number are simply out of practice, given the above. Skills like storytelling in presentations, objection handling, give-gets, challenger selling, deal qualification, and proper Discovery are falling by the wayside. At the same time, we race to technical validation to let the power of our platform speak for itself.

These skills are also not easy to teach in classrooms because most humans learn by example, and the best models to try and replicate/refine these skills are found in the field. Unfortunately, finding good examples of doing this properly is also very difficult. Because of this, our brand needs to formalize a shadow program where front-line leaders inventory the best and brightest practitioners of specific soft skills and let up-and-comers witness what good looks like in front of a real-world scenario in meetings with customers.

Program Sales Objectives

- Re-align sales engineering expectations of what good looks like within the sales process.
- Develop and refine the core selling skills and techniques desperately needed by some of the sales engineers in the field to help grow/qualify the pipeline and follow sales best practices.
- Help to develop and grow a new generation of leaders within sales engineering by allowing them to mentor and support their fellow SEAC .

Program Details

The Walkabout Program (TWP) was tested within the North America East Enterprise team as a trial to validate the program's effectiveness and then rolled out to the larger organization. The program began by having front-line SEAC managers measure the skill sets of their individual contributors. The measurement was across a range of three high-level skills using both experiences from the field and feedback from individual DMs to identify the most talented technical sellers in three key areas:

Preparation & Planning

- Executes account research prior to engaging.
- Conducts dry runs.
- Develops meeting outlines for answers needed and overall objectives.

Communication Skills

- Commands a room.
- Uses storytelling and persona-based examples.
- Demonstrates our platform with passion and excitement.
- Gets customers excited.
- References customers.

Selling Techniques

- Challenges customers (challenger seller).
- Handles objections well.
- Asks the hard questions sought to qualify the deal.
- Consults rather than sells to customers.

- Manages difficult customers with grace.

They use the skills assessment, which this book will provide as a guide. We compiled a list of SEs with the time, skills, and willingness to coach an SE in a given area. Based on this assessment, SEMs nominated one SE from each territory they feel would benefit from shadowing an SE and what areas need improvement.

Participation Requirements

To participate as a shadower in the TWP, the following requirements must be met:

- Nomination by your SEM and DM for one skill set that needs improvement.
- Shadowing occurs in meetings mutually agreed upon by the customer account team.
- A list of goals and objectives for joining the program in partnership with your SEM.
- Willingness to have your partner SE shadow you in meetings.
- Each meeting will have 15-minute pre and post-mortems.
- Must shadow a minimum of two meetings a month.

To be shadowed in TWP, the following requirements must be met:

- Nomination by both your SEM and DM.
- Sales engineers must be willing to take on additional responsibilities.
- Agrees to a monthly 1:1 sync with their shadower's SEM.
- Agrees to shadow SE on at least two calls a month.

- No more than one SE per person being shadowed.

As an SEM, to have your SE participate in TWP, the SEM must agree to the following:

- Monthly syncs with the SE being shadowed.
- Regular participation in meetings where the shadower is being observed.
- Provide a skills assessment of the SE's skill set in the given area at the beginning and end of the quarter.

The shadow program provided immediate positive results in ramping up new hires and migrating those individuals with strong technical skills to include strong sales presentation skills. We also transitioned those technical SEAC s to participate in a role more aligned with their specialty. These roles included evangelists, product leaders, verticalized specialties, and product SMEs (subject matter experts).

This program allowed participation at multiple levels, allowing more significant leadership exposure for many SEAC s trapped below the radar. Additionally, this allowed the individuals to showcase their specialized talent and be visible to the leadership for future advancements.

The shadow program is not new and has been implemented at several organizations where I have either participated or led the charge inside the company. If you accept an offer at a company, see if they have a shadow program and if not, follow these guidelines, locate a few senior SEAC s and make it happen. You will benefit not just from being shadowed, but leadership should see your initiative as a positive. Thank you, Ben Greene, for spearheading this program.

Workshop

Objective: To implement and practice the shadowing techniques outlined in the Walkabout Program.

Materials Needed:

- Notebooks
- Pens
- Access to virtual meeting platforms (Zoom, Teams, etc.)
- List of shadowing partners and their meeting schedules

Duration: 2 hours

Steps:

1. Introduction (15 minutes)
    - Explain the goals of the workshop.
    - Provide an overview of the Walkabout Program.
2. Role Assignment (15 minutes)
    - Pair participants with shadowing partners.
    - Assign roles for the exercise (SE, shadow SE, customer).
3. Scenario Planning (30 minutes)

- Create realistic customer meeting scenarios.
    - Outline objectives and potential challenges for each scenario.
4. Shadowing Simulation (1 hour)
    - Conduct mock customer meetings with one SE leading and the shadow SE observing.
    - Perform pre- and post-meeting briefings.
5. Debrief and Feedback (30 minutes)
    - Discuss observations and feedback.
    - Highlight key takeaways and areas for improvement.

Book Recommendations

1. "The Challenger Sale" by Matthew Dixon and Brent Adamson
    - **Reason:** This book outlines effective selling techniques that challenge customers and provide value through insight.
2. "SPIN Selling" by Neil Rackham
    - **Reason:** A classic on how to use the SPIN (Situation, Problem, Implication, Need-Payoff) technique to improve sales conversations and outcomes.
3. "To Sell is Human" by Daniel H. Pink
    - **Reason:** Explores the art and science of selling, emphasizing the importance of moving others and understanding their perspectives.
4. "The Trusted Advisor" by David H. Maister, Charles H. Green, and Robert M. Galford
    - **Reason:** Focuses on building trust with clients, which is crucial for effective sales engineering.

5. "Selling to the C-Suite" by Nicholas A.C. Read and Stephen J. Bistritz
    - **Reason:** Provides insights into how to engage and sell to senior executives, a valuable skill for sales engineers aiming to influence decision-makers.

Quiz

1. What are the three high-level skills measured in the Walkabout Program?
    - A) Preparation & Planning, Communication Skills, Selling Techniques
    - B) Technical Knowledge, Product Features, Presentation Skills
    - C) Customer Engagement, Account Management, Sales Strategy
2. Which of the following is NOT a requirement to participate as a shadower in the TWP?
    - A) Nomination by your SEM and DM
    - B) Completion of a sales training course
    - C) Willingness to have your partner SE shadow you in meetings
3. How often must a shadower participate in meetings?
    - A) Once a month
    - B) Twice a month
    - C) Weekly
4. What is one of the key benefits of the shadow program?
    - A) Immediate positive results in ramping up new hires
    - B) Guaranteed promotions
    - C) Decreased workload for SEs
5. Who needs to provide a skills assessment of the SE's skill set in the TWP?
    - A) The customer
    - B) The SEM
    - C) The shadower

Answers

1. A) Preparation & Planning, Communication Skills, Selling Techniques
2. B) Completion of a sales training course
3. B) Twice a month
4. A) Immediate positive results in ramping up new hires
5. B) The SEM

Chapter 23: The Rest of the Organization

After establishing a strong foundation with your initial setup and understanding the compensation structure, it's crucial to dive into the internal workings of various organizational teams. Developing a solid relationship with these teams will not only enhance your knowledge but also foster collaborative success. Let's explore the training organization, professional services, support, and how a consumption model impacts your role.

"An investment in knowledge pays the best interest." - Benjamin Franklin

Training Organization

The training team is excellent to work with as you onboard yourself with the technology. Contact the customer training coordinator to identify the class schedule. Typically, you have no cost to audit a class; the challenge may be getting approval for travel. This classroom-based training is a fantastic way to learn the product. Plus, you get a chance to take a customer out to lunch. I would match many of my new hires with the training team. We had an excellent relationship since an equal benefit to them will be my SE organization will promote the training organization during a sales cycle. Since they attended the classes, they can use this knowledge to convince customers to participate in future courses. In most, if not all, cases, positioning training is never part of a compensation plan. However, if you can successfully launch your customer onto your

Platform, you have a great chance of upselling them later. The class audited is an excellent give/get for helping position future training sales. You can use this give/get in justification for your attendance and possibly the travel and expense costs.

Professional Services

When the timing is reasonable, try to embed yourself in the professional services team. You want to engage in the field with professional services to hear about the challenges they may have with implementations. Understand that the professional services teams are typically on the hook to deliver what you sell. Too often, the presales teams will over-promise to help close a deal and are not there to help pick up the pieces. Now, this is not always the case; however, as an SE, having the ability to let customers know you have participated in previous implementations builds immediate credibility. Not to mention, you gain direct knowledge on deploying your Platform in a real-world situation.

As a leader, I would look to negotiate with Professional Services to rotate a few SEAC s into their teams for at least thirty days. The relationship value between PS and SEAC teams increased tremendously. The investment benefits outweighed the thirty-day loss time in the field. The direct relationships developed will benefit future customer situations and allow for early PS entry into the sales cycles. Unfortunately, you will not likely be paid for professional services sales like training. However, again each successful implementation will drive increased cross-sell and upsell opportunities. These opportunities you do get paid on and will benefit you long term.

Support Organization

The support organization is another team to understand the inner workings within the first six months of your onboarding. You will find that most organizations have migrated from on-prem installations to the cloud. The migration to the cloud has completely changed the game regarding selling solutions. You have to keep the customer happy to get a renewal. You will get paid on renewals, and as such, you will need to work with the one team that will help you keep your customer active. The support teams are grossly underappreciated for the work they have to do. Understand that they have to sift through situations you may have established an expectation in the customer's mind.

There are all types of situations that could break a customer's implementation. The professional services team may have written custom code to implement the solution. Instead, the product management team rolled out a new update that broke the customer's version. The customer could have hired a team who never took the time to learn the product. The worst is having a delivery partner who sold, implemented, and wrote custom code into a small line of business at one of your biggest customers. All of these scenarios must be cleared through the support organization and will likely escalate to senior leadership. Things that escalate typically fall back down to you in the SEAC organization. This is one of the best reasons to connect with this team and get to resolutions quickly.

Take the time and get to know these teams; they will bail you out someday. They used to be centralized, but now most are decentralized across the globe, working from remote offices. I remember when at Jetform, I would purchase pizzas for the team in Ottawa when I visited. I made a deal with the pizza guy down from the office, and he would deliver pizzas when I was in the states. Every time I went to the Ottawa office, I would find the person who helped me in the field and take them to lunch. In addition, I would buy bagels and coffee for the floor when visiting. The bottom line, take care of these teams and understand your future sales revenue depends on it.

Consumption Model

In a consumption-based model, going live is critical because you make no money until they start consuming the technology. For example, you were selling electricity, and they had nothing inside their storefront or home to burn electricity. Guess what? You're not consuming anything. You're not making money. You will find the Go-Live date will be critical for your success. The best way to do that is to sell training work with professional services and work with the partner. Read through a great book - Consumption Economics, to understand how this will impact your operations with presales. I have a full webcast on this topic and recognize that the presales world is changing due to this industry shift.

Workshop:

Title: Cross-Functional Collaboration Workshop

Objective: Enhance collaboration between SEACs and internal teams such as Training, Professional Services, and Support.

Materials Needed:

- Post-it notes
- Voting dots
- Whiteboard or large paper sheets
- Markers

Duration: 2 hours

Step-by-Step Instructions:

1. Introduction (10 minutes)
    - Briefly introduce the purpose of the workshop and the importance of cross-functional collaboration.
2. Ice Breaker (10 minutes)
    - Participants introduce themselves and share one positive experience they had with another team.
3. Identify Challenges (30 minutes)
    - Split participants into groups.
    - Each group lists challenges faced in collaborating with other teams.
    - Write each challenge on a Post-it note.
4. Prioritize Challenges (20 minutes)
    - Groups place their Post-it notes on the whiteboard.
    - Use voting dots to prioritize the challenges.
5. Develop Solutions (30 minutes)

-
  -
    - Groups brainstorm potential solutions for the top challenges.
    - Document the solutions on large paper sheets.
6. Share and Discuss Solutions (20 minutes)
    - Each group presents their solutions.
    - Open discussion on the feasibility and impact of each solution.
7. Action Plan (20 minutes)
    - Create a list of actionable items based on the solutions.
    - Assign responsibility and set deadlines.
8. Wrap-Up (10 minutes)
    - Summarize key takeaways.
    - Thank participants for their time and collaboration.

Books to Recommend and Reason:

1. "Consumption Economics: The New Rules of Tech" by J.B. Wood, Todd Hewlin, and Thomas Lah
    - Provides a comprehensive understanding of the shift towards consumption-based models and its implications on sales strategies.
2. "The Challenger Sale: Taking Control of the Customer Conversation" by Matthew Dixon and Brent Adamson
    - Offers insights into effective sales techniques, particularly useful for SEAC s looking to adopt a challenger mindset.
3. "Crossing the Chasm: Marketing and Selling Disruptive Products to Mainstream Customers" by Geoffrey A. Moore
    - Essential reading for understanding the adoption lifecycle of new technologies and how to effectively market and sell them.

Quiz:

1. What is a primary benefit of auditing a training class?
    - A) Learning the product
    - B) Free travel opportunities
    - C) Networking with competitors
    - D) None of the above
2. How can embedding with the professional services team benefit an SEAC ?
    - A) Reduces workload
    - B) Builds credibility with customers
    - C) Guarantees higher sales commissions
    - D) None of the above
3. Why is it important to build a relationship with the support organization?
    - A) They can provide direct sales leads
    - B) They help maintain customer satisfaction and renewals
    - C) They handle marketing promotions
    - D) None of the above
4. In a consumption model, what is crucial for earning revenue?
    - A) Initial product sale
    - B) Customer go-live and usage
    - C) Providing free training
    - D) None of the above
5. What should be included in a cross-functional collaboration workshop?
    - A) Identifying challenges
    - B) Developing solutions
    - C) Creating an action plan
    - D) All of the above

Answers:

1. A) Learning the product
2. B) Builds credibility with customers
3. B) They help maintain customer satisfaction and renewals
4. B) Customer go-live and usage
5. D) All of the above

These resources will enhance your understanding and skills in sales engineering, ensuring you are well-equipped to navigate and excel in your role.

Chapter 24: OFF YOU GO !

Hold on to the Safety Bar

To recap, within your first 30 and 60 days, you've completed your HR requirements. You have your communication systems up. You have the who's who listed on the wall and printed out the org chart. You know where people are and what they do. You worked with your sherpa to build out your demonstration and master the standard demonstration. You are fine-tuning your elevator pitch. You continue to work through the why buy anything, why buy now, and why buy the brand.

With some training wheels, you are now ready to be let loose into the wild. I recommend you embrace failing; you will often fail these next few months and maybe even years. I fail often; the key is to fail quickly, learn from that experience, and don't fail again.

Welcome to your new career as a presales solution engineer, sales engineer, sales consultant, solution consultant, solution architect, or specialist!

The next book will discuss the Day In the Life of an SEAC . We will cover the following:

- Day in the life
- Working with Partners | Service | Marketing | Support
- Organizing your calendar
- Training your dragon (aka Sales Rep)
- Rocking the Stage
- Art and Science - Discovery
- SEAC Negotiation / Objection Handling

- Lead SE Training
- In-Person Meeting Best Practices
- Zoom Best Practices
- Story Telling
- Presentation Best Practices
- Developing Relationships
- Career Options
- How to Get Ahead
- What to Plan For
- Your Next Five Years
- Taste of Management

Summary and What is Next

As you close this book, it's important to reflect on the key takeaways and the journey ahead.

Key Takeaways:

1. **Understanding Compensation:** Grasp the importance of negotiating your salary and benefits effectively, knowing the midpoints, and strategically positioning yourself for growth within the compensation matrix.
2. **Building Relationships:** Cultivate strong relationships with cross-functional teams such as Training, Professional Services, and Support to enhance collaboration and customer satisfaction.
3. **Continuous Learning:** Embrace the various learning opportunities provided by your organization, including training sessions, shadow programs, and professional services rotations.
4. **Effective Communication:** Develop and refine your communication skills, both internally and externally, to effectively convey your value and foster teamwork.
5. **Adapting to Change:** Stay flexible and open to feedback as you navigate the evolving landscape of the sales engineering field. Embrace failure as a learning opportunity and continuously improve your skills.
6. **Leveraging Resources:** Utilize the resources and tools provided by your organization, from learning management systems to support teams, to maximize your effectiveness and efficiency.

7. **Personal Development:** Invest in your personal growth by setting goals, seeking mentorship, and staying informed about industry trends and best practices.
8. **Customer-Centric Approach:** Always prioritize the customer's needs and success. Your role as a sales engineer is to provide value, build trust, and drive customer satisfaction.
9. **Strategic Planning:** Plan your career trajectory with a focus on long-term growth, skill development, and positioning yourself for leadership opportunities.
10. **Networking and Mentorship:** Engage with peers, mentors, and industry leaders to expand your network, gain insights, and support your professional development.

What's Next:

Head over to my website and make a request for a free e-published book, "SE Worklife – My Journey." This is a quick read that will guide you through my entire career from when I started at my father's business to my current state. I will give you access to all the things I learned, both done wells and do betters through my journey.

Thank you, Dad, for helping me understand that hard work will pay off and never forget who you work for! Hey sister, thanks for being there every day in my life.

Glossary of Terms and Acronyms

A

- **AACV (Annual Contract Value)**: The total value of renewable SaaS divided by the contract's length (in years).
- **ACID (Atomicity, Consistency, Isolation, Durability)**: A set of properties that ensure database transactions are processed reliably.
- **AE (Account Executive)**: The primary sales representative responsible for managing customer accounts.
- **API (Application Programming Interface)**: A set of protocols for building and interacting with software applications.

B

- **Base Salary**: The fixed amount of money paid to an employee, not including bonuses, benefits, or other compensation.
- **BI (Business Intelligence)**: Technologies and strategies used by enterprises for data analysis of business information.
- **Bio for the Boss**: A brief biography provided by an employee for their manager, highlighting personal and professional details.
- BMANTR (Budget, Authority, Need, Timeline, Method, Risk): An extended sales qualification framework.
- **Bookings**: Total value of all eligible products sold on a contract.
- **BANT (Budget, Authority, Need, Timing)**: A sales qualification framework to determine the readiness of a potential customer.

C

- **Challenger Seller**: A sales technique where the seller challenges the customer's way of thinking and presents unique insights to add value.
- **Commission**: Earnings based on a percentage of sales made by an employee.
- **Compensation Matrix**: A structured outline of salary ranges and other compensations based on employee levels and roles.
- **Consumption Model**: A pricing strategy where revenue is based on the actual usage of the service or product by the customer.
- **CRM (Customer Relationship Management)**: A technology for managing a company's relationships and interactions with potential customers.

D

- **DBs (Dry Runs)**: Practice sessions where the sales team rehearses their presentation or pitch before the actual meeting.
- **Decision Maker (DM)**: The person in an organization with the authority to make purchasing decisions.
- **Discovery**: The process of gathering information to understand a customer's needs and challenges.
- **DW (Deal Workouts)**: Sessions where sales teams plan and strategize for upcoming deals.

E

- **Enablement Schedule**: A calendar of training and development activities designed to onboard and educate new employees.
- **ESPP (Employee Stock Purchase Plan)**: A company-run program in which employees can purchase company stock at a discounted price.
- **Executes Account Research**: The process of gathering detailed information about a potential customer's business to tailor the sales approach.

F

- **FTE (Full-Time Employee)**: An employee who works full-time hours as defined by their employer.

G

- **Give-Gets**: Negotiation technique where one side offers something in return for a concession from the other side.

H

- **HR (Human Resources)**: The department responsible for managing employee-related functions.
- **HRM (Human Resource Management)**: Systems and processes used to manage employees, including their personal information, performance, and benefits.

I

- **IC (Individual Contributor)**: An employee who contributes to the company's goals without managing other employees. Levels indicate seniority (e.g., IC3, IC4, IC5).

- **IPO (Initial Public Offering)**: The first time a company offers its stock for public sale.

K

- **Kickoff Meeting**: An initial meeting that marks the start of a project or initiative, often used to align the team and set goals.
- **KPI (Key Performance Indicator)**: A measurable value that demonstrates how effectively a company is achieving key business objectives.

L

- **Learning Management System (LMS)**: Software used to deliver, track, and manage training and education programs.

M

- MEDDPICC (Metrics, Economic Buyer, Decision Criteria, Decision Process, Paper Process, Identify Pain, Champion, Competition): A sales qualification methodology.
- **Midpoint**: The middle value in a compensation range, used as a reference point for salary negotiations.
- **Mindtickle**: A learning management system used for sales training and enablement.

N

- **Non-Recoverable Draw**: Advance payments made to an employee that are not required to be paid back if future commissions do not meet the advance amount.

O

- **Objection Handling**: Techniques used to address and overcome customer objections during the sales process.
- **OPEX (Operating Expenses)**: Expenses a company incurs through its normal business operations.
- **OTE (On-Target Earnings)**: The expected total earnings of an employee, including base salary and commission, if they meet their sales targets.

P

- **PCR (Personal Commission Rate)**: The rate at which an employee earns commission, personalized based on their individual agreement.
- **Pre-Mortem**: A strategy session before a meeting to anticipate and plan for potential challenges.
- **Post-Mortem**: A review session after a meeting to assess what went well and what could be improved.

Q

- **Quota**: The sales target assigned to a sales team or individual within a specific period.
- **QBR (Quarterly Business Review)**: A meeting to review business performance over the past quarter.

R

- **RSU (Restricted Stock Unit)**: A form of compensation issued by an employer to an employee in the form of company shares, subject to vesting criteria.
- **Ramp Period**: The initial period when a new hire is getting up to speed and not yet fully productive.

- **RFP (Request for Proposal)**: A document that solicits proposals, often through a bidding process.

S

- **Sales Engineer (SE)**: A professional who supports the sales team with technical knowledge and expertise.
- **SE Summit**: A large meeting or conference for sales engineers to learn, network, and align on strategies.
- **Shadow Program**: A program where less experienced employees observe and learn from experienced colleagues in real-world scenarios.
- **Sherpa**: A guide or mentor assigned to help new hires navigate their new role and responsibilities.
- **SPIF (Sales Performance Incentive Fund)**: A bonus or incentive given to salespeople to motivate them to achieve specific targets.
- **Solution Selling**: A sales methodology that focuses on addressing the specific needs and challenges of the customer.
- **Storytelling**: Using stories or narratives to communicate key messages in sales presentations.

T

- **Technical Validation**: The process of verifying that a technical solution meets the requirements and expectations of the customer.
- **TWP (The Walkabout Program)**: A shadow program designed to help sales engineers improve their skills by observing experienced colleagues.

W

- **W4**: A tax form used in the United States to indicate employee's tax situation to the employer.

Z

- **Zoom**: A video conferencing tool often used for virtual meetings and presentations.

Additional Terms

- **Consumption Economics**: A recommended book for understanding shifts in the presales world due to the consumption-based business model.
- **Joint Execution Plans**: Plans that outline joint activities between teams to achieve a common goal.
- **MUD (Meaningful, Unique, Defensible)**: A principle for evaluating solutions in a competitive market.

Notes

- BMANTR and MEDDPICC are extended qualification frameworks useful for deep diving into the customer's needs and readiness for purchasing.
- **Consumption Economics** is a highly recommended book for understanding shifts in the presales world due to the consumption-based business model.

This glossary includes the key terms and acronyms from the document and should cover most, if not all, of the important terminology used throughout the book.

SE Worklife - My Journey

Lessons Learned

Disclaimers

The content contained within this book may not be reproduced, duplicated or transmitted without direct written permission from the author or the publisher. Under no circumstances will any blame or legal responsibility be held against the publisher, or author, for any damages, reparation, or monetary loss due to the information contained within this book. Either directly or indirectly. You are responsible for your own choices, actions, and results.

Legal Notice:

This book is copyright protected. This book is only for personal use. You cannot amend, distribute, sell, use, quote or paraphrase any part, or the content within this book, without the consent of the author or publisher.

Disclaimer Notice:

Please note the information contained within this document is for educational and entertainment purposes only. All efforts have been executed to present accurate, up-to-date, and reliable, complete information. No warranties of any kind are declared or implied. Readers acknowledge that the author is not engaging in the rendering of legal, financial, medical or professional advice. The content within this book has been derived from various sources. Please consult a licensed professional before attempting any techniques outlined in this book. By reading this document, the reader agrees that under no circumstances is the author responsible for any direct or indirect losses incurred as a result of the use of the information contained within this document, including, but not limited to, errors, omissions, or inaccuracies.

KDP, Kindle, Kindle Unlimited, and Kindle Select are all registered trademarks of the Amazon Corporation.

FTC Notice: Some links in this book contain affiliate links whereby I will receive a small commission.

Trade Mark # 324R731 - SE Worklife

Copyright Kevin R Kunz 2022 All rights reserved.

ISBN : 9798362636432

Acknowledgements

I must start by expressing my deepest gratitude to Anne Kunz for enduring my workaholic drive and its impact on our family. She has stood by my side unwaveringly, especially when I needed her the most. I am profoundly grateful to her for convincing me to retire early, take my 30 years of experience, and do something meaningful with it. Not to mention, having three amazing children early in our journey provided me with invaluable real-world experience in applying family management skills to everyday work scenarios. Truly exceptional leaders often have a supportive family behind them, serving as the proving grounds for their leadership.

I owe a heartfelt thanks to Lauren, Brian, and Heather, my three wonderful children, for making my life and career journey as thrilling as it has been. I am immensely proud of each of them for following in their parents' footsteps: Lauren leading a team of pre-sales engineers at Veeva Software, Brian coding innovative solutions for a consulting organization, and Heather embarking on her career as a human resources lead for a software startup. Great job to all of you!

A huge thank you goes to those individuals who took a chance on me and made a significant difference in my career as leaders: Seth Lewis at CSR, Dan Shea, Warren Lederer, Steve Corwin, Steve Zimmerman, Tracey Lyons at Moore Business Forms; Rick Allen, Tony Bishop, John Hogerland at JetForm; David Antila, Don Beck, Stacey Box, Johne Brennan, Gloria Chen, Bill Hippenmeyer, Keith Johnson, Nicole Kealey, Thomas Loane, Tracey McDonald, Josee Murray, Karen Richter, Hugh Shannon, Steve Trombetta, Kumar Vora, and Donna Zontos at Adobe; Don Beck at Involver; Tanya Bragin, Anne Krechmer, Steve Mayzak, Ryan McGinty at Elastic; and Brian Daniels, Michael Keaveney, and John Sapone at Snowflake. To keep the book concise, I have only mentioned those in leadership circles. Many more people have influenced my career direction and are left off this list. The key takeaway is that your village will grow over time, and you will quickly discern who is there to help you and who is there to help themselves.

To my review team, who inspired me to start this book series and have painstakingly put the work into reviewing, adding, and editing this content: You, the readers, benefit from each of these leaders' vast experiences. When you combine this team's talent, you are looking at over 274 years of combined experience. Don't worry; I have a few 25-year-olds in the mix to keep it relevant. Thanks to Jason Barnett, Anne Kunz, Andrea Middleton, Greg Robinson, Tracey Sacht, Bill Van Hout, John Palazzolo, Neal Wadhwani, and others. You are all remarkable leaders in your roles, and I am deeply humbled by your support in this effort.

As you will see from my career journey section, my father and sister had a tremendous impact not just on my life but also on how I accelerated my career. The understanding that the people who work for an organization are far more valuable than the executives is a fundamental principle my father lived by. Take the time to understand what each person works for and how you can help them get there as a leader. Also, understand that hard times will cycle, and you may need to make tough choices to ensure the business's survival. But don't stop there; use your network to find those people jobs. In my father's business, he would find jobs for people if he had to reduce work, and I followed this same approach during my Adobe career. Thanks, Dad and Sister, for being there when it counted the most.

SE Worklife

A Journey Through Tech Leadership

Overview:

Embark on an exhilarating journey through the dynamic world of technology and sales engineering with "SE Worklife: A Journey Through Tech Leadership." This compelling narrative chronicles Kevin R. Kunz's 30-year career, filled with transformative experiences, invaluable lessons, and powerful insights that will captivate aspiring professionals, seasoned executives, and tech enthusiasts alike.

Why You Should Read This Book: (Reviewers Insight)

Unveil the Secrets of Tech Giants

Ever wondered what it's like to navigate the corridors of power at tech titans like Adobe, Oracle, Elastic, and Snowflake? Dive into firsthand accounts of high-stakes mergers, revolutionary IPOs, and the relentless pursuit of innovation. Discover how industry leaders steer their ships through turbulent waters and learn the strategies that keep them at the forefront of technology.

Master the Art of Leadership

From building cohesive teams to fostering a culture of excellence, this book offers a masterclass in leadership. Kevin shares his personal journey of growth, revealing the challenges and triumphs that shaped his leadership style. Gain insights into effective team management, employee motivation, and the importance of empathy and adaptability in today's fast-paced business world.

Navigate Career Transitions with Confidence

Whether you're eyeing your first big break or contemplating a mid-career shift, "SE Worklife" is your roadmap to success. Learn how to leverage your skills, make strategic moves, and seize opportunities that align with your professional goals. Kevin's experiences provide a blueprint for navigating career transitions, from startup excitement to post-IPO challenges.

Build Strong, Lasting Relationships

In an era of remote work and virtual connections, building meaningful relationships is more crucial than ever. This book delves into the nuances of creating and nurturing professional relationships at various levels—from first impressions to deep, enduring connections. Discover practical tips and engaging anecdotes that will help you cultivate a robust professional network.

Achieve Work-Life Balance

Balancing a demanding career with personal commitments is no small feat. Kevin's journey underscores the significance of family, personal well-being, and the pursuit of happiness beyond professional achievements. Learn how to prioritize what truly matters and create a fulfilling work-life balance that sustains long-term success.

Embrace Change and Innovation

The tech landscape is ever-evolving, and staying ahead requires a willingness to embrace change and drive innovation. "SE Worklife" equips you with the mindset and tools to adapt to new technologies, market shifts, and industry trends. Be inspired by stories of resilience, creativity, and the relentless pursuit of excellence.

Interactive Workshops and Practical Insights

The book isn't just a narrative; it's a hands-on guide with practical workshops and actionable steps. Engage in thought-provoking exercises designed to enhance your skills, foster team collaboration, and drive business success. These workshops are crafted to spark discussion, encourage brainstorming, and provide tangible takeaways you can implement in your career.

Introductions

If you are reading this e-book, then you must have purchased one of the SE Worklife series. I began with "How to Become an SE," and if you started there on this journey, then this biography will provide invaluable insights to guide your steps toward success.

Entering this career is possible at various technical skill levels, even with almost no technical skills, provided you have the charisma, drive, and interpersonal capability to tell compelling stories. The ultimate goal is to become a trusted advisor for your customer and identify the critical business and technical issues you can solve.

Chapter 1: Model Homes

"As we reflect on the early years of my journey, the lessons learned in a family business laid the groundwork for understanding the value of hard work, automation, and the importance of a strong team."

"It is not the strongest of the species that survive, nor the most intelligent, but the one most responsive to change." - Charles Darwin

My upbringing set the tone for my future, as it does for so many people. I was born and raised in New Jersey, Exit 22 off Rt 80 and later Exit 11 of Rt 78 - as they say, everyone lives off an exit in NJ. I grew up in an entrepreneurial family, with my father owning several businesses. His most successful venture was Model Homes. We experienced good quarters and some tough quarters in the household. However, we all knew where the money came from; the hard work put in six days a week.

Model Homes was a dollhouse manufacturing warehouse in Boonton, NJ. The store sold thousands of dollhouse kits across America through retailers like FAO Schwartz and JCPenney. It was here that I cut my teeth at the age of 13. Since it was a family business with about 20 full-time employees, you pitched in where you could. I used to work in the wood shop sweeping daily, moving sawdust piles to various containers. Eventually, I graduated to operating the forklift, moving pallets of dollhouse kits and lumber off the side rail. I learned about automation and process design while helping dad set up the assembly lines for packing the kits. I saw firsthand how hard my dad and all the employees worked to be successful.

Eventually, he opened a factory outlet store to the public. The store was unique; he had models built as showcases to the customers, and he was a direct importer of dollhouse miniatures from Taiwan. His creativity and wacky personality shined in creating these miniature room shadow boxes to showcase the furniture. Each shadow box told a story and provided the emotion and inputs necessary for the customers to make a connection. People would come from all over to see the store. He modeled the ideas off of the NY Christmas store window displays. People would gather daily in NY to see the latest window and creativity on display. He was a true marketer and brilliant businessman. I enjoyed how he would run through each room's story with me and ask me to point out the wacky things like the little mouse on the floor or the hidden beer can behind the young boy's bed.

As we are familiar with Black Friday in retail, so was the factory outlet's Black Friday sale. I remember when we had our first big sale, full-page ads in the Bergen Record, Herald News, and Star-Ledger. These ads were my first experience with marketing. He used coupons with unique codes to track which paper did the best for drawing people to the store. It's funny to think about Eloqua and Response software today doing this tracking. The first sale was called the carnival sale. He had the Shriners with their clowns and big tents outside to draw even more people. He was a true showman, and it paid off.

I remember driving early that Friday at four am with dad in his old 1973 Super Beetle (The car I learned to drive on by the way) to arrive at a massive line wrapping around the building. The police were notified and had to close down the main street to the factory. It was crazy. The store opened up, and off we went. I was in charge of running to pick merchandise off the shelves. Remember, there was no automation back then; you had to fill out a form, and we processed the ticket. We ran for hours, but then at 1 pm, dad shut it all down - forcing people to wait an hour. You may be asking why shut down in the middle of a sale. Dad would shut down for the employees each day for lunch and purchase these massive hoagies, full beer, soda, and full service. The employees took a complete break together, sharing the stories of the chaos. My dad recognized that the people working there mattered more than just the sales. At the end of the weekend, he would have a huge gathering for all the employees and their families. I carried this tradition into my management style, as we will discuss later.

Here is a story that illustrates how deeply my father cared for his employees: I was chatting with my sister while preparing for this book, and she reminded me of another thing my dad did that was impactful back then for several reasons. My dad used to give every employee a huge turkey or ham for Christmas each year - essentially a full dinner for people to cook at home. Remember, the late 70s and early 80s were a tough period financially for all. This offering was talked about each year and was very special for my father to be able to do this for his team. Unfortunately, the business had a bad year, and he had to change the end-of-year Christmas gift and instead had to pull the offer. This sent shockwaves through the organization; all types of things were being discussed. "How could he do this? Why is this happening? We were counting on this Christmas gift." He was able to turn it around with the employees later at Easter, but the damage was done. He really had some hard emotions internally, fighting with the fact that, "Don't these employees know how hard it is to keep a business working? Why are they not supporting me?" Lots of emotions and attitudes drove the behaviors on all sides. It was a huge lesson learned and one where I would see happen over and over again.

This lesson became especially relevant later in my career. At Involver, a startup, they had free breakfast each day for their employees. Then the owner saw the employees started to pack stuff up and take home with them. He cut the program down by two days, and the place, just like Dad's employees, was upset. This also happened at Adobe when the leadership decided to reduce the number of Sales Engineers who could qualify for Club. Though in this case, they made that decision at a Vegas sales conference. Employees' names who overachieved did not show up on the slide and ended up not going to Club. I had over 20 people upset with the company and felt cheated. It was so difficult to try to calm the situation. It got to the point where when the next Club was announced for the new year, no one believed it, and the carrot quickly became a stick. The intent of these programs is to keep people motivated to win deals, sacrifice weekends and evenings on the hope of taking their significant other to Club. I am sure if Tom Loane and John Hogerland are reading this, they all remember those conversations!

Sorry for the squirrel moment—a reference from the movie Up. Let's continue with Model Homes: After returning from break, doors opened again, and off we went. This time I had a chance to help out on the floor. Moving to the sales floor was a big step for me. I started helping people figure out what house they could afford and that met their requirements. I would walk up to folks hovering around the house models with my Model Homes work apron on, with a big, bold sticker saying "KEVIN." I watched the other sellers and how they approached people. It became natural for me, and I immediately fell in love with selling things.

Interestingly, I never considered a career in selling; I came to it as helping people with decisions that met their needs. I gave tips and tricks on how to build the kits. I never sold the most expensive houses, but I used to sell the hell out of the furniture. Since the likelihood of a buyer putting together this kit by Christmas was crazy, you had to have something under the tree; I crushed it and was number three out of five salespeople on the floor. My reward was counting the piles of cash late that evening at our kitchen table. That night I counted about 75K in bills. My sister was responsible for the credit card receipts.

As the years progressed, so did my selling abilities and my dad's investments in automation. Enter the Radio Shack TRS80 Model 4 with 64K core memory. At the time, I was tinkering with a Commodore 64 with a disk drive, doing basic programming to make games. His investment in the TRS80 allowed me to feed my technology habit. His programmer Ray Egatz, our neighbor, helped build an inventory system, accounting ledger system, payroll, and time cards, all the things necessary to run the business. The green bar paper and the label sheets would print all day from the special room called "computer room" on the door. Thanks to Ray, I learned much about the computer and the "why" it was beneficial. At the time, mailing advertisement cards were big; remember, this was before email and the internet. Yes, I am that old! One of the most significant advantages of the computer was that Zip + 4 presorted saved about 3 cents per mailing. The postal savings add up when you are processing thousands of cards.

Working with the computer and learning data entry started my first entry into business for me. My dad set me up in the "Computer Room" to do data entry for other companies/brands who wanted to do zip plus four sorting. Seeing how you could reuse all these names from the white pages was great. Oh, the white pages were these six-inch thick telephone books, where you could look up people's names and numbers. People used to use them as highchairs for their kids. Yep, you guessed it, my dad, sister, and I used to sit in front of this computer and type in one page at a time. All of these names into this thing called a database that Ray built. I must think about it today and how my iPhone has so much more capability than that machine did in 1983.

I learned so much from my father and did not realize it until much later in my career journey. One of the biggest takeaways is his relationship with his people. Dad was a boss that cared about individuals and their families. During significant sales events, as mentioned, he would deliver a full buffet for the employees and their families to the factory. These people would walk through fire for my father, and I believe how he treated them made a difference. This is a mandatory requirement for my leadership style, and you will read about this during my Adobe tenure with a fantastic human, Scott Hamlow.

Lessons Learned: Model Homes

- Meticulous Planning: Thorough planning is essential for navigating complex projects.
- Adaptability: Be ready to adapt to changing circumstances and requirements.
- Automation: Understand the value of automating processes to improve efficiency.
- Relationship Building: Build and maintain strong relationships with employees and customers.
- Marketing Creativity: Use creativity and storytelling in marketing to engage customers.
- Employee Appreciation: Recognize and reward employee efforts to foster loyalty.
- Impact of Reward Programs: Understand the significant impact reward programs have on employee morale, and the potential negative effects if those rewards are removed.

Applying Lessons to Modern Business Culture

"Good to Great" by Jim Collins

- **Meticulous Planning**: Thoroughly plan your projects and ensure all aspects are considered to navigate complex challenges effectively.
- **Relationship Building**: Invest in building and maintaining strong relationships with employees and customers to enhance loyalty and satisfaction.
- **Employee Appreciation**: Regularly recognize and reward your employees' efforts to foster a positive work environment and enhance employee retention.

Why Read "Good to Great": This book explores why some companies make the leap to greatness while others do not. It offers valuable insights into leadership and organizational behavior, emphasizing the importance of disciplined people, thought, and action.

"Measure What Matters" by John Doerr

- **Adaptability**: Cultivate a mindset of flexibility and adaptability to thrive in dynamic business environments.
- **Automation**: Implement automation tools and technologies to streamline operations and increase productivity.
- **Marketing Creativity**: Utilize creative marketing strategies and storytelling to create emotional connections with customers and differentiate your brand.
- **Impact of Reward Programs**: Carefully design reward programs to maintain employee motivation, and consider the implications before making any changes to these programs.

Why Read "Measure What Matters": This book introduces the concept of Objectives and Key Results (OKRs), a goal-setting framework that has helped major companies achieve significant growth. Understanding OKRs can help you implement effective performance tracking and goal achievement strategies in your business.

Workshop Topic: Building Strong Teams

- **Objective**: To understand and implement the key qualities that make a strong team.
- **Materials Needed**: Post-it notes, voting dots, whiteboard or large paper sheets, markers.
- **Duration**: 2 hours

Step-by-Step Instructions:

1. Introduction (10 minutes):
    - Start by explaining the objective of the workshop: building strong teams.
    - Highlight the importance of teamwork in achieving business success.
2. Brainstorming Session (20 minutes):
    - Provide each participant with Post-it notes and a marker.
    - Ask participants to think about the qualities that make a strong team and write each quality on a separate Post-it note.
    - Encourage them to think broadly and include qualities such as communication, trust, collaboration, diversity, and leadership.
3. Posting and Grouping (15 minutes):
    - Have participants post their notes on a whiteboard or large paper sheets.
    - As a group, start grouping similar qualities together to identify common themes.
4. Prioritizing (10 minutes):
    - Give each participant a set of voting dots.

- Ask participants to vote on the qualities they believe are the most important for building a strong team by placing dots on the grouped qualities.
5. Discussion (30 minutes):
    - Facilitate a discussion based on the results of the voting.
    - Ask participants why they think the top-voted qualities are important and how they can be cultivated within their teams.
    - Share personal anecdotes or examples from the Model Homes experience to illustrate the impact of these qualities.
6. Action Planning (25 minutes):
    - Divide participants into small groups.
    - Ask each group to choose one or two top-voted qualities and develop a plan to implement or enhance these qualities within their teams.
    - Encourage groups to think about specific actions, timelines, and metrics for success.
7. Readout and Commitments (10 minutes):
    - Have each group present their action plans to the entire workshop.
    - Encourage participants to commit to at least one action they will take to build stronger teams in their workplace.
8. Wrap-Up and Resources (10 minutes):
    - Summarize the key takeaways from the workshop.
    - Provide additional resources or readings that participants can explore to further their understanding of building strong teams.
    - Examples:

- "The Five Dysfunctions of a Team" by Patrick Lencioni
- "Team of Teams" by General Stanley McChrystal

Chapter 2: Crazy Bobs

Crazy Bob's Cookie Store: Learning the Basics

"Moving from a family business to launching my own entrepreneurial venture provided invaluable insights into the complexities of running a business and dealing with unforeseen challenges."

"Do or do not. There is no try." - Yoda, Star Wars

Starting Crazy Bob's Cookie Store

As I prepared to head off to college, my dad had some candid advice for me. He believed college was largely a societal requirement—a piece of paper that said you were qualified. If I really wanted to learn about business, he said, I should start one. So, we did just that.

My dad always dreamed of opening a business on Long Beach Island, NJ. As kids, we vacationed on the island, and the Kunz family owned a few houses there. We found the perfect spot in Beach Haven, right next to Fantasy Island amusement park. Welcome to Crazy Bob's Cookie Store, home of the cookie with a bite taken out of it. We sold the bites separately in a bag of Bob's Bites, much like Dunkin' Donuts' Munchkins. We also had a blue soda called "Blew Up" and an ice cream called "Gahbage," which was a blend-in ice cream before blending was popular.

The Best Learning Experience

Opening Crazy Bob's was one of the best experiences of my life. My dad was right—I learned more about running a business than any college class could have taught me. I had to figure out how to open a food business, build a storefront, acquire equipment, market our products, hire and train employees, manage supplies, and navigate local politics. My sister ran the books, payroll, and purchasing, which was a blessing since I was terrible at it. Be nice to your sister, folks, and remember that social security numbers are critical in payroll.

Dealing with Local Politics

One of my favorite lessons learned was dealing with local politics. We found the best location on the island, a clam shack next to the only amusement park on Long Beach Island, "Fantasy Island," owned by Big Ed. My dad called it Ed's Kingdom. We renovated the building in early winter to prepare for a May opening.

However, if you renovated a building by more than 50%, you had to put the building on pilings. Pilings are telephone pole-sized structures drilled into the sand to raise the building, allowing hurricane water to run underneath. We wanted to stay below the 50% threshold to avoid this, but we received a "stop work" order in May, just before the summer season started. The building commission claimed we had renovated more than 50%, though we hadn't. It turned out the mayor's son owned a piling company. Welcome to local politics. We ordered four pilings at $2,000 each, drilled them next to the building, and put picnic tables on top. Two weeks later, we received our occupancy certificate. If you're ever in Beach Haven during a hurricane, tie yourself to one of those picnic tables—they're not going anywhere.

Training and Operations

Training was a colossal battle. We hired college kids at the beginning of the season and high schoolers after the college kids left in late July. Training these employees, especially for tasks like cutting lemons into eight equal parts for lemonade, was challenging. I had to draw a storyboard showing each step. Step 1 – whole lemon – Step 2 – Cut lemon in half, Step 3 – Cut half in half etc. Oh, put in container and put container in fridge after putting a date on it. Sounds Simple right, not for these folks! This simple but effective method ensured everyone understood the task.

The business operated on a 10-week season, which allowed me to attend Rider College in Lawrenceville, NJ, where I majored in marketing and fine arts. I made money by tutoring statistics and working in the computer lab. Back then, computers were large, expensive pieces of equipment, and I worked on a VAX system while IBM personal computers were becoming popular.

Facing Environmental Challenges

We managed the business for four years until the late nineties when medical waste washed up on the Jersey shores, severely impacting tourism and our business. This taught me that some factors, like environmental issues, are beyond your control and can significantly affect your business.

I went full circle, opening a business with my family, dealing with operations, vendors, politics, and environmental issues. This experience offered me a final chapter in Crazy Bob's journey. Later in my career, I discovered the acronym PESTLE (Political,

Economic, Social, Technical, Legal, Environmental), which impacts all aspects of business.

I graduated from college with honors in 1992, ready to take on the world. Unfortunately, it was during a massive recession, making it difficult for graduates to find jobs. Marketing positions were essentially sales jobs. I didn't panic; I used the STOP (Stop, Think, Observe, and Plan) method to figure out my next steps. I enjoy acronyms; my team used to call them Kunzisms. Networking paid off, and I met Seth Lewis, a Rider alumni at Computer Systems Repair, who gave me my first big break as a sales manager.

Lessons Learned: Crazy Bob's Cookie Store

- **Location is Key**: A prime location is crucial for business success.
- **Local Politics**: Be prepared to navigate local politics and regulations.
- **Hiring and Firing**: Learn the processes of hiring, training, and if necessary, firing employees.
- **Training**: Develop clear and effective training programs for your employees.
- **Family Involvement**: Working with family can be beneficial—take care of your sister.
- **Supply Chain Management**: Understand the intricacies of managing your supply chain.
- **Marketing**: Effective marketing strategies are essential for attracting customers.
- **Business Hardships**: Owning a food business is challenging and requires resilience.
- **Employee Management**: High-achieving students may lack practical common sense.

- **Environmental Impact**: External environmental factors can significantly impact your business.

Applying Lessons to Modern Business Culture

"Never Split the Difference" by Chris Voss

- **Local Politics**: Stay informed about local regulations and political dynamics to avoid unexpected obstacles.
- **Hiring and Firing**: Implement thorough hiring processes and training programs to ensure a competent workforce.

Why Read "Never Split the Difference": This book, written by a former FBI hostage negotiator, teaches negotiation techniques that can be applied to business. Understanding negotiation is crucial when dealing with local politics and hiring processes.

"The Lean Startup" by Eric Ries

- **Location is Key**: Choose your business location wisely to maximize customer footfall.
- **Supply Chain Management**: Develop a robust supply chain management system to ensure smooth operations.
- **Marketing**: Invest in creative marketing strategies to stand out in the market.

Why Read "The Lean Startup": This book introduces a methodology for developing businesses and products. It focuses on efficient operations, marketing, and decision-making, which are essential for a startup.

"Good to Great" by Jim Collins

- **Training**: Use clear, step-by-step training materials to effectively onboard new employees.
- **Family Involvement**: Leverage family support and skills in your business endeavors.
- **Business Hardships**: Prepare for the challenges of running a business, especially in the food industry.

Why Read "Good to Great": This book explores why some companies make the leap to greatness while others do not. It offers valuable insights into leadership and organizational behavior, emphasizing the importance of disciplined people, thought, and action.

Workshop Topic: Navigating Local Politics and Regulations

- **Objective**: To understand and effectively navigate local politics and regulations to ensure business success.
- **Materials Needed**: Post-it notes, whiteboard or large paper sheets, markers, internet access for research (optional).
- **Duration**: 2 hours

Step-by-Step Instructions:

1. Introduction (10 minutes):
   - Start by explaining the objective of the workshop: navigating local politics and regulations.
   - Highlight the importance of understanding and managing local politics in achieving business success.
2. Brainstorming Session (20 minutes):
   - Provide each participant with Post-it notes and a marker.
   - Ask participants to think about potential political and regulatory challenges they might face in their business and write each challenge on a separate Post-it note.
   - Encourage them to think broadly, including zoning laws, building codes, permits, and local business practices.
3. Posting and Grouping (15 minutes):
   - Have participants post their notes on a whiteboard or large paper sheets.
   - As a group, start grouping similar challenges together to identify common themes.

4. Research and Discussion (30 minutes):
    - Divide participants into small groups.
    - Assign each group a common theme to research and discuss strategies for navigating these challenges.
    - Groups should consider the following:
        - Understanding local regulations and requirements.
        - Building relationships with local officials and stakeholders.
        - Preparing for unexpected regulatory changes.
    - Encourage groups to share personal experiences or hypothetical scenarios to illustrate their points.
5. Action Planning (25 minutes):
    - Have each group develop a plan to address their assigned theme, including specific actions, timelines, and metrics for success.
    - Plans should include steps such as:
        - Conducting regular regulatory audits.
        - Establishing a local advisory board.
        - Engaging with local business associations.
    - Groups should be prepared to present their plans to the entire workshop.
6. Readout and Commitments (10 minutes):
    - Have each group present their action plans to the entire workshop.
    - Encourage participants to commit to at least one action they will take to better navigate local politics and regulations in their business.
7. Wrap-Up and Resources (10 minutes):
    - Summarize the key takeaways from the workshop.
    - Provide additional resources or readings that participants can explore to further their

understanding of navigating local politics and regulations.
- Examples:
  - "The Art of War" by Sun Tzu (for strategic thinking)
  - Local government websites for regulatory updates
  - Business associations for networking opportunities

Chapter 3: CSR

Starting the Corporate Journey

"With the lessons learned from my formative years at Crazy Bob's Cookie Store, I ventured into the corporate world, where new challenges and opportunities awaited."

"The only way to do great work is to love what you do." - Steve Jobs

Starting at CSR

My first real corporate job was at CSR (Computer Systems Repair) in Secaucus, NJ. As a sales representative, I was tasked with managing two territories: Washington State and Oregon, as well as North Carolina and South Carolina. This role marked a significant transition from my hands-on experience at Crazy Bob's to the structured environment of a corporate job.

Customer Relationships and Product Knowledge

In this new role, I quickly understood the importance of building strong customer relationships. Unlike the familiar and personal environment at Crazy Bob's, CSR required a more professional and strategic approach to client interactions. I dedicated myself to learning everything I could about our products and services, ensuring I could answer any questions and provide solutions tailored to each client's needs.

The Value of Mentorship

At CSR, I was fortunate to be mentored by Seth Lewis, a seasoned professional with extensive experience in the industry. Seth taught me the importance of listening to clients, understanding their pain points, and providing value beyond the product itself. His guidance was instrumental in shaping my approach to sales and client relationships.

Navigating Corporate Politics

Corporate politics was a new challenge. Understanding the influence of various stakeholders and the importance of alliances was crucial. I learned that successful project execution often depended as much on managing internal relationships as it did on technical expertise.

The Power of Persistence

Sales cycles at CSR were often long and challenging. Securing a contract could take months of negotiation, multiple presentations, and continuous follow-ups. I learned to stay patient, maintain a positive attitude, and keep pushing forward despite setbacks. Persistence, I discovered, was key to closing deals and achieving targets.

Balancing Territories

Managing two geographically distant territories required meticulous planning and time management. I had to balance my efforts between Washington and Oregon on the one hand, and North Carolina and South Carolina on the other. I had to wake up early to get my NC account discussions completed and then work late into the evening for the West Coast. In addition, I had to deal with cultural differences – one world was "hey you big hoser " and the other was How Ya all doing today, god bless". These experiences taught me the importance of efficient scheduling, effective communication, and the ability to juggle multiple priorities simultaneously.

Adapting to Different Markets

Each territory had its unique market dynamics and customer preferences. I had to adapt my sales strategies to meet the specific needs of clients in each region. This adaptability was crucial for my success at CSR and helped me develop a more flexible and responsive approach to sales.

Technical Passion and Process Improvement

My passion for technology continued to grow while at CSR. I was always looking for ways to improve sales processes, customer inventory management, and automation tools. At CSR, I worked with an old guy in the basement who ran the Fortran code for our inventory systems. I started designing process workflows on FileMaker Pro. For instance, I had to fill out a form for every fuser toner cartridge, which would then be re-keyed by the front office manager. This paper process drove me nuts, knowing we had the technology to solve it. So, I built an automation process to enter information into FileMaker Pro and print out the filled-in form.

Initially, I faced resistance as people were used to the old ways. Seth Lewis encouraged me to involve the team members in designing the process. By getting their input, they felt ownership of the new system, leading to smoother adoption. The old guy in the basement even helped me connect the data files to merge the data nightly. It was fascinating to see how far we've come with systems like Salesforce, Big Machines, ServiceNow, and other automation tools today, considering we had almost nothing in the 90s.

Lessons Learned: CSR

- **Relationship Selling**: Building and maintaining strong relationships with clients is crucial for successful sales.
- **Identify and Solve Problems**: See opportunities to fix inefficiencies and take initiative to implement solutions.
- **Customer Focus**: Spend time in front of your customers to understand their needs better.
- **Collaborative Change**: Encourage team involvement in process changes to foster ownership and acceptance.
- **Mentorship**: Seek guidance from experienced mentors to navigate the corporate environment.
- **Persistence**: Stay persistent and maintain a positive attitude, even when facing long sales cycles and setbacks.
- **Adaptability**: Be ready to adapt your strategies to meet the unique needs of different markets.
- **Technology and Innovation**: Embrace technology to improve processes and efficiency.
- **Respecting Tradition**: Understand the balance between implementing new processes and respecting established methods.

Applying Lessons to Modern Business Culture

"Let's Get Real or Let's Not Play" by Mahan Khalsa

- **Relationship Selling**: Invest time in building and nurturing strong client relationships.
- **Customer Focus**: Prioritize face-to-face interactions with customers to gain deeper insights.

Why Read "Let's Get Real or Let's Not Play": This book offers a practical guide to client-centric selling, emphasizing the importance of honesty and integrity in building long-lasting customer relationships.

"The Lean Startup" by Eric Ries

- **Identify and Solve Problems**: Proactively look for inefficiencies and implement innovative solutions.
- **Technology and Innovation**: Continuously explore and adopt new technologies to enhance business operations.

Why Read "The Lean Startup": This book introduces a methodology for developing businesses and products. It focuses on efficient operations, marketing, and decision-making, which are essential for a startup.

"Good to Great" by Jim Collins

- **Collaborative Change**: Foster a culture of collaboration by involving team members in decision-making processes.
- **Mentorship**: Seek and provide mentorship to develop skills and navigate career challenges.
- **Respecting Tradition**: Balance innovation with respect for established processes and methods.

Why Read "Good to Great": This book explores why some companies make the leap to greatness while others do not. It offers valuable insights into leadership and organizational behavior, emphasizing the importance of disciplined people, thought, and action.

Workshop Topic: Building Strong Customer Relationships

- **Objective**: To understand and implement the key qualities that make strong customer relationships.
- **Materials Needed**: Post-it notes, voting dots, whiteboard or large paper sheets, markers.
- **Duration**: 2 hours

Step-by-Step Instructions:

1. Introduction (10 minutes):
    - Start by explaining the objective of the workshop: building strong customer relationships.
    - Highlight the importance of strong customer relationships in achieving business success.
2. Brainstorming Session (20 minutes):
    - Provide each participant with Post-it notes and a marker.
    - Ask participants to think about the qualities that make a strong customer relationship and write each quality on a separate Post-it note.
    - Encourage them to think broadly and include qualities such as trust, communication, understanding, and value.
3. Posting and Grouping (15 minutes):
    - Have participants post their notes on a whiteboard or large paper sheets.
    - As a group, start grouping similar qualities together to identify common themes.
4. Prioritizing (10 minutes):

- Give each participant a set of voting dots.
- Ask participants to vote on the qualities they believe are the most important for building strong customer relationships by placing dots on the grouped qualities.

5. Discussion (30 minutes):
   - Facilitate a discussion based on the results of the voting.
   - Ask participants why they think the top-voted qualities are important and how they can be cultivated in their customer interactions.
   - Share personal anecdotes or examples from the CSR experience to illustrate the impact of these qualities.

6. Action Planning (25 minutes):
   - Divide participants into small groups.
   - Ask each group to choose one or two top-voted qualities and develop a plan to implement or enhance these qualities in their customer interactions.
   - Encourage groups to think about specific actions, timelines, and metrics for success.

7. Readout and Commitments (10 minutes):
   - Have each group present their action plans to the entire workshop.
   - Encourage participants to commit to at least one action they will take to build stronger customer relationships in their workplace.

8. Wrap-Up and Resources (10 minutes):
   - Summarize the key takeaways from the workshop.
   - Provide additional resources or readings that participants can explore to further their understanding of building strong customer relationships.

- Examples:
  - "The Trusted Advisor" by David H. Maister, Charles H. Green, and Robert M. Galford
  - "Customer Centricity" by Peter Fader

Chapter 4: Moore

Moore Business Forms:

"After gaining valuable experience at CSR, I transitioned to Moore Business Forms, where I encountered new challenges and opportunities that further developed my professional skills."

"Imagination is more important than knowledge." - Albert Einstein

Moore Business Forms: Expanding Horizons

I enjoyed my tenure at CSR, though companies were not repairing computers as much as they were just dumping them to make way for new hardware, which was faster and, in some cases, cheaper to purchase than repair. I was lucky enough to move my career to Moore Business Forms. Moore was one of the largest paper form manufacturers in the world. Some of their competitors were NCR - National Cash Register, Wallace, and Uarco. Moore was in the big leagues; the company had about 60,000 employees worldwide.

Moore was another critical component in my business education journey. I started as an account manager at Moore, primarily in pharmaceutical, light manufacturing, and commercial sectors. I did struggle to work in this business, though again, I had great people around me. Dan Shea took me under his wing; he was a seasoned sales professional. I conducted a ride-along where you go on a call and say nothing; it was just a learning experience. Dan was a master of relationships; his gift was not overselling, being that trusted advisor for a customer. He always made the customer feel like he worked on their team for them. Dan was the number one sales rep in the region year over year and constantly went to Club. Dan and I worked very closely on all deals, and as Dan moved up the ladder, he helped me move with him.

The forms industry was very competitive. With the advent of laptop technology, many of the old printed flip books migrated to overhead projector RGB displays you would connect to a computer. Again, my computer hobby was in high demand since many of these sales executives had no formal PC training. In addition, my marketing and arts degree finally started to pay off. I worked with applications like Harvard Graphics, Corel Draw, and other presentation software to create excellent content. Customers were in awe of my presentations, and the printed copy truly represented Moore's brand. My brand was recognized and sought after by regional and then national executives.

The combination of sales, technology, storytelling, and artistic background redefined my career. But then, our regional office's strategic customer services team moved me from the field. Warren Lederer gave me my break and pulled me into the financial services team for special technical projects. Warren recognized that my technical talents could help his financial customers like Prudential, Bank of NY, New York Life, and John Hancock. These were all multi-million dollar brands assigned to his team. So I headed a project called POND, Production on Demand.

Production on Demand

Production on Demand was the first print-on-demand solution from employee desktops down to the manufacturing level across the US and Canada. Our test customer was Prudential Insurance. The project was to have an employee log into the Prudential inventory system and request a package of forms, booklets, etc. Instead of pulling them off a shelf, they would be produced off DocuTech 6135s—these colossal printer copier machines at the warehouse—and shipped locally. The most significant benefits were faster delivery, cheaper delivery, no expired inventory thrown out, and compliance. Many of these were legal forms where the terms and conditions would change frequently; using the wrong form would result in non-compliance and the risk of massive fines.

I worked closely with Prudential and an executive, Sal Bassio, who managed the project from PSI (Prudential Securities). Sal was so hard to please; I learned much from this experience—his demands always felt beyond the scope. He would push hard on ROI metrics for this project. We had to go through every hard dollar and soft dollar metric before Sal would sign off on anything. He was an enormous pain in the ass to deal with during this project. I am so grateful Sal was part of my career journey. Sal taught me the value of not just crossing T's and dotting I's but looking under every rock and then looking under that. Never satisfied with a yes, check and double-check everything you do. Sal hardened me to understand that perfection is not easy but rewarding with successful implementations.

From Print to Digital

Our project at Prudential was an early adopter in this new technological evolution. We migrated from POND - Production on Demand to POD Print on Demand to MPOD, Merge Print on Demand. Remember, I love acronyms, and so did Sal. This project morphed into the realization that maybe we did not even need to print these documents. Perhaps we could just create a free reader to open these templates, allowing the end user to fill in the data, merge the data, and ship them via email for consumption and action.

Welcome Jetform to the discussion – who was advanced to the market's first data form entry systems and workflow solutions. Cigna was one of the first insurance providers to embrace fillable forms. Cigna saved tremendous money both in production costs and claims processing time. Not to be overshadowed by Cigna, Prudential wanted to go further and apply a signature to these documents. At the time, Wacom and other signature pad companies entered the business. I worked on one of the first e-signature solutions. Prudential purchased over 10 million dollars in signature pads to outfit all field agents. We received several awards for this program at Moore and Jetform. You are welcome for all those signature pads you take for granted today. We started that trend and continued with things like thumbprint recognition, etc. I remember at Comdex in Vegas, asking questions to the vendors. So all I need to do is cut someone's Thumb off and use that? - replied: nope, the pad senses the Thumb's temperature. So since I am a guy from Jersey, all I have to do is put the Thumb in a microwave? Replied, nope got you there; we check to see if it has a pulse. Drop the mic moment for that vendor.

My success at Prudential and Cigna's projects allowed me to build long-lasting relationships with folks inside Moore Business Forms and, most importantly, inside Jetform with the product engineering and management teams. The next project I worked on was at Kodak for a technology that empowered SAP to generate documents outside their product. If you remember, we talked about Jetform Central, which allows you to merge data into templates and how those templates are generated out as PCL/PostScript. This was during the time frame of Y2K when we all made a tremendous amount of money because somebody back in 1985 only had 2 Bit character sets. Unfortunately, the 2 Bit Char did not have enough digits for the complete 00 to move to 2001.

The risk was that anyone not in compliance by 2000 might have dire circumstances. Simple calculations would impact things like elevators not working and automated pumps at nuclear power plants that rely on the correct date and time. So, there was a lot of concern back then, which made many consulting jobs available. For example, I had a project at Kodak using SAP as their warehouse management solution and financial invoicing package. Unfortunately, at Kodak, when they deployed generic sap, the actual invoices generated never looked like the old invoices. These invoices didn't have a logo, didn't have formatting, didn't have the font type; literally, it was just an invoice. The results were that customers weren't paying their invoices because they thought they were coming from somebody other than Kodak. Kodak lost millions of dollars a month because customers weren't paying their bills. So Jetform worked on a solution with the SAP scripts to generate the required PostScript header that we used to predefined templates designed in our Jetform designer end and generated invoices representing the brand—fixing the invoicing problem, saving them millions of dollars in receivables.

One thing I learned there was how to work with SAP script. At the time, SAP consultants were making $1,500 an hour, which was perfect money back in the day. The other thing that I learned was how much you would count on the Jetform support teams. I ended up building solid relationships with them. Many SAP systems implemented were on Unix, and I was not a Unix guy, so I became friendly with the Ottawa support team. I quickly understood that these people were critical to my success and underappreciated. So I made a point of ensuring that we built a long-lasting relationship. Anytime I went to Ottawa, I would go to the support floor and meet face-to-face with all the people working with me on Kodak, Panasonic, and a couple of other accounts. I made sure that I took him out to lunch. There were times when they helped me in the field, and I would order a pizza to be delivered from the local pizza parlor down the road, with whom I made a deal with who contracted with him to ensure that he would accept my credit card payments from the states. This relationship was so fruitful not just for me but also for my customers because I was able to solve problems quickly. Bonus—I ended up learning more by watching the mechanics work on the car so that I could fix it next time.

Having mastered the electronic forms business via Moore Business Forms, it was time to think about changing careers and expanding my wallet share. Unfortunately, being at a company for more than five years, you tend to fall into the 1-2% increase per year cycle, maybe with a promotion here or there. But you're not going to move up from a financial perspective quickly.

One day, I was at the Four Seasons in Philadelphia, giving a presentation on Jetform Technology. I played to my background working with Kodak, Cigna, and Prudential, telling compelling stories with the classic beginning, middle, end, and aha moments that mattered. My presentation was not just about technology; more importantly, it was about people, processes, and technology. The aha moment that mattered was the value realization.

Lessons Learned: Moore Business Forms

- **Everything We Know in College Is an Integral Part of Our Careers**: My degrees in fine arts and marketing played significant roles.
- **Hobbies Can Turn Into Careers**: My passion for computers and technology evolved into a central part of my professional life.
- **Life Lessons From Early Jobs**: Selling dollhouses on a factory floor taught me invaluable lessons about hard work and customer interaction.
- **Don't Miss Learning From PITA Customers**: Pain in the Ass (PITA) customers, like Sal Bassio, teach you to be thorough and meticulous.
- **Look Under Every Rock**: When you find something, dig deeper. There's always more to discover.
- **Technology Continues to Evolve**: Stay ahead of the curve by continually researching and learning.
- **Be a Technical Advisor**: Understand your client's needs deeply and provide well-researched, thoughtful solutions.

Applying Lessons to Modern Business Culture

"The Lean Startup" by Eric Ries

- **Look Under Every Rock**: Proactively look for inefficiencies and implement innovative solutions.
- **Technology Continues to Evolve**: Continuously explore and adopt new technologies to enhance business operations.

Why Read "The Lean Startup": This book introduces a methodology for developing businesses and products. It focuses on efficient operations, marketing, and decision-making, which are essential for a startup.

1. "Good to Great" by Jim Collins
    - **Life Lessons From Early Jobs**: Apply the fundamental lessons from early job experiences to your professional life.
    - **Learn From Difficult Clients**: Embrace challenging clients as opportunities to improve your skills and processes.
    - **Be a Technical Advisor**: Build trust with clients by being a knowledgeable advisor.

Why Read "Good to Great": This book explores why some companies make the leap to greatness while others do not. It offers valuable insights into leadership and organizational behavior, emphasizing the importance of disciplined people, thought, and action.

Workshop Topic: Handling Difficult Situations and Objection Handling

- **Objective**: To equip participants with strategies to effectively handle difficult situations and objections in a business setting.
- **Materials Needed**: Post-it notes, whiteboard or large paper sheets, markers, role-play scenarios.
- **Duration**: 2 hours

Step-by-Step Instructions:

1. Introduction (10 minutes):
    - Start by explaining the objective of the workshop: handling difficult situations and objections.
    - Highlight the importance of these skills in maintaining client relationships and achieving business success.
2. Brainstorming Session (20 minutes):
    - Provide each participant with Post-it notes and a marker.
    - Ask participants to think about common difficult situations or objections they face in their business interactions and write each one on a separate Post-it note.
    - Encourage them to think broadly, including client objections, internal conflicts, and challenging project demands.
3. Posting and Grouping (15 minutes):
    - Have participants post their notes on a whiteboard or large paper sheets.

- As a group, start grouping similar situations and objections together to identify common themes.
4. Role-Play Preparation (10 minutes):
    - Divide participants into small groups.
    - Assign each group a common theme identified in the brainstorming session.
    - Ask each group to prepare a role-play scenario based on their assigned theme, including the roles of the client and the employee handling the situation.
5. Role-Play Execution (30 minutes):
    - Have each group perform their role-play scenario in front of the workshop.
    - Encourage all participants to observe and take notes on the strategies used to handle the situation or objection.
6. Discussion (20 minutes):
    - Facilitate a discussion based on the role-play scenarios.
    - Ask participants to share their observations and insights on the strategies that were effective and those that could be improved.
    - Share personal anecdotes or examples from your experience at Moore Business Forms to illustrate the impact of effective objection handling and conflict resolution.
7. Action Planning (25 minutes):
    - Have each group develop a plan to implement effective objection handling and conflict resolution strategies in their business interactions.
    - Encourage groups to think about specific actions, communication techniques, and follow-up strategies.
8. Readout and Commitments (10 minutes):

- Have each group present their action plans to the entire workshop.
- Encourage participants to commit to at least one action they will take to improve their handling of difficult situations and objections in their workplace.

9. Wrap-Up and Resources (10 minutes):
   - Summarize the key takeaways from the workshop.
   - Provide additional resources or readings that participants can explore to further their understanding of handling difficult situations and objections.
   - Examples:
     - "Crucial Conversations: Tools for Talking When Stakes Are High" by Kerry Patterson, Joseph Grenny, Ron McMillan, and Al Switzler
     - "Never Split the Difference: Negotiating As If Your Life Depended On It" by Chris Voss

Chapter 5: Jetform

The Transition to Technical Sales

"With the lessons learned from my time at Moore Business Forms, I transitioned to Jetform, where I encountered new challenges and opportunities that further developed my professional skills."

"If you can't explain it simply, you don't understand it well enough."
- Albert Einstein

Jetform: The Transition to Technical Sales

So, I remember Rick Allen walking up to me after my presentation. I was in the back of the room, and he said, "Wow, what an excellent presentation. Have you ever thought about working for Jetform directly?" At the time, I was very flattered. For me, it wasn't really about how I gave a presentation. It was to ensure the people in the auditorium were left satisfied. My wife and I were thinking of having another child at the time. We were thinking of expanding the household; sure enough, this came at the best time. So I said to him, "Sure, always interested in looking at an opportunity."

Here was my first chance to make a career move after being at Moore Business Forms for five years. Unfortunately, like all of us, we consistently undervalue who we are and what we're worth to an organization. I had a phenomenal coach and mentor at Moore Business Forms. I remember him telling me that I'm worth $125,000 a year. I was happy with $75,000; at the time, I was only making $55,000. My coach worked with me for two days role-playing the interview. We covered the hard questions, how to ask questions, and understand what to do when closing the conversation.

Rick Allen set up an interview with Brian Palazzi out of the DC office. Brian talked about a role that was called presales. I had never heard of this role before; remember, this is 1992. So I got in my white Mercury Sable, drove to Washington, DC, and met with Brian Palazzi. The presentation reviewed my working technical knowledge and my ability to position the technology for average business people. We got to the end of the presentation, and just as I practiced, Brian asked, "OK, how much do you want to make?" I chuckled to myself as this was exactly how my coach prepared me for the session.

I was so excited about this opportunity that I didn't want to lose it. I remembered what my coach told me, and he said to tell him, "What can you offer?" So I said, "OK, well Brian, what can you offer?" and I sat back and didn't say a word. It was a little bit awkward, probably about five minutes. Brian finally submits and says, "Well, I can probably give you $95,000 a year." I was blown away, lost all thought—I was happy with $75,000. Now I had a chance to make $95,000. I had to hold back the resistance to jump at it because I was about to blow the opportunity to negotiate. So instead of asking for $125,000, which I know all of you are probably thinking about right now, I said fine, but can you give me an extra two weeks' worth of vacation? He said yeah, no problem, four weeks. I said, is there a chance I can work out of NJ so I don't get double taxed in New York and New Jersey. He said that's easy. Most of us work from home. OK, will I get all my equipment set up? Yep absolutely, even get a gym membership. I had nothing else to ask, so I said, "Let's make this happen." On my drive home, I called my wife and said, "I got the job." Her first response was, wait for it, "You got $125,000?" I replied, "No," in a discouraged voice, "I got $95,000, but I got an extra couple of weeks' vacation and all the other perks." The job was life-changing money for us; we went from $50,000 to $95,000, which changed the entire direction of my career.

Lessons Learned: Jetform

- **Take care of those who take care of you**: Service Teams are invaluable.
- **Build your internal network**: Brand recognition within the company is crucial.
- **Have internal advocates**: They can help you advance your career.
- **Be humble, be yourself**: Authenticity is key.
- **Have a personal coach**: Preparation is vital for success.
- **Don't underestimate your value**: The first rule in negotiation is that you can always go down, but you can't go up!
- **Don't leave money on the table**: Give/Get—get something in return, like vacation time, if you can't get the salary you want.
- **Work-life balance**: It's crucial for long-term happiness and success.

I had no idea what a presales solution engineer role was when I took the Jetform job. The presales role in 1995 was probably about a 60/40 split—60% technical and 40% business—so they were looking for people who knew how to talk to both business and technical customers. In addition, they needed people to ensure that the rep would not oversell what the product did or did not do. This job was tailor-made for my background. If you remember, computers were my hobby, but I love sales and marketing.

Compensation Models

When looking at compensation models back in 1995, they are still similar to today's comp programs. The compensation model at $95,000 wasn't a pure $95,000. Remember, you're also a salesperson, so I had a comp plan that was a 70/30 split. Of that $95,000, 70% was guaranteed, and 30% was at risk. What does at risk mean? At risk is called PCR or personal commission rate. The formula is to take 30% of your OTE—On Target Earnings—and then calculate that against your quota to achieve your commission rate. Let's say you have a $1 million quota. This means if you reached $1 million in sales, you received 100% of that 30 at risk. To help you with the math, let's say I received $100K OTE—on a 70/30 plan—I was risking $30,000 as a commission. If I attained 100% of my quota, I would receive $30 grand. However, if I overachieved that number, there's this thing called accelerators; I could realize 2x my commission and up to 3x my commission. In my first year at Jetform, I crushed it and made my base $66,500 plus 100% of my risk $28,500—but since I was in accelerators, I overachieved and made an additional $73K—for a total of $168K. Just one year prior, I was making about $60K.

Presales' career was a perfect role and the best of all worlds. But, think about it, what's that risk? Your sales rep has a 50/50 plan, so that's 50% commission and 50% base. So they have more risk and take more rewards. Unfortunately, when the sales rep doesn't make their number at the end of the quarter, they're at risk of being fired. Though a pre-sale SE has a significantly lower risk of being terminated. Keep this in mind as you approach your Sales/SE relationships. The sales job is not easy; many factors can cause harm to a deal. Many of those are sales prevention teams like legal and finance. You should walk in the AE's shoes one day and see how painful and rewarding it is to respect the role.

The SE and AE Working Relationship

The SE and AE working relationship was subservient to the account executive. The hierarchy challenges became increasingly noticeable as the account team approached week six in the current quarter. The company had no rules of engagement outlined. In our absence, we had no consistent sales motion across the team. Some SEs were too pleased to just do demo after demo. They did not participate in Discovery calls to identify the client's needs and power sponsorship. They were happy to conduct proof offerings, investing hundreds of hours at a customer with no scope and end date. We had some SEs who would even discuss pricing when asked. Some SEs would showcase roadmap items and not sell what was on the truck. The SE organization did not know how to push back on sales where necessary, and Sales did not know how to weaponize the SE to gain a hunting license to power sponsorship.

The current sales and system engineering relationship were very frustrating. I figured I could take a lot of whatever I had already learned at Moore Business Forms to apply it to a very young start-up-minded company. So I had to leg up when conducting interviews and discovery questions. I finally approached my Account Executives and landed on a rough expectations outline. We agreed to conduct discovery calls together before any onsite meeting. This allowed me to ask questions that, if requested by the sales rep, would have been responded to differently. In the eyes of the customer, we all know the Salesperson is only after one thing: close business. I, as the Systems Engineer, am to be that trusted advisor. We sat down to outline our first sales motion draft:

- **Construct Discovery Questions**: Qualify in or out quickly the individual we worked with.

- **Never Discuss Pricing**: EVER!
- **Avoid Roadmap Items**: Don't position future roadmap items, which typically will extend the sales cycle.
- **Participate in Prospecting**: Help with prospecting weekly.
- **Divide and Conquer**: Divide tasks when going onsite.
- **Offer Demos Sparingly**: Offer demos as a last resort.
- **Get Something in Return**: Only offer something if we get something in return for our investment.
- **Customize Demos**: Generate customized demos based on those items identified in the pre-call.
- **Expense All Meals**: Ensure all meals are expensed by the AE.

You start to realize that success drives success, and my AE's and I worked collaboratively to accomplish closing business. Our working relationship was very different from my peers, who continued to demo, extend sales cycles, and talk about pricing. They were willing to pull together a three-week proof of concept with no attached give/get or exit date.

Good Examples

I remember walking into a Bank of New York (BONY) with my sales executive Mark Solazzo one day. Mark would go left, and I would go right when walking into the lobby. After that, I typically would go to the basement—where the server rooms would be. Yes, this is way before cloud computing:

1. I would talk to the technical communities and identify critical projects with fun code names like Road Runner or Death Star.
2. Mark and I would meet for lunch and review what we discovered. The significant part of those code names, you

knew it was a budgeted project when Mark referenced the same code names from the business discussions.
3. Mark and I would compare our notes and piece together the who, what, and when.
4. Mark knew the essential details about the tasks outlined by the business that the technical teams either had faith in or not.

I always discovered more truthful information from the technical teams than the business would let on. Eventually, Mark and I ended up having security badges at New York Life, Guardian Life, MetLife, and others across the city. Mark would negotiate an office onsite for us to work out of. So I would walk into these companies like a regular employee. Working in New York City allowed me to be at a different customer office each day of the week. I ultimately got invited to those last-minute meetings involving any electronic form project. Eventually, the customer thought I was working for them, to the point where I was invited to the Christmas parties, retirement parties, lunch parties, and after-hours events. This process worked so well; when companies wanted to go out to bid, they would come to me to help write the RFP—request for proposal. Side note on RFPs: unless you are writing them for the client, do not respond to the RFP—you are probably column fodder.

Another Great Working Relationship

Another example of a great working relationship was Tiffany Weisert. We talk about powerful women in the workforce today as a new thing. Tiffany blazed paths for so many successful women. She also was in the top 10 reps I had the pleasure to work with. Tiffany was always about relationships and never gave away anything without getting something in return. When it came to her system engineer, she would always negotiate for access to this resource. She would defend her SE to the point of walking out of a meeting. I remember a meeting at Polo in Secaucus, NJ. The client was abusing the lead SE, Jason Barnett. Tiffany stopped the session, thanked them for their time, and said, "We will not do business with you in this manner," and walked out! It was a fantastic thing to see. Tiffany had the tenacity and mindset to understand that she was in control.

Another lesson learned working with Tiffany is that it is OK to say, "I don't know." These are the three most challenging words for an SE to say. We typically want to know everything. For example, I was in a meeting with K Hovnanian, a national home builder, discussing SAP integration. The customer team was trying to stump the chump with questions. I was holding my own, and then out of nowhere, I snapped. Instead of saying I don't know, I flipped it back and hit it with something like, "Well, tell me what ABAP stands for." Tiffany was quick to help me off the ledge to save the meeting. Again, a lesson learned for the remainder of my career, especially when hiring people.

Lessons Learned: Jetform

- **GIVE/GET**: Never give anything up without getting something in return.
- **Focus on Closing Business**: Always remember your primary goal.
- **Avoid Extending the Sales Process**: Be cautious with roadmap items that can extend the sales cycle.
- **Quota and Skin in the Game**: Understand your combined quota and your skin in the game.
- **Value Your Role**: Never be subservient to sales; you are a costly and valuable asset.

- **Partnership**: Build a strong, understanding relationship with your AE.
- **Celebrate Wins**: Celebrate your wins loudly to build momentum and recognition.
- **"I Don't Know"**: It's okay to admit when you don't have an answer.
- **Set Ground Rules**: Establish clear expectations and ground rules with your AE.
- **Fail Fast, Learn Fast**: Embrace failures as learning opportunities.
- **Relationships**: Build strong internal and external relationships.
- **Know Your Customer**: Understand your customer's needs deeply.
- **Respect Your AE**: They have a tough job and deserve your respect.

During this time, I first encountered my next mentor, John Hogerland, who was in the process of writing up the SE Worklife requirements. He saw the gaps I saw in my first few months on board. John used this manifesto as his way of breaking into a leadership role. I remember my first meeting with John at Bank of Boston, which later became Summit Bank and Bank of America. Bank of Boston was a premier account with some technical challenges with Jetform Central and eForms routing. I conducted my interviews with all parties and wrote a considerable document outlining cause and effect, along with all correspondence between sales, service, and support. I understood that objection handling is first agreeing with the client to defuse the situation and then pivoting to resolution. Thank you, Moore Business Forms for negotiation 101 courses. With this being my first meeting, I knew I was the third chair in essential people. John took the lead; I watched and was very impressed with how he handled the customer's challenges. At the time, I didn't know John was a NA SE director veteran at Novell networks. The Bank of Boston escalation was not his first goat rodeo.

John and I continued to foster a good relationship. Fast forward, one night at the Fairmont Hotel in Ottawa, I discussed the challenges and opportunities I encountered locally. He didn't dismiss me as I would expect an executive from Novell. Instead, John listened and set up additional time to discuss what I saw on the ground. John and I immediately hit it off; his energy and knowledge were infectious. This was the benefit of a small startup—the ability to reach those building the framework and strategy. I spent much time in Ottawa working with John and others around him. He always provided some thought-provoking comments to get you moving in the direction he wanted.

A few months after that first encounter with John, the organization assembled during May at Mt Tremblant, Canada. This beautiful ski resort had all types of spring activities, fishing, biking, etc. For those new bees out there, these are what they call sales conferences. Your first time is so exciting—big jumbotron TVs, screens, stages, speeches, and training sessions. It's a massive boondoggle for salespeople, and yes, you too. I hope COVID doesn't kill this—fast forward, we did a virtual one at Snowflake—fun but missed the best part, and that was meeting people for drinks across the globe. But as you would expect, CFOs like to save money. So in 2022, I flew to Sarasota, watched the virtual event from a pool. Yeah, Florida, Internet, and COVID.

OK Kunz, why are you telling me this about the sales conference? You need to know these are corporate events and keep your head on. Too often, OK, every single sales conference, someone gets

FIRED. I will talk about this through the book—an excellent book to read is **Corporate Confidential**, especially if the company is public vs. IPO. When a company goes public, it must ensure they don't get sued. Human Resources is there to protect the company and its shareholders. If you read my book on How to Become a Sales Engineer, you can read about the challenges in sales conferences.

Let's talk about Mt Tremblant—great time; this ski town had this bar at the bottom of the hill from the hotel called The Mangy Moose. I tell you this because of the crazy nights trying to walk back to the hotel after drinking a few shots. Oh yes, salespeople know how to work hard but play hard as well—some see that as a plus—and it is. Here is the thing, a good career-limiting move is to fill your provided water guns as a fun team sport with Goldschlager. Our Sales leader proceeded to fire his gun at everyone—nope, not me—well, a little later, the VP of Sales and Ops was going table to table doing water gun shots! Note to self, a few people got out of hand and pulled the fire alarm. Yep, the next day on Air Canada flight 1135—seat 22E—middle seat with a hangover. This ruined a good friend, but I get it! That lesson was learned early. ALWAYS, ALWAYS remember you are at a corporate event, and people are watching. Typically, I will have a few gin and tonics, move to just tonic and lime in the glass. No one knows you are not drinking, and added plus—you get to watch those who are messed up—so much fun, especially at that first breakfast the next day.

Lessons Learned: Jetform

- **Speak Up**: When with an executive, remember they are people too.
- **No Risk, No Reward**: Take calculated risks.
- **Startups**: They are fun and full of opportunities.

- **Sales Conferences**: They are a blast, but be mindful of your behavior.
- **Misbehave**: You will get fired.
- **Corporate Confidential**: A must-read for understanding corporate dynamics.

This was my first chance to meet fellow SEs on the team and SE leaders across the globe. Indeed a fantastic amount of talent in that one room. One thing that stuck out immediately was the diversity in this talent pool. Some individuals were complete 90/10's—90% technical and not much personality; others were 60/40's—some 70/30's. Not surprisingly, the SE team tended to sit together, and the sales folks sat at their selected chairs; marketing and partners also continued that trend. I felt that was odd; I ended up sitting with my account executives the first day to plan out the weekly education tracks. We planned out the week; it was clear that this event was for the account executive, not the sales engineer.

It was great to spend a full day learning about solution selling, nine-box evaluations, pricing, and how to conduct discovery questions. But I saw a significant gap in not providing agenda items on helping the SEs do their job. For example, how to use the product and position the product with solution overviews, aka demos, POCs, success stories, and equally essential failures.

To close this gap, I took the initiative and discovered that the main hall upstairs was available. I found the restaurant staff and requested a bunch of food and beer to be delivered. Then, I socialized with my fellow SEs to meet upstairs for a whole night's working session. We found the necessary hardware to set up an NT Server on a laptop, with ethernet connections to a hub, so we could share files, demo content, and presentation material. We essentially set up a full working technical workshop out of scraps and Microsoft developer-licensed CDs.

We took a quick poll of all the attendees, and many needed to know how to implement and use Central, the ins and outs of workflow, designing forms, and network implementation on NT, Linux, Solaris, and AS400. Many folks stood up front to present their go-to demo for each product. This was the beginning of the demo and story-sharing. It was a huge success and helped many of the SEs that struggled to understand how to parse out postscript headers, map data to templates, and generate workflow solutions. In addition, everyone left with at least one great story and one great demo to put in their bag.

The next day, you would expect a big room meeting after breakfast to take stock of the week and provide some announcements. Some of the execs got word of our evening and recognized me and others for taking the initiative. I was not looking for recognition, just to be better as a team, collectively sharing. Many SEs that day came up to me and thanked me for the opportunity to sit in on that night's event.

Lessons Learned:

- **See Something, Do Something**: Take action when you see an opportunity.
- **Beer and Food**: Always essential for gatherings.
- **Best Practices**: Sharing best practices and the art of storytelling empowers people.
- **Natural Recognition**: Don't look for recognition; it will happen naturally.
- **Seize the Moment**: Establish your brand identity.

As a result of that one event and sales conference, I defined my brand, established a global people network, took home a treasure of knowledge, and defined what a pre-sales SE role should be from that moment forward. For Jetform, it was the responsibility of the SE organization to close business by shortening sales cycles by achieving a technical win in the eyes of our prospects. Well, that's what I thought until John Hogerland came into my life and career.

By the way, a technical win is when you have completed your proof offering/questioning, and you ask the client, "Have you selected Jetform as the approved vendor to move forward?" This is a yes or no question. Then you follow that up with, "Will you sponsor us to the executives as a completed technical evaluation?" and finally, "What was it specifically that you thought was a key differentiator from our competition?" This will allow you to paint the customer in a box. I know; sorry for squirreling (reference from the movie UP). I figured it was a good time to understand/define a technical win.

John Hogerland approached me and a few others to congratulate us on our work that evening. He was very impressed and wanted to know more. But John was not about really patting people on the back; he was more trying to get you to think harder about what else you could have done or do. I hated that and loved that about John. He said, "So what? What about the rest of the country or the globe? Think bigger, Kunz; understand that this is a global company with unique challenges. How would you apply this enablement to others around the world?" Then he would hit you with, "What does your 30/60/90-day plan look like? How would you measure success?" I was like, "Damn, this is a lot to think about," but thinking bigger is what he was encouraging his team to do.

For the next three years, I worked closely with John and others on the team to be the best I could be. I always looked at the job and tried to see how to move up in the business. Take on more prominent roles and opportunities. I worked with a wide variety of sales leadership and account executives, all along the way refining and fine-tuning so many things about this complex role. How to help shorten sales cycles, not waste my time, reps, and most importantly, the customer's time. Too often, I and others would get called up 24 hours before an agreed-on meeting with the AE and client to show up and do the standard pitch. No pre-call, no understanding of the customer's business issues. Not even the basics—what are you using today, what do you like about it, and if wishes were for free, what would be the ideal solution? I quickly saw the reps who understood how to hunt for opportunities and weaponize my talent to get to the power sponsor. I also saw representatives happy to live on their base, have me show up, and throw up everything on the screen to see what stuck. Shocking to type this and understand how this has not changed much since 1995.

Career growth was certainly on my radar, and I had the opportunity to start work with other future JetForm leaders. My core teammates were Karl Taylor, Tom Loane, and Brian Polizzi across the country. To define some basic rules of engagement. Thankfully we had excellent SE leadership with John Hogerland, and he aligned with the sales organization. The SE and AVP sales relationship helped immensely when we looked to push back on sales. Rick Allen was the sales executive; he had a fantastic working relationship with his sales team and SE teams. He understood the classics—time kills all deals, we enable bad behavior by giving away resources with nothing in return, and no plan is a plan to fail. Sounds simple right? Well, not simple to enforce, especially in week 8 of the quarter, when your forecast accuracy is written in blood.

We started to incorporate things that you today see as fundamentals. For example, we would not go on-site to any customer without having a pre-call before the meeting. We would not have a pre-call until we had an internal sales team discussion outlining the why and so what factors. More on the three W's later in the book—why buy now, why buy anything, and why buy JetForm. When we agreed to go onsite, we had to have a dry run and ensure what the desired outcome of the meeting was. What role would the sales rep, SE, and client have in the meeting? Sounds simple, right? Even to this day, twenty-five years later, we are still trying to get some of these fundamentals.

As mentioned earlier, sales and SE leadership were in lockstep together. This made our job so much easier, and we became more productive in the field. Unfortunately, we did not have any CRM systems back then, like Siebel, Salesforce, or Sales Cloud. I believe most of us had ACT software for your desktop-siloed sales systems. Otherwise, we could see the metrics—SE time invested in closing rates to the deal size when adequately worked. We did have Excel, and as we all know, spreadsheets are so much fun, unfortunately still widely used today.

I continue into my fourth year at Jetform, working closely with my sales teams, local leadership, and executives in Canada. A true startup mentality, innovation, creativity, and openness to try new ideas. You mattered as an employee and made significant impacts. I helped hire and onboard SEs and participated in high-profile account relationships. I traveled every week across the US and monthly to Canada to meet with the executives and discuss field-level strategy. I was in my element and never expected what would come next. Then, for some crazy reason, they decided to make me a manager.

Sometimes, as a company is growing well, what do they do with successful salespeople or sales engineers? In this case, they make them a manager. Not because you're going to be a good manager; they just make you a manager because you've been there longer than others. I was so excited to move up my career. I wanted to prove to the world that I was successful. But unfortunately, I was the worst manager. Think of the worst manager you ever worked for; that was me. One of my challenges was that I could not let go of the job I enjoyed so much, which was solving customers' technical problems and being that individual contributor. The second and most significant issue was my ego; I always would do my team's work and treat them as my workers vs. their leader. Attitude happens to many new managers, especially those trying to prove something to the world.

I remember John flew down to New York from Ottawa, Canada, to have a meeting. He sat me down in the New York office, which was in Times Square's great office. He says flat out, "You know it's not about you, Kunz, right?" My response was, "John, what do you mean it's totally about me? I'm doing great. I'm crushing my number, my SEs are doing great, my salespeople love me." He responded, "No, it's not about you; it's about your people, and your job is to get rid of your people." I said, "Now wait a minute, get rid of my people, why the hell would I get rid of my people?" His response, "Your job is to help coach and mentor your people to identify their five-year career goals and paths. When they move on in their career and are successful, you are measured based on their success. When they are asked by their new employer, 'Wow, you are doing a great job; where did you learn how to do this?' They answer, 'I used to work for Kevin Kunz'; that's when you're weighed and measured." I'll tell you, I have had many lightbulb moments in my life, and that was one that completely changed my entire thinking around management and leadership. Thank you, John, for allowing me to understand the difference between management and leadership.

Don't worry; I will write a book on SE leadership since I was an individual contributor—manager, senior manager, director, senior director, and VP. I have been very fortunate to hold great pride in helping people who worked for me and have moved up in their careers. When interviewing for Snowflake, I had a slide with about 12 photos of people who worked for me and now are executives at many top organizations. That is called leadership, folks, not managers who just get the job done. I have worked for a few of those in my career, and not a great place to work when you have to deal with those people (you know whom I am talking about if reading this book—hope you are doing well—say hello to Karma for me).

So here I am, Jetform, a first-time manager working with fellow leaders like Tom Loane, Karl Taylor, and John Hogerland. I enjoyed my leadership role. I was fine-tuning my leadership craft. Unfortunately, another recession occurred; these can be times that test your abilities. Jetform began restructuring; as a leader, I had to stack rank my team and cut the lower two on that stack. Lesson learned again: this is not easy; honestly, it shouldn't be easy. If it's easy, you didn't do your job in creating the best of the best on your team. The company was in a tough place, and it looked like we would potentially go out of business. This is where your leadership, trust, and loyalty come into the fold. I found jobs for all those whom I let go.

To prevent collapsing, they rebranded from Jetform to Accelio— new logos, business cards, etc. By the way, that is never a good sign! Good news, though—we were ultimately sold to a company called Adobe. Yes, Adobe Acrobat Photoshop, Illustrator. Adobe saw that the shrink-wrap business was slowing and wanted to get into the enterprise business. At the time—SAAS software as a service / SOA—the server-oriented architecture was becoming a real solution. Adobe purchased Accelio for a good reason—our workflow solutions were a SOA foundation and had PDF Form technology for routing. Our print production technology incorporated merging data with PDF output. In fact, for those who enjoy getting a folio/invoice receipt PDF from, say, Marriott or Chase—you are welcome!

Lessons Learned: Jetform

- **GIVE/GET**: Never give anything up without getting something in return.
- **Focus on Closing Business**: Always remember your primary goal.
- **Avoid Extending the Sales Process**: Be cautious with roadmap items that can extend the sales cycle.
- **Quota and Skin in the Game**: Understand your combined quota and your skin in the game.
- **Value Your Role**: Never be subservient to sales; you are a costly and valuable asset.
- **Partnership**: Build a strong, understanding relationship with your AE.
- **Celebrate Wins**: Celebrate your wins loudly to build momentum and recognition.
- **"I Don't Know"**: It's okay to admit when you don't have an answer.
- **Set Ground Rules**: Establish clear expectations and ground rules with your AE.
- **Fail Fast, Learn Fast**: Embrace failures as learning opportunities.

- **Relationships**: Build strong internal and external relationships.
- **Know Your Customer**: Understand your customer's needs deeply.
- **Respect Your AE**: They have a tough job and deserve your respect.
- **Leverage Relationships**: Internal relationships are crucial for career growth.
- **Think Bigger**: Always ask, "So what?" and "Why do I care?"
- **Plan**: Write down and plan out your 30-60-90 day goals.
- **Proofread**: Have someone proofread your work.
- **Attitude**: Drives behavior which drives results—experiences drive attitude.
- **It's Not About You**: It's about your people. Your job is to help them succeed.
- **Loyalty**: It's a two-way street.
- **Management vs. Leadership**: It's about helping your people grow and succeed.
- **Find Jobs for Those You Let Go**: It shows your character and builds loyalty.

Applying Lessons to Modern Business Culture

Recommended Reading: "Never Split the Difference: Negotiating As If Your Life Depended On It" by Chris Voss

Recommended Reading: "Good to Great: Why Some Companies Make the Leap... and Others Don't" by Jim Collins

- **Focus on Closing Business**: Always remember your primary goal.

- **Value Your Role**: Never be subservient to sales; you are a costly and valuable asset.
- **Partnership**: Build a strong, understanding relationship with your AE.
- **Celebrate Wins**: Celebrate your wins loudly to build momentum and recognition.
- **Plan**: Write down and plan out your 30-60-90 day goals.
- **Management vs. Leadership**: It's about helping your people grow and succeed.
- **Find Jobs for Those You Let Go**: It shows your character and builds loyalty.
- **Think Bigger**: Encourage a mindset of thinking bigger and questioning the status quo.
- **Proofread**: Ensure accuracy and clarity by having important documents reviewed.

Recommended Reading: "Measure What Matters: How Google, Bono, and the Gates Foundation Rock the World with OKRs" by John Doerr

- **Quota and Skin in the Game**: Understand your combined quota and your skin in the game.
- **Avoid Extending the Sales Process**: Be cautious with roadmap items that can extend the sales cycle.
- **Leverage Relationships**: Internal relationships are crucial for career growth.
- **Plan**: Write down and plan out your 30-60-90 day goals.

Recommended Reading: "Solution Selling: Creating Buyers in Difficult Selling Markets" by Michael T. Bosworth

- **Focus on Closing Business**: Always remember your primary goal.

- **Know Your Customer**: Understand your customer's needs deeply.
- **Relationships**: Build strong internal and external relationships.
- **Partnership**: Build a strong, understanding relationship with your AE.
- **Fail Fast, Learn Fast**: Embrace failures as learning opportunities.

Corporate Confidential: Why You Should Read It!

Book Summary:

"Corporate Confidential" by Cynthia Shapiro is an eye-opening guide that reveals the hidden truths of the corporate world. Drawing from her extensive experience as a former human resources executive, Shapiro uncovers the unspoken rules, covert strategies, and hidden agendas that drive corporate decisions. This book aims to equip employees with the knowledge and tactics needed to navigate their careers successfully and avoid common pitfalls.

Key Insights:

Understanding Corporate Agendas: Shapiro demystifies the underlying motives and priorities of corporate management. She explains how decisions are often influenced by factors that employees might not be aware of, such as financial goals, market pressures, and internal politics.

Protecting Your Career: The book provides practical advice on how to safeguard your job and career trajectory. Shapiro shares strategies for maintaining job security, including how to avoid common mistakes that can jeopardize your position and how to stay valuable to your employer.

Navigating Office Politics: "Corporate Confidential" delves into the complex world of office politics. Shapiro offers insights into recognizing and handling power dynamics, understanding the importance of alliances, and effectively managing workplace relationships.

Maximizing Performance Reviews: Shapiro explains how to prepare for and navigate performance reviews to ensure they work in your favor. She highlights the importance of documenting your achievements and aligning your goals with the company's objectives.

Advancing Your Career: The book provides tips on how to position yourself for promotions and career advancement. Shapiro emphasizes the importance of visibility, networking, and continuous learning to stay ahead in a competitive environment.

Recognizing Red Flags: Shapiro teaches readers how to identify warning signs that may indicate trouble within the company or potential threats to their job security. This includes understanding corporate restructuring, financial instability, and shifts in company strategy.

Why a Leader or Individual Contributor Should Read This Book:

Enhanced Awareness: For leaders, "Corporate Confidential" provides a deeper understanding of the dynamics at play within their organization. This awareness can help them make more informed decisions, anticipate challenges, and better navigate corporate landscapes.

Career Protection: Individual contributors can benefit from the practical advice on protecting their careers and ensuring job security. By understanding the hidden rules of the corporate world, employees can avoid pitfalls and position themselves for success.

Strategic Advantage: Both leaders and individual contributors can gain a strategic advantage by learning how to effectively navigate office politics, build strong workplace relationships, and maximize their performance reviews.

Proactive Management: Leaders can use the insights from the book to proactively manage their teams, recognizing the factors that influence employee satisfaction and productivity. This can lead to a more engaged and motivated workforce.

Career Advancement: For those looking to advance their careers, the book offers valuable strategies on how to stand out, gain visibility, and secure promotions. Understanding the corporate mindset can help employees align their efforts with the company's goals.

Risk Mitigation: Recognizing red flags and potential threats within the organization can help both leaders and employees take proactive steps to mitigate risks. This foresight can be crucial in maintaining career stability and organizational health.

Conclusion:

"Corporate Confidential" is an essential read for anyone navigating the complexities of the corporate world. Cynthia Shapiro's insider knowledge provides invaluable insights that can help leaders and individual contributors alike protect their careers, navigate office politics, and achieve their professional goals. By understanding the unspoken rules and hidden agendas of the corporate environment, readers can make more informed decisions, build stronger workplace relationships, and strategically position themselves for long-term success.

Workshop Topic: Mastering Negotiations and Solution Selling

Objective: To equip participants with strategies to effectively conduct negotiations and apply solution selling techniques to close deals.

Materials Needed: Post-it notes, whiteboard or large paper sheets, markers, role-play scenarios, copies of "Never Split the Difference" by Chris Voss, and "Solution Selling" by Michael T. Bosworth.

Duration: 2 hours

Step-by-Step Instructions:

1. **Introduction (10 minutes)**:
   - Explain the objective of the workshop: mastering negotiations and solution selling.
   - Highlight the importance of these skills in achieving business success and maintaining client relationships.

2. **Brainstorming Session (20 minutes)**:
   - Provide each participant with Post-it notes and a marker.
   - Ask participants to think about common negotiation challenges and solution selling scenarios they face and write each one on a separate Post-it note.
   - Encourage them to consider various aspects, including client objections, internal conflicts, and challenging project demands.

3. **Posting and Grouping (15 minutes)**:
    - Have participants post their notes on a whiteboard or large paper sheets.
    - As a group, start grouping similar situations together to identify common themes.

4. **Role-Play Preparation (10 minutes)**:
    - Divide participants into small groups.
    - Assign each group a common theme identified in the brainstorming session.
    - Ask each group to prepare a role-play scenario based on their assigned theme, including the roles of the client and the employee handling the negotiation or solution selling situation.

5. **Role-Play Execution (30 minutes)**:
    - Have each group perform their role-play scenario in front of the workshop.
    - Encourage all participants to observe and take notes on the strategies used to handle the situation.

6. **Discussion (20 minutes)**:
    - Facilitate a discussion based on the role-play scenarios.
    - Ask participants to share their observations and insights on the strategies that were effective and those that could be improved.
    - Share personal anecdotes or examples from your experience at Jetform to illustrate the impact of effective negotiation and solution selling techniques.

7. **Action Planning (25 minutes)**:

    o Have each group develop a plan to implement effective negotiation and solution selling strategies in their business interactions.
    o Encourage groups to think about specific actions, communication techniques, and follow-up strategies.

8. **Readout and Commitments (10 minutes)**:

    o Have each group present their action plans to the entire workshop.
    o Encourage participants to commit to at least one action they will take to improve their negotiation and solution selling skills in their workplace.

9. **Wrap-Up and Resources (10 minutes)**:

    o Summarize the key takeaways from the workshop.
    o Provide additional resources or readings that participants can explore to further their understanding of negotiation and solution selling.
    o Examples:
        - "Never Split the Difference: Negotiating As If Your Life Depended On It" by Chris Voss
        - "Solution Selling: Creating Buyers in Difficult Selling Markets" by Michael T. Bosworth

Chapter 6: Adobe

Navigating Corporate Culture & Innovation

"Following my tenure at Jetform, I embarked on a transformative journey with Adobe, a move that introduced me to the intricacies of navigating a vast corporate landscape while pioneering innovations in enterprise sales."

"Innovation distinguishes between a leader and a follower." - Steve Jobs

I will not attempt to chronicle the entirety of my thirteen-year tenure at Adobe; such an endeavor could fill a book on its own. Instead, I will highlight the significant moments—both triumphant and challenging—that defined this journey. The aim of this section is to impart the profound lesson that spending thirteen years at a single company is often too long. Every story has its beginning, middle, and end, with its share of villains, heroes, and unexpected twists. This chapter is no different, with its villains being culture, product misalignment, brand identity crises, lack of accountability, and economic pressures. The acronym PESTLE (Political, Economic, Social, Technical, Legal, Environmental) encapsulates the multifaceted challenges I faced. The heroes of this narrative are exceptional leaders who upheld accountability and navigated us through turbulent times.

Fortunate Beginnings and Uncertain Mergers

At the onset, I was fortunate not to fall into the lower echelons of the leadership stack ranking, which allowed me to retain my managerial role in the New York office. The initial phase of the merger was fraught with discomfort as we were handed the reins with little direction from Adobe, the acquiring company. This discomfort was palpable during the first mixer at Adobe's offices, where longstanding Adobe employees, including the founding fathers of Photoshop, had to relinquish their cherished corner offices due to the merger. This period highlighted the crucial lesson of not assuming that others are fully informed. The adage "ASSUME makes an Ass out of U and Me" held true as we learned the hard way to communicate openly and find common ground. The merger taught us to bridge gaps with transparency and mutual understanding.

Adobe had always been my dream job—a powerhouse of creativity and innovation. Joining as employee number 1567, in what has grown to nearly 20,000 today, was exhilarating. My advice: if you ever get a chance to work at Adobe, seize it! But perhaps, avoid staying for thirteen years as I did.

The Emotional Turbulence of Mergers

The first six months post-acquisition were intensely challenging. The emotional toll was significant, akin to inviting an unfamiliar family to live in your home, dictating your living arrangements. This scenario was demoralizing, highlighting what to do and avoid during such transitions. Throughout my career, I have witnessed this pattern repeatedly in various mergers and acquisitions, underscoring the need for a masterclass on conducting effective mergers.

Initial Struggles and the Power of Communication

During a pivotal sales conference, non-legacy Adobe leaders attempted to instruct legacy Adobe staff on new methods and sales tactics. This clash was a cultural shock, as Adobe, a well-established brand, needed no introduction or justification. I vividly recall the marketing executive unveiling the Livecycle enterprise suite with grandiosity akin to selling shrink-wrapped software. The incongruity of presenting complex enterprise solutions in a boxed format highlighted the cultural disconnect and added friction in the field.

A Hero Emerges: Don Beck

In the midst of this turmoil, a hero emerged. Don Beck, with his unassuming demeanor, sat amongst us during a conference. Initially oblivious to his significance, I candidly shared my frustrations, only to realize later that he was responsible for all Livecycle sales in North America. His patient and empathetic approach to my candid feedback was a turning point. Don's wisdom underscored the importance of over-communication and humility. I remember sitting next to this thin, older gentleman in a blue suit who stood out amongst the crowd. He casually asked for my opinion on the event. Unaware of his identity, I unloaded my candid thoughts on the lack of direction and confusion. He listened attentively, occasionally nodding, before asking, "How would you solve that?" I enthusiastically laid out my ideas, feeling empowered. After our conversation, I nervously introduced myself, only to discover he was Don Beck, the head of all Livecycle sales for North America. My heart sank, fearing I had overstepped, but he graciously thanked me and expressed interest in further discussions. That was a pivotal moment, teaching me the value of thoughtful communication and the importance of humility.

Tech Insights: Measuring What Matters for the SE Community

We were far advanced in SEAC metrics, and the technologies today still do not match the ability that this tool allowed our leaders and field people to manage their businesses. This was my first understanding of how powerful data insights would be in managing a global business. The SEAC team could, with a high level of accuracy and data to back it up, tell a story to our leadership on sales predictability. In addition, we had the opportunity to share best practices immediately across the world, helping fellow SEAC s with projects and tested demonstration content, saving SEAC time.

Reflecting on this milestone, we were advanced in thinking beyond just trying to achieve a technical win. As a result, we had insights that no other software company had on the SEAC impact on the sales journey. I am still impressed by how the SEAC journey data capture and the advancements in CRM tools have not advanced as fast as expected. The homegrown tools, like ElasticSearch observability, and Snowflake, combined with Sigma visualization, helps to predict potential sales success roadblocks.

Macromedia Acquisition Impacts

As you would expect, I was on the other side of this acquisition, just like Karen when Adobe acquired Accelio. New leadership and this leadership was very ego-driven. I felt for the creative teams. Fortunately, the enterprise and sales teams were merged into the Livecycle enterprise suite. Of course, all the same issues we had with the Accelio merger happened with Macromedia. The Macromedia and Adobe employees circled the wagons, with political positioning and jockeying for positions. The good news is that I was prepared for all the changes and had the curse of knowledge to deal with what came my way. Understand that many things are out of your control, and you need to make peace with that.

With these changes came an addition to the team - Bill Hippenmeyer. He followed Don Beck to Adobe and was a great business partner. He was a military man with eighteen kids in Ohio. Sorry Bill, I am sure I screwed that up. But I learned from his deep faith, experience, and discipline. I had a long-standing relationship with Tom Loane and was worried about Bill at first, but thanks to time, I had experienced so much change that I was ready for Bill. Bill was a great leader, very protective of the SEAC team but balanced with closing business. The lesson from Bill was that patience, accuracy, and empathy go a long way in your career. Ensure that if you have the opportunity to work with someone like Bill, you take advantage of their willingness to work with you and your career. I honed my career development skills at an executive level with Bill.

Sometimes Things Are Out of Your Control

In 2007-2008, you may recall that AIG, Bear Stearns, and others overextended the financial loan systems, leading to a market crash and massive layoffs. These moments in a career define you as a leader or just a manager. A manager focuses solely on the business's demands, whereas a leader prioritizes the well-being of individuals. This period was particularly challenging for me, as I viewed my team as family and dreaded the thought of letting thirteen people go just before Thanksgiving and Christmas.

One crucial takeaway is understanding that Human Resources is there to protect the company, not the employee. "Corporate Confidential" is an excellent book that sheds light on HR's true role. Despite the bleak job market, I worked tirelessly with Tom Loane and others to find positions for as many team members as possible. This involved behind-the-scenes bargaining, finding alternative headcounts, and even arranging demotions or role changes. Remember, you work for yourself and your family, not the company.

I was fortunate to keep my job and help many team members find new positions at companies like Oracle, Salesforce.com, Pega Systems, and various implementation partners. This was a collective effort, and to this day, some of these individuals have returned to work with me or recommended me to other companies.

These years were incredibly stressful, especially with three kids and constant travel. My wife bore the brunt of the burden, dealing with snowstorms and managing the household while working full-time herself. This experience taught me not to let fear dictate my decisions. Staying in one job for too long can lead to stagnation and becoming out of touch with industry trends. Always ask yourself, "Who do you work for?" and "What is your five-year plan?"

Lessons Learned

- **Acquisitions Are Challenging**: Both sides of an acquisition face significant challenges and emotional tolls.
- **Culture as a Villain**: Mergers often fail due to cultural clashes and misalignment.
- **Communication is Key**: Over-communicate and seek to understand the perspective of others.
- **Humility in Feedback**: Always be humble and considerate when providing feedback, especially to senior leaders.
- **Building Trust**: Focus on building trust as relationships and roles can change.
- **Data Insights**: Leverage data for predictive insights and better decision-making.
- **Career Resilience**: Prepare for economic downturns and be proactive in securing new opportunities.
- **Patience, Accuracy, and Empathy**: These qualities are essential for leadership and career growth.
- **HR's Role**: Understand that HR is there to protect the company, not the employee.
- **Network and Support**: Build a strong professional network to support team members in finding new opportunities during tough times.

- **Work-Life Balance**: Prioritize your family and personal well-being alongside your career.
- **Continuous Learning**: Stay updated with industry trends and continuously seek new opportunities for growth.

Applying Lessons to Modern Business Culture

- **Acquisitions and Mergers**: Foster open communication and cultural integration to smooth transitions during mergers.
- **Change Management**: Promote a culture that embraces change and provides the tools and support needed for smooth transitions.
- **Data-Driven Decision Making**: Implement tools and practices that allow for the collection and analysis of data to drive business decisions.
- **Mentorship Programs**: Develop mentorship programs to support employee growth and development.
- **Resilience Building**: Create programs to help employees build resilience and adaptability in the face of economic and organizational challenges.

Workshop: How to Measure Value in Sales Engineering

Objective: Equip participants with the skills and tools to measure and articulate the value of their contributions to the sales process effectively.

Materials Needed: Laptops, projectors, whiteboards, markers, post-it notes, voting dots.

Step-by-Step Guide:

1. **Introduction and Objectives**:
   - Briefly introduce the workshop objectives and the importance of measuring value in sales engineering.
   - Share real-life examples and case studies to illustrate the impact of effective value measurement.

2. **Understanding Value**:
   - Define what value means in the context of sales engineering.
   - Discuss different types of value (e.g., financial, operational, strategic) and how they impact the business.

3. **Identifying Key Metrics**:
   - Brainstorm key metrics that can be used to measure value in sales engineering.

- Categorize these metrics into quantitative and qualitative measures.

4. **Tools and Techniques**:
    - Introduce tools and techniques for data collection and analysis (e.g., CRM systems, analytics platforms).
    - Demonstrate how to use these tools to track and measure key metrics.

5. **Developing a Measurement Framework**:
    - Guide participants in developing a customized framework for measuring value in their specific roles and organizations.
    - Use templates and worksheets to facilitate this process.

6. **Case Study Exercise**:
    - Provide a case study and have participants apply their measurement frameworks to evaluate the value of a hypothetical sales engineering project.
    - Encourage group discussions and presentations to share insights and approaches.

7. **Action Plan and Implementation**:
    - Help participants create an action plan for implementing their measurement frameworks in their daily work.
    - Discuss potential challenges and solutions for effective implementation.

8. **Q&A and Wrap-Up**:
    - Open the floor for questions and provide additional resources for further learning.
    - Summarize key takeaways and encourage participants to continuously refine their value measurement practices.

By the end of this workshop, participants should have a clear understanding of how to measure and communicate the value of their contributions, ultimately enhancing their impact on the business.

Chapter 7: Involver

Embracing the Startup Mindset

"Leaving behind the corporate structure of Adobe, I entered the fast-paced world of startups with Involver, where the dynamics of a smaller team and limited management layers presented new opportunities and challenges."

"Success is not the key to happiness. Happiness is the key to success. If you love what you are doing, you will be successful." - Albert Schweitzer

As summer drew to a close, I found myself contemplating my next career move. The vibrant world of technology beckoned, and I began exploring workflow solutions like Pega, SaaS giants such as Salesforce.com, innovative mobile tools like AppDynamics, and the ever-evolving social media landscape with players like Buddy Media and Facebook. Just as I was weighing my options, I received a call from Don Beck, who was now at the helm of a promising startup called Involver, renowned for its pioneering Social Markup Language (SML).

Don's voice crackled with enthusiasm over the phone, "So, what are you doing?" After sharing my story, he promptly replied, "No, you are working for me now. You are tailor-made for this company." Without much hesitation, I joined Involver as the VP of Solution Engineering. As is often the case with startups, my role quickly expanded to include professional services and training.

The energy at Involver was infectious, a stark contrast to the corporate world I had known. The startup atmosphere, with its dynamic pace and innovative spirit, was exhilarating. Later in this book, I will delve deeper into the different phases of a company's lifecycle, from startup to IPO, post-IPO, and beyond. Each stage has its unique challenges and complexities, shaping the type of companies you might want to join. One critical lesson I learned is that the limited management layers in a startup allow for a more active voice in the company's direction. Regular meetings with Don and the executive team were not just about business strategy but also about fostering relationships and keeping a pulse on the industry.

I immersed myself in the company, leveraging my network to build a strong team. I brought in trusted colleagues like Allen Levine and David Jones, understanding that leadership often prefers to surround themselves with familiar faces to build trust quickly. This practice, though beneficial, also highlights the challenges for those outside the "Club" (SAP, EMC, Salesforce, Oracle, IBM, Business Objects, HP, Compaq, to name a few).

The social media industry was ablaze, with Facebook's public offering on the horizon and emerging platforms like Pinterest, Instagram, and Twitter gaining traction. However, the business model for monetizing social relationships was complex. While advertising revenue and user data were valuable, market saturation was a looming concern. The landscape shifted dramatically when Salesforce.com acquired Buddy Media for about half a billion dollars. This acquisition was a game-changer, prompting Don to work with me on my employment contract, particularly concerning stock options and acquisition scenarios.

Here's a crucial lesson for anyone in the early days of a startup: always negotiate for stock acceleration upon acquisition. It was a concept I hadn't considered until Don coached me through it. In many startups, only three out of ten make it to a public offering. Often, they are acquired by larger organizations, and without stock acceleration clauses, your unvested shares can become worthless overnight.

Following Buddy Media's acquisition, the social media market began consolidating. Oracle moved swiftly, acquiring Vitrue, a Facebook page design company, Collective Intellect, a sentiment analysis firm, and finally, Involver, an audience management platform. I vividly remember April 12th, 2012, the day final negotiations for Involver were completed at Oracle headquarters. It was also the day my BMW convertible was rear-ended by a dump truck en route to the airport. Despite losing the car, I made the flight and sealed the deal.

Lessons Learned

1. **Always Follow Great Leaders**: Trust in proven leadership is worth the risk.
2. **Negotiate Stock Acceleration**: Always ensure your stock options include acceleration upon acquisition.
3. **Surround Yourself with Great People**: Building a strong, trusted team is invaluable.
4. **Startups = Fun, Active Voice, Strategic Direction**: Enjoy the dynamic environment and your active role in shaping the company's direction.
5. **Watch Out for Dump Trucks**: Life's unpredictability requires resilience and quick adaptation.

Applying Lessons to Modern Business Culture

From "Measure What Matters" by John Doerr:

Follow Great Leaders: Leaders set the vision and tone. Their experience and networks can open doors and provide critical guidance.

Strategic Direction: Be part of a company's strategic planning to understand the bigger picture and contribute effectively.

From "The Lean Startup" by Eric Ries:

Stock Acceleration: Protect your financial interests by negotiating favorable terms in your contract.

Startups = Fun and Strategic: Embrace the excitement and strategic influence you can have in a startup environment.

From "Good to Great" by Jim Collins:

Surround Yourself with Great People: Hiring and working with the right people is crucial for building a successful organization.

Leadership Matters: Strong leadership drives organizational success and fosters a positive culture.

From "Who Moved My Cheese?" by Spencer Johnson:

Adapt to Change: Be ready to adapt and thrive in a rapidly changing environment, especially in dynamic industries like social media.

Chapter 8 : Oracle

Merging Ambitions and Cultivating Change

Transitioning from a startup to a corporate giant like Oracle brought with it a whirlwind of experiences, challenges, and invaluable lessons. This chapter explores the intricate process of merging different cultures and technologies to create a cohesive, innovative environment.

"If something is important enough, even if the odds are against you, you should still do it." - Elon Musk

My journey at Oracle began with a new employee number: 157,231. Oracle had pulled together three social media startups to form a comprehensive social relationship management platform, aiming to create a product offering similar to CRM. Oracle was already renowned for Siebel, an on-prem CRM solution acquired for 5.85 billion dollars in 2005. Around this time, Salesforce.com was revolutionizing the industry with its Software as a Service (SaaS) cloud solutions, which included their acquisition of Buddy Media for half a billion dollars.

Integrating Cultures and Teams

Unlike previous mergers, this one involved integrating three startups into Oracle. I recall our initial meetings in San Francisco, where a sales rep from Vitrue, unaware of Oracle's magnitude, casually remarked, "So, how does it feel to be acquired by Vitrue?" This comment highlighted a common misconception about the hierarchy and power dynamics within large organizations. The lesson here is to approach such situations with humility and a willingness to listen rather than assume superiority.

Armed with my experience from Adobe, I was prepared to navigate the complexities of another major acquisition. My primary responsibility was to integrate the presales teams from the three acquired companies and educate Oracle's existing teams on the new social technologies. This integration process involved extensive travel to major Oracle locations, including New York, Chicago, Salt Lake City, Denver, Seattle, Atlanta, Austin, Dallas, and San Francisco. Despite Oracle's sometimes negative reputation, I found the people there to be incredibly talented and eager to learn.

Diving Into the Social Wave

My first task was to dive headfirst into the world of social media technologies, understanding each startup's unique offerings. Involver, with its Social Markup Language (SML), was a trailblazer in creating custom social experiences. Vitrue excelled in social marketing and page design, while Collective Intellect specialized in sentiment analysis. Integrating these distinct capabilities into a cohesive platform was both a challenge and an exhilarating opportunity.

The early days were filled with a blend of excitement and chaos. I remember organizing the first series of training sessions, where we brought together teams from the startups and legacy Oracle employees. The energy in these rooms was palpable. We had seasoned Oracle veterans eager to absorb new knowledge and startup employees passionate about sharing their innovative ideas. These sessions were more than just training—they were cultural exchanges where each side learned to appreciate the other's strengths.

Lessons Learned

1. **Check Your Attitude at the Door**: Always approach new environments with humility and a willingness to learn.
2. **Be Open-Minded**: Embrace the changes and the diverse perspectives that come with them.
3. **Embrace Change**: Adaptability is crucial in dynamic environments.
4. **Provide Immersive Training**: Build long-lasting relationships through comprehensive training programs.

Guidance from Seasoned Executives

I was fortunate to work alongside seasoned executives like Tim Loomis, Eric Verderber, Jim Moss, David Pacheco, Greg Robinson, and my good friend Hugh Shannon. These executives provided invaluable insights and mentorship. However, transitioning from a startup environment to a massive enterprise required adjusting my expectations and understanding my role within the larger corporate structure. I leaned on my colleagues, David Jones, Greg Robinson, Allen Levine, and Hugh Shannon, to navigate this new landscape.

Innovative Training Programs

To ensure a smooth integration, we developed innovative training programs tailored to bridge the gap between the startups and Oracle's vast resources. One of the most memorable programs involved an immersive training experience where startup employees and Oracle veterans collaborated on real-world projects. These projects not only facilitated knowledge transfer but also fostered a sense of camaraderie.

I vividly remember a training session in Chicago where we organized a hackathon. Teams were formed with members from different backgrounds—startup engineers, Oracle sales reps, and presales consultants. The goal was to create a prototype that leveraged social media data to enhance customer relationship management. The results were astounding. Not only did we come up with several viable solutions, but the bonds formed during this event laid the foundation for a cohesive team moving forward.

A New Challenge: Customer Experience Architects

As the social media integration phase concluded, I transitioned to a new role, managing the Customer Experience Architects. This presales group was responsible for creating cohesive technical stories across various products. Initially, I found this role daunting as it seemed removed from direct revenue generation. However, the importance of presenting a unified message to clients soon became apparent.

To illustrate the complexity, imagine a meeting with representatives from Oracle's MDM team in suits standing alongside the marketing team in casual attire. This dissonance could confuse customers, and our job was to present a unified front. We achieved this through Customer Experience Journey Mapping, a process inspired by Stanford Design School thinking, which focused on understanding and improving customer interactions.

Journey Mapping: A Game-Changer

Journey Mapping transformed our approach to business and life. This process involves mapping out customer personas and their interactions with our brand, identifying pain points, and developing solutions. A memorable example involved a marketing team, where a disagreement between the CMO and the field marketing manager highlighted the need for better alignment and understanding. This methodology, encapsulated in the acronym CASH (Critical Business Issues, Access to Power, Shorten Sales Cycles, Hunting License to the Line of Business), became a cornerstone of our strategy.

Lessons Learned

1. **Invest in Value-Adding Programs**: Programs like Journey Mapping can provide deep insights and significant value.
2. **Leverage Solution Exhaust**: Use the byproducts of solutions to generate additional revenue.
3. **CASH Framework**: Focus on critical business issues, access to decision-makers, shortening sales cycles, and obtaining a hunting license to the line of business.
4. **Attitudes Drive Results**: Positive attitudes lead to better behaviors and outcomes.
5. **Post-It Notes**: These simple tools can be more powerful than sophisticated technology in brainstorming sessions.

Innovative Messaging Techniques

As part of continuous change at Oracle, I was allowed to pull together a messaging team in addition to the CX Journey Mapping group. Our messaging team at Oracle was innovative, focusing on customer-centric presentations and storytelling. A notable example involved a presentation to Lululemon, where our team wore Lululemon attire and used their corporate presentation templates. This approach demonstrated our commitment to understanding and aligning with the customer's brand.

We also developed Day in the Life (DIL) videos, which illustrated the potential benefits of our solutions through relatable customer stories. One team member, Alex Dombroski, was particularly adept at engaging audiences with his captivating presentations. His ability to connect with customers was so impressive that a CMO once considered hiring him on the spot.

Health Scare and Life Lessons

In March 2017, I experienced a health scare that underscored the importance of balancing work and life. Despite feeling unwell, I attended a crucial meeting in Vancouver, only to later discover I had multiple heart blockages requiring immediate surgery. This experience was a wake-up call, emphasizing the need to manage stress and prioritize health.

Lessons Learned

1. **Journey Mapping**: This process can transform your approach to business.
2. **Customer-Centric Messaging**: Always tailor your presentations to resonate with your customer.
3. **Storytelling**: Stories are far more memorable than mere facts.
4. **Listen to Your Body**: Stress can have serious health consequences, so manage it effectively.

Final Thoughts on Oracle

Reflecting on my five years at Oracle, the journey was filled with ups and downs, challenges and triumphs. The experience enriched my professional life and provided invaluable lessons. From integrating startups into a corporate giant to managing innovative training programs and health scares, each experience contributed to my growth.

Lessons Learned: Oracle

1. **Humility**: Approach new environments with an open mind and a willingness to learn.
2. **Adaptability**: Embrace change and adjust to new circumstances.
3. **Training and Integration**: Invest in immersive training programs to build cohesive teams.
4. **Customer Focus**: Always tailor your messaging to resonate with the customer.
5. **Health and Well-being**: Prioritize your health and manage stress effectively.
6. **Innovation**: Leverage innovative techniques like Journey Mapping to drive business success.
7. **Storytelling**: Use stories to make your presentations more engaging and memorable.

Applying Lessons to Modern Business Culture

Books:

"The Lean Startup" by Eric Ries - This book provides insights into how to navigate the complexities of startup culture and integrate innovative practices into larger organizations.

"Measure What Matters" by John Doerr - Emphasizes the importance of setting and measuring objectives and key results (OKRs) to drive success.

"Switch: How to Change Things When Change Is Hard" by Chip Heath and Dan Heath - Offers strategies for managing change and overcoming resistance.

"The Art of Scalability" by Martin L. Abbott and Michael T. Fisher - Guides on scaling technology and business practices efficiently.

Workshop Title: Navigating Mergers and Acquisitions

Objective: To provide participants with strategies and tools to successfully navigate the complexities of mergers and acquisitions, ensuring smooth integration and cultural alignment.

Total Duration: 4 hours

Materials Needed:

- Whiteboards and markers
- Post-it notes
- Handouts on M&A best practices
- Case studies of successful and unsuccessful mergers
- Projector and screen for presentations
- Notebooks and pens for participants

Agenda:

1. Introduction (15 minutes)
    - Welcome and overview of the workshop objectives
    - Brief discussion on the importance of effective M&A integration
    - Icebreaker activity to engage participants
2. Case Study Analysis (45 minutes)
    - **Activity (15 minutes):** Present two case studies—one successful and one unsuccessful merger. Provide handouts with details of the case studies.
    - **Group Discussion (30 minutes):** Break participants into small groups to discuss what

worked and what didn't in each case. Each group will appoint a spokesperson to share their findings.
- Questions to Initiate Discussion:
  - What were the key factors that led to the success/failure of the merger?
  - How were cultural differences managed?
  - What could have been done differently?
  - What were the major challenges faced during the integration process?
  - How did leadership impact the outcome of the merger?

3. Cultural Integration (1 hour)
   - **Presentation (15 minutes):** Provide strategies for aligning different corporate cultures, emphasizing communication and conflict resolution.
   - **Role-Playing Exercise (30 minutes):** In pairs, participants will role-play scenarios involving cultural conflicts and practice resolution techniques.
   - **Group Reflection (15 minutes):** Reconvene and discuss insights and lessons learned from the role-playing exercise.
   - Questions to Initiate Discussion:
     - What strategies were effective in resolving conflicts?
     - How can these strategies be applied in real-life situations?
     - What are the most common cultural clashes during M&A?
     - How can open communication help in cultural integration?
4. Break (15 minutes)
5. Change Management (1 hour)

- **Presentation (15 minutes):** Share techniques for managing change and addressing resistance during M&A.
- **Interactive Session (30 minutes):** In small groups, participants will develop a change management plan for a hypothetical merger scenario provided by the facilitator.
- **Group Sharing (15 minutes):** Each group presents their change management plan and receives feedback from peers and the facilitator.
- Questions to Initiate Discussion:
  - What are the main sources of resistance during M&A?
  - How can you effectively communicate change to employees?
  - What strategies can help in overcoming resistance?
  - How can you measure the success of a change management plan?

6. Best Practices in M&A (45 minutes)
   - **Presentation (20 minutes):** Overview of best practices in mergers and acquisitions. Provide handouts summarizing these practices.
   - **Group Brainstorming (25 minutes):** Participants brainstorm on how to apply these best practices in their own organizations. Use whiteboards and post-it notes to capture ideas.
   - Questions to Initiate Discussion:
     - Which best practices are most relevant to your organization?
     - How can you implement these best practices in your M&A strategy?

- What challenges might you face in applying these best practices?
- How can you ensure continuous monitoring and improvement during M&A?

7. Action Plan Development (45 minutes)
   - **Individual Work (20 minutes):** Participants create an action plan for navigating M&A in their organizations, using a provided template.
   - **Pair and Share (15 minutes):** Participants pair up to share and discuss their action plans, providing constructive feedback to each other.
   - **Group Feedback (10 minutes):** Volunteers present their action plans to the group for additional feedback and refinement.
   - Questions to Initiate Discussion:
     - What are the key components of your action plan?
     - How will you measure the success of your action plan?
     - What potential obstacles might you face in implementing your action plan?
     - How can you ensure that your action plan is adaptable to changing circumstances?
8. Conclusion and Q&A (15 minutes)
   - Summarize key takeaways from the workshop
   - Open floor for questions and additional discussion
   - Provide additional resources and reading materials for further learning

Detailed Step-by-Step Instructions:

1. Introduction (15 minutes)

- Greet participants and briefly introduce yourself and your background in M&A.
- Explain the objectives of the workshop and what participants can expect to learn.
- Conduct an icebreaker activity such as "Two Truths and a Lie" related to participants' experiences with M&A to foster engagement and interaction.

2. Case Study Analysis (45 minutes)
    - Activity:
        - Project a summary of each case study on the screen.
        - Distribute detailed handouts of the case studies to participants.
    - Group Discussion:
        - Divide participants into small groups of 4-5.
        - Assign each group one case study to analyze.
        - Provide guiding questions such as:
            - What were the key factors that led to the success/failure of the merger?
            - How were cultural differences managed?
            - What could have been done differently?
            - What were the major challenges faced during the integration process?
            - How did leadership impact the outcome of the merger?
        - Allow each group 20 minutes to discuss.
        - Reconvene and have each group's spokesperson share their findings with the entire workshop (10 minutes per group).
3. Cultural Integration (1 hour)

- Presentation:
  - Discuss the importance of cultural integration in M&A.
  - Highlight strategies such as open communication, cultural assessments, and team-building activities.
  - Provide real-world examples of successful cultural integrations.
- Role-Playing Exercise:
  - Pair up participants and give each pair a scenario involving a cultural conflict in a merged company.
  - Allow 15 minutes for role-playing, where one participant plays the role of an employee from the acquired company and the other as a manager from the acquiring company.
  - After the role-playing, have each pair reflect on the exercise and discuss what worked and what didn't.
- Group Reflection:
  - Gather all participants and facilitate a discussion on key insights from the role-playing exercise.
  - Ask questions like:
    - What strategies were effective in resolving conflicts?
    - How can these strategies be applied in real-life situations?
    - What are the most common cultural clashes during M&A?
    - How can open communication help in cultural integration?

4. Break (15 minutes)
5. Change Management (1 hour)
    - Presentation:
        - Discuss common challenges in change management during M&A.
        - Introduce techniques such as the ADKAR model (Awareness, Desire, Knowledge, Ability, Reinforcement) for managing change.
        - Provide examples of successful change management initiatives.
    - Interactive Session:
        - Present a hypothetical merger scenario with several potential change challenges.
        - Divide participants into small groups and have each group develop a change management plan for the scenario.
        - Provide a structured template for the plan, including sections for identifying change impacts, communication strategies, and training programs.
        - Allow 20 minutes for group work.
    - Group Sharing:
        - Each group presents their change management plan (3-5 minutes per group).
        - Facilitate a feedback session, encouraging constructive critique and suggestions for improvement.
    - Questions to Initiate Discussion:
        - What are the main sources of resistance during M&A?
        - How can you effectively communicate change to employees?

- What strategies can help in overcoming resistance?
- How can you measure the success of a change management plan?
6. Best Practices in M&A (45 minutes)
    - Presentation:
        - Outline key best practices in M&A, including due diligence, integration planning, stakeholder engagement, and continuous monitoring.
        - Share success stories and lessons learned from real M&A cases.
    - Group Brainstorming:
        - Have participants brainstorm in groups on how these best practices can be applied to their own organizations.
        - Use whiteboards and post-it notes to capture ideas and encourage creative thinking.
        - Each group appoints a scribe to record and later present their ideas.
        - Allow 20 minutes for brainstorming and 5 minutes for each group to present their ideas.
    - Questions to Initiate Discussion:
        - Which best practices are most relevant to your organization?
        - How can you implement these best practices in your M&A strategy?
        - What challenges might you face in applying these best practices?
        - How can you ensure continuous monitoring and improvement during M&A?
7. Action Plan Development (45 minutes)

- Individual Work:
    - Distribute action plan templates.
    - Guide participants through the process of developing their action plans, focusing on the key components such as goals, strategies, timelines, and metrics.
    - Allow 20 minutes for participants to work on their plans individually.
- Pair and Share:
    - Have participants pair up and share their action plans with each other.
    - Encourage them to provide constructive feedback and suggestions for improvement.
- Group Feedback:
    - Select a few volunteers to present their action plans to the group.
    - Facilitate a group discussion to provide additional feedback and refinement.
- Questions to Initiate Discussion:
    - What are the key components of your action plan?
    - How will you measure the success of your action plan?
    - What potential obstacles might you face in implementing your action plan?
    - How can you ensure that your action plan is adaptable to changing circumstances?

8. Conclusion and Q&A (15 minutes)
    - Summarize the key takeaways from each session.
    - Highlight the importance of effective M&A integration and continuous improvement.

- Open the floor for any remaining questions and additional discussion.
- Distribute additional resources and reading materials for further learning.
- Thank participants for their engagement and encourage them to apply the lessons learned in their own organizations.

This comprehensive workshop aims to provide participants with a deep understanding of the complexities involved in M&A and equip them with practical tools and strategies to ensure successful integrations.

Chapter 9: Elastic Search

Embracing Open Source

"In open-source, we feel strongly that to really do something well, you have to get a lot of people involved." — Linus Torvalds

Elasticsearch: A New Chapter

After a summer of re-evaluating my career path, I decided it was time for a change. With my kids' college costs and our house paid off, I felt the pull to return to the excitement of startups. This time, I landed on the open-source technology of Elasticsearch.

What is Elasticsearch? Elasticsearch is a search engine based on the Lucene library. It offers a distributed, multitenant-capable full-text search engine with an HTTP web interface and schema-free JSON documents. Developed in Java, Elasticsearch is dual-licensed under the source-available Server Side Public License and the Elastic license. According to the DB-Engines ranking, Elasticsearch is the most popular enterprise search engine.

A Brief History of Elasticsearch Shay Banon created the precursor to Elasticsearch, called Compass, in 2004. Realizing the need for a scalable search solution, he built Elasticsearch from the ground up to be distributed and to use JSON over HTTP, making it suitable for various programming languages. The first version was released in February 2010.

Elastic NV was founded in 2012 to provide commercial services and products around Elasticsearch. By June 2014, the company had raised $70 million in a Series C funding round, bringing total funding to $104 million. Elastic went public in October 2018 with an estimated valuation between $1.5 and $3 billion.

Joining Elastic Elastic was a pre-IPO company with a bottom-up sales approach, focusing on open-source technology for a technical community. Although I knew little about open source or search technology, I was drawn to the company by its dynamic leaders. Steve Mayzak, VP of Solution Architects, and Ryan McGinty, head of sales for the East, both impressed me with their vision and experience.

The mission at Elastic was to hire quickly, build a robust management structure, educate sales and engineers on positioning technology, and establish processes in preparation for the IPO. This involved creating programs for career development, partner engagement, hiring best practices, and sales strategies.

The Role of a Solution Architect in Open Source Selling open-source technology requires a different skill set compared to packaged solutions. A Solution Architect needs an 80/20 split of technical expertise and sales acumen. The open-source community is deeply connected to the technology, which means the sales motion often involves educating users who may not be paying customers.

Typical experience requirements include:

- IT architecture, infrastructure, and cloud development
- Engineering and software architecture design
- DevOps practices
- Network administration and data security
- Business analysis techniques
- Various operating systems and database management

- Coding proficiency in multiple languages

Certifications often needed include:

- AWS Certified Solutions Architect
- Microsoft Certified Azure Solutions Architect Expert
- Google Professional Cloud Architect
- CISSP Information Systems Security Architecture Professional
- Professional Cloud Solutions Architect Certification

Lessons Learned

- The bottom-up sales motion is unique and challenging.
- Open-source companies operate differently from traditional engineering-led companies.
- Solution Architects are 80% technical and 20% sales/business.
- Community involvement is crucial and infectious.
- Pre-IPO periods are free of politics and filled with collective effort.
- Post-IPO challenges often favor leadership from established brands, making transitions difficult.
- Individual contributors should proactively bridge gaps between solution architects and account executives.

Workshop: Bridging the Gap Between SEs and Account Executives

Objective: Improve collaboration and understanding between SEs and Account Executives to enhance sales performance and customer satisfaction.

Materials Needed:

- Whiteboard and markers
- Post-it notes
- Voting dots
- Printed copies of customer scenarios

Duration: 2 hours

Step-by-Step Instructions:

1. **Introduction (10 minutes)**
    - Explain the purpose of the workshop.
    - Highlight the importance of collaboration between SEs and AEs.

2. **Icebreaker (15 minutes)**
    - Have participants share their biggest challenge in working with their counterpart (SE or AE).

3. **Scenario Analysis (30 minutes)**
    - Divide participants into small groups.
    - Provide each group with a customer scenario.

- Ask them to outline how they would approach the scenario, focusing on collaboration between SEs and AEs.

4. **Role-Playing (30 minutes)**

    - Groups present their approach to the larger group.
    - Other participants role-play as the customer, providing feedback and objections.
    - Encourage constructive criticism and alternative strategies.

5. **Brainstorming Solutions (20 minutes)**

    - Use the whiteboard to list common challenges identified during role-playing.
    - Have participants suggest solutions, writing them on Post-it notes and placing them on the board.

6. **Voting and Discussion (15 minutes)**

    - Use voting dots to prioritize the most critical challenges and solutions.
    - Discuss the top-voted items as a group.

7. **Action Plan (10 minutes)**

    - Summarize key takeaways.
    - Develop an action plan for improving SE and AE collaboration.
    - Assign follow-up tasks to ensure implementation.

By addressing the unique dynamics of selling open-source technology and fostering collaboration between SEs and AEs, you can navigate the challenges and capitalize on the opportunities in this

Chapter 10 Snowflake

Embracing Challenges and Building a Future

Snowflake's journey was marked by monumental achievements and significant challenges. As I transitioned from Elastic to Snowflake, I brought with me the lessons learned from navigating post-IPO transitions, understanding that leadership changes often shift a company's culture and strategic direction. Snowflake was no exception.

"Great companies thrive on adaptability and the relentless pursuit of innovation, even amidst unprecedented challenges." - Satya Nadella, CEO of Microsoft

In the face of a global pandemic, we all found ourselves grappling with new realities and unexpected challenges. For me, leaving my job just before the pandemic hit meant navigating a period of uncertainty, self-discovery, and resilience. This journey ultimately led me to Snowflake, where I experienced firsthand the intricacies of building remote relationships and adapting to a rapidly evolving business landscape.

Background on Snowflake:

Snowflake Inc., a cloud computing–based data cloud company founded in Bozeman, Montana, in July 2012, publicly launched in October 2014 after two years in stealth mode. Offering cloud-based data storage and analytics services, Snowflake allowed corporate users to store and analyze data using cloud-based hardware and software. The company had been running on Amazon S3 since 2014, on Microsoft Azure since 2018, and on the Google Cloud

Platform since 2019. Ranked first on the Forbes Cloud 100 in 2019, Snowflake's IPO raised $3.4 billion, making it one of the largest software IPOs in history.

My introduction to Snowflake was through a series of Zoom calls with various people, including a sharp-minded hiring manager, several team members, and sales leaders like Brian Daniels and Michael Keaveney. Finally, I spoke with the SVP Global Solution Engineering for Snowflake. It was clear that this was no ordinary startup; executives from SAP and EMC were already embedded in the company.

COVID delayed my offer, but it eventually came through, and I was thrilled to start. However, the company made some changes, and I ended up working with the west coast VP, who had previously worked with the Global VP in an SAP setting. To add to the excitement, the global VP went on maternity leave, leaving my VP to take over some of her duties. She helped me ramp up quickly, giving me the freedom to run my business as needed.

Key Focus Areas:

Hiring: We focused on hiring and unifying the Eastern S.E. organization with Canada. By the end of my first year, we expanded from five to eight managers and doubled our S.E. headcount. We met our headcount numbers with the help of an amazing H.R. team and committed S.E. managers.

Team Culture: We worked on integrating teams from the northeast, Canada, and the southeast, who had not previously collaborated across regions. Virtual meetings helped grow relationships and team spirit, leading to remarkable success even during COVID.

Sales Consulting: Snowflake shifted towards value selling with a 70/30 tech-to-sales split. With a fantastic technical bench to onboard those with stronger sales backgrounds, Snowflake proved to be a good path for individuals with a solid sales understanding and a willingness to learn the technology.

The IPO and Post-IPO Challenges

Snowflake's IPO was a monumental event, the largest in software history. This success brought both opportunities and challenges. Post-IPO, we faced growing pains, particularly in managing the SE and sales relationships. The intense competition from companies like Databricks exposed weaknesses within our sales process, emphasizing the need for accountability and engagement rules.

Dealing with Employees Who Became Millionaires After the IPO

One unique challenge that arose post-IPO at Snowflake was managing employees who became instant millionaires. The IPO was one of the largest in software history, and many early employees saw significant financial windfalls. This newfound wealth can be a double-edged sword in a corporate environment.

The Challenge

When employees suddenly find themselves with substantial financial security, their motivations and priorities can shift dramatically. Some might lose the drive to work hard, feeling they've already "made it." Others might begin to pursue passion projects or side ventures, reducing their focus on their primary job. This change in dynamics can impact team productivity, morale, and the overall drive to achieve corporate goals.

Strategies for Management

Open Communication: It's crucial to have open and honest conversations with these employees. Understand their new priorities and find ways to align their personal goals with the company's objectives. For example, someone interested in philanthropy might be motivated by leading a corporate social responsibility initiative.

New Challenges: Many newly wealthy employees still crave intellectual stimulation and personal growth. Offering them new challenges, leadership roles, or opportunities to innovate within the company can keep them engaged. They need to feel that their contributions are still valuable and necessary.

Flexible Roles: Consider creating flexible roles that allow for part-time commitments or remote work arrangements. This can help retain talent that might otherwise leave due to their newfound financial freedom. Flexibility can also enable these employees to balance their work with personal pursuits.

Equity-Based Incentives: While they might not need the money, equity-based incentives can still motivate wealthy employees. Stock options and other long-term financial incentives can align their success with the company's continued growth and prosperity.

Mentorship Programs: Leverage the experience and knowledge of these financially secure employees by involving them in mentorship programs. Their insights can be invaluable to new hires and those looking to advance their careers within the company.

Recognition and Purpose: Beyond financial rewards, recognition, and a sense of purpose can drive engagement. Highlighting their contributions and aligning their work with meaningful outcomes can rekindle their passion for the job.

Corporate Governance: Implement policies that ensure all employees, regardless of their financial status, contribute equitably to the company's success. This might include performance reviews that consider both individual and team contributions.

Bold Leadership – Remove CSM Teams

Snowflake's decision to eliminate the Customer Success Manager (CSM) team was another significant shift. Initially skeptical, I soon realized the logic behind this move. The CSM role often attracted individuals who either aspired to be salespeople or had transitioned from sales to a more stable position. Without clear engagement rules, the burden fell on SEs and SDRs, stretching their capacity.

Adapting to Change and Preparing for the Future

As Snowflake continued to grow, we encountered the same post-IPO challenges that affected Elastic. The influx of new leadership from larger enterprise companies brought significant changes. The fabric of Snowflake's culture began to shift, reflecting the influence of new executives and their trusted colleagues. This dynamic created both opportunities and challenges, forcing us to adapt and evolve.

IPO and Growth:

Snowflake had the largest IPO in history, and we prepared the team for massive changes post-IPO. We faced growing pains with S.E.

and Sales relationships and needed to follow a structured sales process to avoid wasting time and losing deals.

Customer Success Management (CSM):

Snowflake made the bold move to remove its CSM team, an unusual step for a SaaS company. The burden often fell on S.E. shoulders or the SDRs. As the company grew, managing S.E. time became challenging. Engagement rules and a proper compensation plan were critical.

Lessons Learned

1. Ask how companies measure success and failure.
2. Ensure the system used by sales teams is the same as the one used by sales consultants.
3. Understand the level of adoption, accountability, and enforcement for these systems.
4. Be aware that spending 10 hours a week entering data to report to management does not make you more productive.
5. Find out if the company has a CSM team and the rules of engagement.
6. Understand how the company measures success.
7. Know how closely coupled the sales and S.E. teams are, including data reporting.
8. Expect the unexpected.
9. Get a great financial planner.

Applying Lessons to Modern Business Culture

To effectively apply these lessons, here are some recommended readings that can provide deeper insights into handling these challenges:

Drive: The Surprising Truth About What Motivates Us by Daniel H. Pink - This book delves into what truly motivates people beyond financial incentives.

Leaders Eat Last: Why Some Teams Pull Together and Others Don't by Simon Sinek - Focuses on the importance of leadership in fostering a cooperative and motivated team environment.

Workshop: Building Relationships in a Remote World

Duration: 4 hours

Materials Needed:

- Post-it notes
- Dots for voting
- Whiteboard or large sheets of paper
- Markers
- Printed handouts of the story and discussion prompts

Workshop Agenda:

1. Introduction and Icebreaker (30 minutes)

- **Introduction:** Briefly introduce the workshop and its objectives. Emphasize the importance of building strong relationships in a remote work environment.
- **Icebreaker Activity:** Participants share their most unexpected skill learned during the pandemic.

2. Story Presentation (30 minutes)

- **Story Presentation:** Provide a detailed recounting of experiences in building remote relationships, highlighting challenges and successes.

3. Building Relationships in a Remote World (1 hour)

- **Level 1 Relationships: First point of contact.**
    - **Discussion Prompt:** "What are the key elements of a strong first impression in a virtual meeting?"

- - **Brainstorming Questions:**
      - What is one effective way to introduce yourself in a virtual setting?
      - How can we make new team members feel welcome during their first remote meeting?
      - What are some icebreakers that have worked well for you in virtual meetings?
  - **Examples:**
      - Use personalized introductions that include interesting facts about oneself.
      - Create a welcoming slide with everyone's names and roles.
      - Start meetings with a quick round of fun, light-hearted questions to break the ice.

- **Level 2 Relationships: Continued relationship with blurred business and personal lines.**
  - **Discussion Prompt:** "How do you maintain professional boundaries while developing a deeper connection?"
  - **Brainstorming Questions:**
      - How can we create opportunities for informal interactions in a remote environment?
      - What are some ways to show empathy and understanding to colleagues you've never met in person?
      - How do you balance sharing personal updates with maintaining professionalism?
  - **Examples:**
      - Set up virtual coffee breaks or casual chat sessions.

- - Use empathy maps to understand colleagues' feelings and perspectives.
  - Schedule regular check-ins that allow for both professional updates and personal sharing.

- **Level 3 Relationships: Full-on relationships, borderline friends.**

    - **Discussion Prompt:** "What are the benefits and challenges of becoming friends with colleagues?"
    - **Brainstorming Questions:**
        - What activities or initiatives can help foster deeper connections in a remote team?
        - How can we support each other personally and professionally while working remotely?
        - What boundaries should we set to ensure professional relationships remain effective?
    - **Examples:**
        - Organize virtual team-building activities like online games or shared hobby sessions.
        - Create a buddy system where colleagues pair up to support each other.
        - Establish clear guidelines for work-related communication to maintain professional boundaries.

4. Interactive Activity: Relationship Building (1 hour)

- **Activity:** Participants use post-it notes to write down examples of L1, L2, and L3 relationships from their experience.

- **Dot Voting:** Identify the most common and impactful strategies for each level.
- **Group Discussion:** Analyze results and discuss strategies to implement these in their own teams.
- **Brainstorming Questions:**
    - What new ideas can we implement to improve remote team bonding?
    - How can we ensure regular and meaningful interactions among team members?
    - What virtual team-building activities have you experienced that were particularly effective?
- **Examples:**
    - Use collaborative tools like Miro or Jamboard for interactive brainstorming sessions.
    - Incorporate team recognition moments in meetings to celebrate achievements and milestones.
    - Rotate the role of meeting facilitator to give everyone a chance to lead.

5. Actionable Readout and Q&A (1 hour)

- **Summary:** Summarize the key points from the discussion.
- **Action Steps:** Develop a set of actionable steps to enhance relationship building in their teams.
- **Q&A:** Open floor for additional insights and questions.
- **Brainstorming Questions:**
    - What immediate steps can we take to improve our remote work relationships?
    - How can we measure the success of our relationship-building efforts?
    - What support or resources do you need to foster better relationships remotely?
- **Examples:**

- Implement regular team feedback surveys to gauge the effectiveness of relationship-building efforts.
- Establish a mentorship program to pair new hires with experienced team members.
- Schedule quarterly virtual retreats to foster team cohesion and alignment.

Additional Brainstorming Techniques and Questions

Techniques

1. **Mind Mapping**
   - **Question:** How can we visually map out our team's relationship-building strategies?
2. **SCAMPER Technique**
   - **Question:** How can we modify our current practices to better suit a remote environment?
3. **SWOT Analysis**
   - **Question:** What are the strengths, weaknesses, opportunities, and threats related to our current remote relationship-building efforts?

General Brainstorming Questions

- What challenges have you faced in building relationships remotely, and how did you overcome them?
- What tools or technologies have you found most effective for maintaining connections in a remote setting?
- How can we create a sense of community and belonging in a virtual workspace?
- What are some innovative ways to celebrate team achievements remotely?
- How can we ensure that new hires feel integrated and supported in a remote environment?

By following this structured approach, you can create a comprehensive understanding of how to build and maintain relationships in a remote world, ensuring that your team thrives despite the challenges posed by the modern business landscape.

Personal Note:

My journey was further impacted by a prostate cancer diagnosis in October. The team was supportive, and I eventually needed surgery. Thanks to Snowflake, Elasticsearch, and my financial planner Jason, I can afford to take a break.

Conclusion: Lessons Learned from My Journey

"In conclusion, my journey has taken me to this point in life where I finally realize what is important. That is Family, Customer, Employees, Leadership, and Brand!" - Kevin R. Kunz

Introduction

Reflecting on my career, I am reminded of the wisdom of Albert Einstein: "Life is like riding a bicycle. To keep your balance, you must keep moving."

My professional journey has been a series of moves—some calculated, some unexpected—that have collectively shaped my understanding of what truly matters in business and life. Each step has offered valuable lessons, and it's time to share these insights, hoping they will guide you in your journey.

The Importance of Family

Family has been the cornerstone of my life and career. The support and understanding from my loved ones have enabled me to pursue my professional ambitions. Balancing work and family life is crucial, and this balance often requires tough decisions and sacrifices.

For instance, during my tenure at Snowflake, the COVID-19 pandemic brought home the importance of being there for my family. Navigating remote work while ensuring my family felt supported was challenging, yet it underscored the need to prioritize family without compromising on professional responsibilities.

Key Lessons:

Support System: Your family is your primary support system. Their encouragement and understanding provide the strength needed to navigate professional challenges.

Balance: Strive for a healthy work-life balance. Prioritizing family does not mean neglecting your career; it means finding a way to excel in both areas.

Quality Time: Make time for family activities and be present during these moments. This strengthens bonds and provides a necessary break from work-related stress.

Customer-Centric Approach

Throughout my career, a customer-centric approach has been pivotal. Understanding the needs and pain points of customers and delivering solutions that address these needs effectively is the bedrock of any successful business. This principle was particularly evident during my time at Elastic and Snowflake, where the focus on providing value to customers was paramount.

Key Lessons:

Listen Actively: Truly understanding customer needs requires active listening and empathy.

Deliver Value: Always aim to exceed customer expectations by delivering value through innovative solutions.

Build Trust: Trust is the foundation of any long-term customer relationship. Transparency and reliability are key to building trust.

Valuing Employees

Employees are the lifeblood of any organization. My experiences have taught me that investing in employees' growth and well-being leads to a more motivated and productive workforce. Whether it was hiring the right talent at Elastic or fostering team spirit at Snowflake, valuing employees has always been a priority.

Key Lessons:

Invest in Development: Provide opportunities for continuous learning and career advancement.

Foster a Positive Culture: A supportive and inclusive work culture enhances employee satisfaction and retention.

Recognize Achievements: Regular recognition and rewards for hard work and achievements boost morale and motivation.

Effective Leadership

Leadership is not just about managing tasks but inspiring and guiding people towards a common goal. Throughout my career, I have encountered various leadership styles and have learned the importance of adaptability, empathy, and decisiveness.

Key Lessons:

Lead by Example: Demonstrate the values and work ethic you expect from your team.

Be Adaptable: The business landscape is constantly changing; adaptability is crucial for effective leadership.

Empathy and Support: Understanding and addressing the concerns of your team fosters loyalty and dedication.

Building a Strong Brand

Brand is more than just a logo or a tagline; it represents the values, mission, and reputation of a company. My journey through various companies like Adobe, Oracle, Elastic, and Snowflake has shown me the power of a strong brand in attracting customers, retaining employees, and driving business success.

Key Lessons:

Consistency: Ensure that all aspects of your business consistently reflect your brand values.

Customer Experience: Provide exceptional customer experiences that reinforce your brand's promise.

Innovation: Continuously innovate to keep your brand relevant and competitive in the market.

The Impact of Professional Relationships

Do not underestimate who you will work with and how they will impact your life for the better or for the worst. Each encounter has its lessons learned over time. Building strong professional relationships has been a cornerstone of my success. From mentors who have guided me to peers who have collaborated with me, every relationship has added value to my journey.

Key Lessons:

Networking: Actively build and maintain a professional network; it opens doors to new opportunities and insights.

Mentorship: Seek mentors who can provide guidance and support throughout your career.

Collaboration: Foster a collaborative environment where knowledge and ideas are freely shared.

Managing Post-IPO Challenges

The transition from a startup to a public company brings its own set of challenges. Employees who become millionaires overnight can experience shifts in motivation and engagement. Managing this transition effectively is crucial to maintaining a productive and cohesive team.

Key Lessons:

- **Address Changes Transparently:** Communicate openly about the changes and what they mean for the team.
- **Maintain Engagement:** Find ways to keep employees engaged and motivated, even after financial windfalls.
- **Foster a Sense of Purpose:** Reinforce the company's mission and values to keep employees aligned with the organizational goals.

Applying Lessons to Modern Business Culture

The insights gained from my experiences can be applied to modern business culture to foster growth and success. Here are some practical applications of these lessons:

Focus on People

Family First: Ensure a healthy work-life balance for yourself and your employees. Flexibility and support can lead to higher productivity and job satisfaction.

Customer Centricity: Always put the customer at the center of your business decisions. Regular feedback and customer engagement are key.

Employee Development: Invest in training and development programs. Recognize and reward employees regularly to boost morale and retention.

Build Strong Relationships

Networking: Encourage employees to build professional networks. Provide opportunities for team-building and cross-departmental collaboration.

Mentorship Programs: Implement mentorship programs to help employees grow and develop their careers.

Transparency and Communication: Maintain open lines of communication within the organization. Transparency builds trust and fosters a positive work culture.

Embrace Change

Adaptability: Encourage a culture of adaptability and resilience. The business landscape is constantly changing, and flexibility is essential.

Innovation: Foster a culture of innovation. Encourage employees to think creatively and provide the resources needed to turn ideas into reality.

Continuous Improvement: Implement a continuous improvement mindset. Regularly review and refine processes and strategies to stay competitive.

Final Thoughts

In conclusion, my journey has been a tapestry of experiences, each offering valuable lessons. These lessons have shaped my understanding of what truly matters in business and life—Family, Customer, Employees, Leadership, and Brand. The people you work with and the relationships you build profoundly impact your career and personal growth.

As you navigate your own journey, remember to prioritize these core elements. Embrace change, invest in relationships, and continuously strive for improvement. I am grateful for the opportunities and challenges that have brought me to this point, and I look forward to sharing more insights in the SE Worklife series.

Connect and Continue the Journey

You too can have an amazing journey, and I can help you along the way. Feel free to link in with me at LinkedIn or visit my website at SE Worklife. I welcome all feedback on the entire series—SE Worklife. This is just one out of four books total in the series to help you start, advance, and retire in this industry.

Best of luck to all of you.

If You Need Help, Give Me a Call – I Can Help

Navigating the intricate waters of the startup world can be challenging, and having the right guidance can make all the difference. I am Kevin Kunz, and with over three decades of experience in technical sales, solution engineering, and strategic leadership, I am here to help you succeed.

1. Extensive Experience in Diverse Business Environments: Having worked at industry leaders like Adobe, Oracle, Elastic, and Snowflake, I bring a wealth of knowledge and a proven track record of success. From leading teams through significant mergers and acquisitions to driving growth in both pre-IPO and post-IPO stages, I have seen it all. I understand the unique challenges and opportunities that come with each phase of a company's lifecycle.

2. Bridging the Gap Between Sales and Technology: One of my core strengths lies in bridging the gap between sales and technology. I have developed and implemented training programs, streamlined sales processes, and built cohesive teams that work towards common goals. Whether you need help with sales strategy, technical integration, or building a robust solution architecture, I can provide the expertise you need.

3. Strategic Leadership and Mentorship: Throughout my career, I have been a mentor and leader, guiding teams to achieve their best. My approach focuses on understanding individual strengths and fostering a collaborative environment. If you need guidance on building and leading effective teams, developing a strategic vision, or navigating complex business challenges, I am here to help.

4. Navigating Post-IPO Challenges: The transition from a startup to a publicly traded company brings its own set of challenges. I have firsthand experience in managing these transitions and can help you understand the intricacies involved. From managing new compliance requirements to maintaining company culture and driving innovation, I can offer the insights and strategies needed for success.

5. Focus on Building Relationships: Building strong relationships is at the heart of any successful business. Whether it's with your customers, employees, or stakeholders, I can help you develop and maintain these critical connections. My experience in building relationships in both remote and in-person environments ensures that you can thrive no matter the circumstances.

If you need help navigating the complexities of the startup world, refining your sales strategy, or leading your team to success, I am here for you. Reach out, and let's work together to achieve your business goals. Feel free to connect with me on LinkedIn at linkedin.com/in/kevinrkunz or visit my website at www.seworklife.com.

Best of luck to you – let's win together!

Recommended Reading List

Corporate Confidential:

50 Secrets Your Company Doesn't Want You to Know—and What to Do About Them

Author: Cynthia Shapiro

Why Read: Provides insider knowledge on navigating the corporate world, protecting your career, and understanding the unspoken rules and hidden agendas that drive corporate decisions.

Measure What Matters:

How Google, Bono, and the Gates Foundation Rock the World with OKRs

Author: John Doerr

Why Read: Learn about the OKR (Objectives and Key Results) framework used by top organizations to set and achieve ambitious goals, drive performance, and foster innovation.

Who Moved My Cheese?

An Amazing Way to Deal with Change in Your Work and in Your Life

Author: Spencer Johnson

Why Read: A simple yet profound parable about change in work and life, offering insights into how to adapt and thrive in a constantly changing environment.

The Lean Startup:

How Today's Entrepreneurs Use Continuous Innovation to Create Radically Successful Businesses

Author: Eric Ries

Why Read: Provides a scientific approach to creating and managing successful startups in an age when companies need to innovate more than ever.

The Innovator's Dilemma:

When New Technologies Cause Great Firms to Fail

Author: Clayton M. Christensen

Why Read: Understand why large companies can fail despite doing everything right, and learn how to avoid these pitfalls by embracing disruptive innovation.

The Hard Thing About Hard Things:

Building a Business When There Are No Easy Answers

Author: Ben Horowitz

Why Read: Offers practical advice on building and running a startup, from dealing with competition to managing through tough times, by one of Silicon Valley's most respected entrepreneurs.

Drive:

The Surprising Truth About What Motivates Us

Author: Daniel H. Pink

Why Read: Explores the science of motivation, revealing the mismatch between what science knows and what business does, and how to harness intrinsic motivation for better performance and satisfaction.

Radical Candor:

Be a Kick-Ass Boss Without Losing Your Humanity

Author: Kim Scott

Why Read: Provides a framework for giving constructive feedback that improves team performance and relationships, emphasizing the importance of caring personally and challenging directly.

Good to Great:

Why Some Companies Make the Leap... and Others Don't

Author: Jim Collins

Why Read: Identifies key principles that can turn good companies into great ones, based on extensive research and case studies.

Thinking, Fast and Slow

Author: Daniel Kahneman

Why Read: Nobel laureate Daniel Kahneman delves into the two systems that drive the way we think, offering profound insights into decision-making and problem-solving.

Leaders Eat Last:

Why Some Teams Pull Together and Others Don't

Author: Simon Sinek Why Read: Explores the importance of leadership that prioritizes the well-being of the team, fostering trust and cooperation to create a strong organizational culture.

Start with Why:

How Great Leaders Inspire Everyone to Take Action

Author: Simon Sinek

Why Read: Discusses the importance of identifying and communicating your "Why" to inspire and lead effectively, using examples from successful organizations and leaders.

Crossing the Chasm:

Marketing and Selling Disruptive Products to Mainstream **Customers**

Author: Geoffrey A. Moore

Why Read: Essential reading for tech entrepreneurs and marketers, offering strategies for successfully bringing disruptive innovations to mainstream markets.

Blue Ocean Strategy:

How to Create Uncontested Market Space and Make the Competition Irrelevant

Authors: W. Chan Kim & Renée Mauborgne

Why Read: Provides a systematic approach to making the competition irrelevant by creating a "blue ocean" of untapped market space ripe for innovation.

The Five Dysfunctions of a Team:

A Leadership Fable

Author: Patrick Lencioni

Why Read: Offers a leadership fable that delves into the five dysfunctions that can undermine a team, along with practical advice for overcoming them to build a cohesive and effective team.

Made in the USA
Columbia, SC
13 August 2024